MW01242867

Decode Your Personality

Go Beyond Myers-Briggs
With 64 Brain-Based Subtypes

Dario Nardi, PhD

1712 Pioneer Avenue #120
Cheyenne, WY 82001, USA
www.RadianceHouse.com
service@radiancehouse.com

As always, others have come before me and inspired key ideas
and materials. With great thanks: Dr. Carl Jung, Dr. Linda
Berens, Dr. Victor Gulenko, Dr. Steve Myers, Dr. John Beebe,
Dr. Helen Fisher, and Dr. Mina Barimany.

In addition, I thank the 600 people who've participated in
brain-imaging, and my UCLA lab assistants, notably Erin
Nguyen, and also Joshua Leach for helping with data analysis,
Ben Vaserlan for the bridge to Socionics, my business partner
Adrien Mangeot for the big push with new technology,
Zhihan Cui, PhD for insights into type and Chinese culture,
and Joe Arrigo for encouraging me to finish this!

Also, thank you to the members of The Magic Diamond
online reading group led by Elena Wolf including Alex Booth,
Elise Allan, Nicole Croizier, Ruby Grigsby-Schulte, and
Sandra Etherington.

Special thanks to Antonia Dodge and Joel Mark Witt
at Personality Hacker, and all of my family and friends.

Proofread by Anne Spurrier and Klaus Schepers
Cover design by Yehuda Ben Jehoshua.

Table of Contents

Welcome 5

Quick Start 7

Personality Type Basics 15

The Journey: From 16 Types to 64 Subtypes 35

Subtypes in Action: Four Vignettes 53

The 64 Life Paths
    ESTP 65
    ISTP 79
    ESFP 93
    ISFP 107
    ESTJ 121
    ISTJ 135
    ESFJ 149
    ISFJ 163
    ENTJ 177
    INTJ 191
    ENTP 205
    INTP 219
    ENFJ 233
    INFJ 247
    ENFP 261
    INFP 275

Coaching the Subtypes 289

Navigating Your Neurotic Boundary 305

The Yin and Yang of Type 325

Fulfill Your Aspirations 359

Cognitnive Processes Assessment 383

About the Author 389

Digital Courses at Udemy.com 390

Yet More on the Web 392

Top Books 393

References and Resources 394

Welcome!

What's your personality type—your operating system? And how can you use that to find greater satisfaction in life?

Maybe you've heard of the Myers-Briggs 4-letter type code. That would be ESTJ, INFP, and so on for 16 types total. While 16 types sounds like a lot, really it's not. It's all too common for people to struggle to find a great fit, or they plain can't decide, or they simply need more specificity.

Since 2006, I've worked hands on, conducting brain imaging of people from all over the world, and all walks of life, with different personality profiles. Imagine sitting in a lab, wearing a nylon cap with sensors, and doing a dozen tasks over the course of 40 minutes—in return, you get a report on your brain, skills, and personality. The neuroscience reveals that we all use our brains differently, and brain-wiring correlates with personality, skills, and demographics like career and upbringing.

The neuroscience takes us with confidence beyond 16 types, with 4 neuro-variants of each type, for 64 subtypes total. These subtypes are more than "smaller boxes". They reflect our lives as lived, reflect where we are now, and suggest where we might easily go. They remind us of different facets of ourselves and our potential to grow. Importantly, they give us a map to make life changes and become more fulfilled.

One of the biggest insights: The way we work, day to day, shapes our brains, whatever our personality type. Maybe you are in a leadership position, or you are one of many in a large pool of workers. Or maybe you work one-on-one in a personal way, or you like small creative teams where you can "think different". I've met people who identify with the same personality type who otherwise relate to these different work situations. There are ISTJ CEOs, ISTJ postal clerks, ISTJ musicians, and ISTJ psychologists. The Myers-Briggs type code by itself is not enough to describe someone's life, their passion, or their development. So we need more, and now we can go deeper.

We will start with the basics, cracking the 4-letter code and revealing the underlying framework as defined by the famous Dr. Carl Jung. From there, we get into the meat and potatoes: the story of the subtypes and the opportunity to explore any or all of the 64 profiles. Every profile is based on actual brain-imaging and demographic data. And all along the way, we remember the dynamic nature of personality. People are not just clusters of behavioral traits. We are alive, complex, and multi-faceted with neuroses, energy management issues, hidden aspirations, and particular keys to growth.

As you explore and understand the subtypes, I hope you will find a better path forward in your life. This book is called, "Decode Your Personality", and the word "decode" has two meanings. One is learning the hidden meaning of the letters in a code. The other is going beyond a code, to de-code who you are and return to your organic sense with all of its potential. The point of having a language, or a lens to describe personality is ultimately to step beyond it. Everyone is already in a box of their own and others' making. And, when we are informed and can name what we see, we have a lever to step out and make our lives better.

After you explore the subtypes, you may want to learn about coaching advice, the *yin* and *yang* sides of yourself, and how to navigate the neurotic boundary of each type. That extra stuff is up to you.

To quote Joel Mark Witt of Personality Hacker, "The power of Personality Profiling is not that we simply know your personality type, it's that we know HOW you are your personality type. This gives us the power to help you through coaching and advice."

Thank you for taking the time to listen, read, think, observe, and get to know yourself. The examined life is worth living, and the purposeful life even more so. Let's dive in!

Cheers,
Dario Nardi

1

Quick Start

We're Both Nature and Nurture

"What is my next career step?", "Why is my friend acting so strangely?", or "How am I still not happy?" —Have you ever heard or asked questions like these?

We're each unique. At the same time, there are patterns to how we think, feel, and act. That's our personality. And when we know how we function, we can make wiser choices.

Insights into our own and others´ psychology brings many benefits. We better understand our family, friends, colleagues, and even people we may call "enemies". We can make better choices around our career and lifestyle, like what fits our skills, interests, and style. We learn how to create better relationships—staying open-minded (and open-hearted), showing care, and building trust. Often, we enjoy more positive emotions when things make sense.

In short, when we better understand personality, we:
- spend less time expecting others to be like us,
- spend less time trying to be like others,
- become more flexible when interacting with people who are different from us, and
- get more from being ourselves, enjoying what we do best.

From People Types to Neuro-Variants

Carl Jung's 1921 book, *Psychological Types,* described 8 ways we function. Later, in the 1940s, Isabel Myers and Katherine Briggs packaged his ideas as 16 types to better share with the public. Each of the 16 represents a balanced way to thrive: a pair of cognitive processes that help us, inside and out, to perceive and decide. As many millions of people have discovered: when we know which type fits best—our operating system so-to-speak—we can make the most of our gifts.

As of late, research including brain imaging expands the picture to show how we develop in various ways. We can talk about 4 variants of each of the 16 types, for 64 subtypes total. Each subtype reflects the impact of culture, upbringing, career choice, relationships, and more.

When you know your best-fit subtype, the way ahead tends to get really clear and specific. In a nutshell, the brain-based subtypes are:

Dominant	Creative
More confident and driven. More often in leader roles.	More exploratory and sociable. More often in rebel roles.
Normalizing	Harmonizing
More conventional and dedicated. More often in support roles.	More empathic and reflective. More often in relater roles.

These are not crisp categories. They are like points on a compass. When you know where you and others *currently* sit on the compass, you can more precisely understand others, as well as choose specific career and lifestyle options more in tune with how you operate.

Three Basic Principles

Before jumping to confirm your type and subtype, and find some life suggestions, let's sit a little more with a proverbial glass of wine and talk philosophy, because our attitude, our frame of mind, matters. Here are three simple points to hold on to:

1. *Personality is foremost about persons*, not just theories, traits, or statistics. Every person is a unique, whole, organic being.

2. *We are 50/50 nature and nurture*. Genetics research shows that 40%-60% of personality is inherited, which means half is environment! Similarly, studies show that people's behavior can shift slowly over decades even as a core self remains stable.

3. *Real change equals behavior change*. We are called to do some uncomfortable work and try life changes that will shift who we are.

In this book, you will find a mix—a 50/50 blend of nature and nurture, theory and environment—to better make sense of yourself and others. This will help you see the story of your past more clearly, and you will be empowered to make more satisfying choices going forward. Just switching on a light can be tremendously validating and energizing!

This Book is For You!

Anyone Seeking Self-Understanding and Growth: This book offers tools and concepts for self-awareness, notably through the lens of personality type and subtype. Readers looking to delve deeper into their own nature, nurture, and inherent tendencies will find it valuable.

Career Professionals: Since there's a focus on aligning subtype with one's best-fit career path, this book benefits career counselors, recruiters, human resources professionals, and others who advise individuals on career paths and professional development.

Coaches and Consultants: There is specific advice for coaching the subtypes to help coaches and consultants to better understand their clients and offer more personalized advice, especially around topics like energy management and pursing hidden aspirations.

Psychologists and Therapists: Each type chapter covers cognitive processes, neuroses and similar elements that professionals in mental health and therapy will find useful, especially if they already integrate some personality type theory in their practice.

Students of Psychology and Personality: Those studying psychology, human behavior, and personality theory (formally or out of personal interest) will get their fill from the novel content and research presented.

Individuals Interested in Eastern Philosophy: Given the focus later in the book on yin and yang energies, those who appreciate or study Eastern philosophies will enjoy this holistic approach.

Business Leaders and Managers: Understanding the diverse personalities and subtypes of team members can help leaders to foster better communication, create more harmonious teams, and maximize productivity by aligning tasks with individuals' inherent strengths.

General Readers: Anyone curious about understanding human behavior, personal development, and the intricate dynamics of nature vs. nurture will find this accessible, research-based book enlightening.

A Metaphor for Change

People are living systems, not mechanical or abstractions. Thus, a smart metaphor to understand ourselves is nature. A tree is born and grows according to its genetics and environment, from soil to weather. It has metabolism, like what we call functions in personality type. It has a design, with branches, leaves, fruits, a trunk and roots that follow a sensible pattern. And it has a role (purpose) in the larger environment. A tree also adjusts through the passage of seasons. As you explore the subtypes in this book, you might think of them like the seasons, as places you can visit, with meaning, even if you have a favorite subtype right now.

What's at Stake?

Before you start, consider one big thing that's "at stake" in your life? It might be a relationship, career choice, or anything else that really matters and begs for action. As in, if you don't act, there will surely be problems, maybe big ones? Often, we don't want to think about these things because they evoke dread. But do your best to name one big thing:

Ideally, by the time you get to the final chapter, Fulfill Your Aspirations, you'll be on your way to addressing what's at stake.

Alchemical Magic

Dr. Jung intended his framework to act as a therapeutic and developmental tool. Imagine a well that you can keep returning to, in order to find refreshment and new insight time and again. We can ignore the well, and stay where we are, biased and stuck. Or we can recognize what is at stake and dare to make a change.

So, how can you grow? For one, you can review, reflect on, and discuss the framework: cognitive processes, types, subtypes, and so on. Secondly, every type chapter includes "reminders for growth". You can select some to act on. And third, the final four chapters, six through nine, include activities and advice.

Along the way, you can follow in Dr. Jung's footsteps with "alchemy". Jung observed a central challenge in every person, and in every society: bias. That is, we all become imbalanced, both in our practical affairs and internally, psychologically. To restore balance, he engaged his clients in practices that evoked strange images and feelings, what he called "material" from the unconscious. Then he helped the person express that material, to make something of it. In the act of doing so, the person transformed and balance was restored, eventually. Particularly in the final chapter, you will have opportunities to do this.

The Journey Ahead

Don't know the Myers-Briggs types at all? Uncertain of your type? Already feeling overwhelmed? Here are the key stops in this book.

Chap. 2: Personality Type Basics: Learn about the famous Dr. Carl Jung and his framework of 8 cognitive processes. These are the diverse ways we get information and make decisions, and are validated with over 130,000 people. The result is 16 personality types, from ESTJ to INFP. What are your likely favorite processes and type code?

Chap. 3: From 16 Types to 64 Subtypes: The story continues, based on demographics, brain data, and convergent research from around the world. Learn about four neuro-variants, where 16 types x 4 variants equals 64 subtypes. For every ESTJ or INFP, there is a Dominant, Creative, Normalizing and Harmonizing variant. These are flexible over time and reflect development. Your subtype may start to come into focus here.

Chap. 4: Subtypes in Action: Four Vignettes: Get a better feel for the subtypes through short stories about four people of the same type.

Chap. 5: The 64 Subtype Descriptions: Jump to your type, or explore any or all types. Look at each type from multiple angles: its favorite processes, conversations with people of that type, brain-based portraits of the subtypes, and ways the type shows up as neurotic, unbalanced, and secretly aspirational. There's also advice.

Chap. 6: Coaching the Subtypes: Now that you know your subtype, what's next? Maybe you are a coach, consultant or counselor. Or, maybe you just wish to make the most of where you are now. Reflect on the advice here and form an action plan. Includes body-mind exercises.

Chap. 7: Navigate Your Neurotic Boundary: Everyone gets into trouble, or even goes nuts, in a different and maybe dramatic way. Ironically, our neuroses—forever popping in and out of consciousness—are also our most fertile ground for continued growth.

Chap. 8: The Yin and Yang of Type: Personality is more than behavior. It's energy. What's your energy? Underlying every facet of personality is a subtle bias for *yang* or *yin* energy. Yang is focused, confident, and active. Yin is diffuse, accepting, and reflective. What is your mix of these two primal forces? And how might you rebalance them?

Chap. 9: Fulfill Your Aspirations: This is what we all hope for, a road map or suggestions to identify and get to our deepest aspirations. When we recognize the "inferior" side of our personality, and incorporate it into our career, hobbies, and relationships, we find the secret treasure that we didn't even know we valued.

Appendix: Cognitive Processes Assessment: Go here, or go online to www.keys2cognition.com, to complete a questionnaire to get your personality profile. How much do you use each of the 8 cognitive processes, and what is your likely type code?

2

Personality Basics

Making Sense of Our Diversity

Do you know anyone different from you? Well, of course. Or how about "very different"? You know, the person who shares observations or makes decisions in a way that easily amuses, annoys, awes, or perplexes you? Or maybe there's someone special who is "a sibling from another mother?" In the human kaleidoscope, there is great variation, and we can make sense of it to better help ourselves and others.

A century ago, the famous Swiss psychiatrist Dr. Carl Gustav Jung described in his popular book, *Psychological Types,* the various ways that people function. We possess within us a capacity for all of these ways. Yet like a preference for right- versus left-handedness, we develop preferences—what's automatic, our gifts, biases, blind-spots, and neuroses.

Preference, Bias, or One-Sidedness?

Please try the following exercise.

Sign your name here:

Now sign your name again using your other hand:

Notice how you can sign your name with both hands. However, using your preferred hand is easier, produces better results, and tends to be automatic. That's great. You've specialized and have a useful bias. And, if you decided to only use one hand for everything in life, that would be unfortunate and extremely one-sided. Similarly, in many other ways, you've learned to function mostly with useful biases but also likely with some limitations as well.

To see the big picture of how you work, let's go on a step-by-step tour from two hands to various mental functions to 16 types. Along the way, remember that this is a language that's meant to be useful. The language helps us notice and discuss kindly where we and others may be overly one-sided—and where growth is easiest—rather than to put people in boxes.

Let's Crack the 4-letter Code

One way to name our preferences uses the Myers-Briggs 4-letter code. The code looks like ESTJ, INFP, or such. In the code, the letters stand for preferences that work like handedness. The result is 16 personality options. Let's take a look.

1st letter: Where you find energy

   E—*Extraverting*: Initiate interactions and energized by collaborative activities.

   I—*Introverting*: Focus on inner life and energized by solitary activities.

2nd letter: How you take in information

   S—*Sensing*: Focus on what's tangible, known, concrete, practical for today, and fits experience.

   N—*iNtuiting*: Focus on abstractions, patterns, potential possibilities, imagination, and the future.

3rd letter: How you make decisions

   T—*Thinking*: Organize and decide based on objective impersonal criteria.

   F—*Feeling*: Organize and decide based on harmony, values, and beliefs.

4th letter: How you like to organize

   J—*Judging*: Plan ahead with a drive for completion and closure.

   P—*Perceiving*: Open and engaged with a drive for more input and flexibility.

Notice that the letters stand for verbs such as "E" for Extraverting and "S" for Sensing. A type is not just a collection of outward traits. It reflects an underlying pattern of functioning, or mental processing—how you prefer to metabolize experiences.

Many people know about the 16 types through this coding. However, the codes are pretty limited. They present a static picture. In contrast, the original thinker behind this framework, Dr. Carl Gustav Jung, intended a dynamic picture of human beings. To honor that aim, we need to go a step deeper.

Going Deeper With Functions

The story began with "E" and "I". Dr. Jung noticed early in his practice that his clients varied energetically along a spectrum from more extraverted (E) to more introverted (I). Soon, however, he found that this dimension by itself was too limited. He felt compelled to look deeper.

Next, Dr. Jung asked how people tend to operate. He observed that we rely on a mix of four mental functions, summarized below. These are the second and third letters of the 4-letter code. Everyone uses all of these in some way, but like handedness, we have preferences. What might yours be?

Two Open-Ended CEOs:
What's your bias when gathering information?

Sensing (S)	**Intuiting (N)**
Rely on the five senses first. Focus on concrete, tangible data and what is known, the present, and past experiences. Stay hands-on and act on practical options.	Rely on imagination first. Focus on concepts, patterns, what's hidden, symbols, metaphor, and the future. Ask "what if?" Follow potential possibilities.

Two Goal-Focused CEOs:
What's your bias when organizing and making decisions?

Thinking (T)	**Feeling (F)**
Rely on logic first. Decide and organize based on objective criteria, deduction, models, frameworks, measures, and impersonal, efficient principles.	Rely on values first. Decide and organize based on social and interpersonal appropriateness, beliefs, and the importance or worth of oneself and others.

For the sake of balance, each of us prefers two: either Sensing (S) or Intuiting (N) as our trusted "open-ended" CEO, and either Thinking (T) or Feeling (F) as our trusted "goal-focused" CEO. To paraphrase Isabel Briggs Myers, one hand (or function) is like an army's general and the other is like a faithful lieutenant.

For example: If you prefer Intuiting and Feeling, then you will likely develop those early, and trust and use them often. They are your favorites. Opposing these two are Sensing and Thinking. and like using your non-prefrred hand, you will surely encounter opportunities to use and develop the opposites. Dealing with your non-preferences is where anxiety, drama, dreams, allies, enemies, romance, failure, and growth come in. Maturing to use all four processes is a life-long process.

You may reflect on your preferences now, and you will have plenty of opportunities in the upcoming sections to clarify and go deeper.

The Story of "J" and "P"

Before we finish, you might wonder, what about "J" and "P" in the 4-letter code? Where do Judging and Perceiving fit? It's a bit tricky. This fourth letter was developed by Myers and Briggs as a short-cut, and it does correlate to some aspects of people's behavior. But we won't dwell on this letter going forward.

In a nutshell: If there is a "J" in the type code, it means the world sees the person's goal-focused CEO (Thinking or Feeling). Conversely, if there is a "P" in the code, the world sees the person's open-ended CEO (Sensing or Intuiting). That's all.

Scientific Validity

Jung's framework has been in use for a century, and the Myers-Briggs assessment is the most highly researched personality assessment in the world. In the late 1990s, it was redesigned in line with the "gold standard" of psychometric practices, and there are many millions of users and thousands of published articles, theses, and papers. It is not the favorite for everyone. Nor is it for all occasions. For example, it is not designed to predict performance in specific job roles. There are also related instruments such as the Cognitive Processes Assessment (www. keys2cognition.com) that are also heavily supported by large sample sizes (over 130,000 people) and significant results. That said, no assessment can deliver perfection. At best it provides a starting point only. Moreover, any framework, even one with 64 options, necessarily simplifies. Ultimately, only you can decide who and how you are.

Personality in Action

We can get a better understanding of our psychological preferences when we view them in action. Let's look at what's typical based on the two letters in the middle of the code: How we prefer to take in information (Sensing or Intuiting?) and how we prefer to make decisions (Thinking or Feeling?) The portraits below are based on decades of assessment research results and are not definitive. But they are a nice way to start going deeper.

Sensing-Feeling (SF) Preferences

People who favor Sensing and Feeling tend to be helpful, sympathetic, and friendly as they tackle life's many practical problems. With Sensing, they trust tangible data, particularly what they know first-hand, such as the signs others give off about their needs and emotions. With Feeling, they tend to set goals and make decisions based on their values, weighing what matters personally to themselves and for others.

Generally, whatever the situation, these people attend to concrete information about people, such as others' specific likes and dislikes, back-stories, and current life situations. They easily notice people's de facto behavior such as body language, attitude, and time spent helping. They tend to focus on how people interact with each other based on their roles, needs, and drives. For example, did someone lend an ear or hand in a time of need? Did someone put in extra hours at work or remember to give a nice holiday gift? And so forth. They are very realistic this way.

On the job, these individuals offer practical help and encourage an enjoyable atmosphere. They are often adept with customers in day-to-day operations and do their best to bring a happy smile. Except for the most introverted, they like teams or at least collaborating with or being inspired by someone. They seek others' input on problems. As leaders, they like to consult with the people involved, hear what's going on for them, their opinion, and then, ideally, engage in some kind of shared process to find and implement a solution. Career wise, they gravitate to social service, healthcare, craftwork, and the fine and performing arts, though they can work in any field. What's important is that their work has a human application and is not overly abstract or impersonal.

In relationships, people who prefer Sensing and Feeling want a down-to-earth, caring partnership. Ideally, each person constantly keeps in mind what the other prefers and needs and is readily available with concrete and heart-felt support. They like romantic gestures and can be highly passionate. When there is a problem, they like to talk it out, though they tend to gather advice from friends and family first. When under stress, especially when feeling impatient or unheard, they may engage in excessive theatrics and catastrophizing rather than painful self-analysis or thoughtful, forward-looking problem solving.

With strengths comes one-sidedness. These individuals tend to discount what they don't know personally, especially regarding future hypotheticals, and they may easily find themselves out of their element in unfamiliar and impersonal situations. Under stress, they can suddenly get cold and critical, contrary to their usual personal warmth, and they can get caught up in a really confused picture of others' intentions and behaviors, contrary to their usual perceptiveness.

At mid-life or earlier, these individuals experience a gentle push to develop Intuiting and Thinking. This can show up several ways, such as interest in technology, scientific research, spiritual practices, or business management. Ideally, the activity includes a practical human element. For example, an interest in media technology might be about visually telling real people's dramatic stories. An interest in research might be about gathering and analyzing data about human behavior. Or an interest in spirituality might involve teaching a body-mind practice like yoga. Whatever their path, they must often deal with obstacles to growth such as family obligations, questions of self-worth and capability, or a desire to simply enjoy life's comforts.

Sensing-Thinking (ST) Preferences

People who favor Sensing and Thinking tend to be realistic and matter-of-fact with a business-like approach to life's many practical challenges. With Sensing, they trust tangible data, particularly what they can observe and measure, from a car's idling sound to a company's bottom-line profit. With Thinking, they tend to logically assess the facts of a situation, reasoning from cause to effect, premise to conclusion, and relying on methods that are clear and relevant.

Generally, whatever the situation, these people are interested in concrete technical information, such as cost, weight, typical cycles, and performance metrics like number of customers. They tend to view people as another kind of resource, and they evaluate others based on their behavior and the results they produce, often weighing pros and cons. For example, even if a colleague is difficult to deal with sometimes, exceptional performance makes his or her presence manageable until the person shapes up or someone better fitting is found.

On the job, these individuals are data- and task-oriented. They collect and verify information, and then analyze it in an objective way to complete a task or solve a problem. For example, they will look for tables with numbers to inform decisions, they will trust their experience and observations over abstractions, and they limit risks to areas they know well. As leaders, they tend to apply incentives for people to modify their behavior to fit with the key principles and procedures. Career wise, they gravitate to banking, business, law, manufacturing, the military, land management, and anything hands-on and technical from car repair to surgery to software coding, though they can work in any field. What's important is that the work affords real-world problem-solving and tangible rewards.

In relationships, people who prefer Sensing and Thinking want a down-to-earth, respectful partnership. Together, the couple is doing fun activities, divvying up and carrying out responsibilities, and solving life's problems in a thoughtful way with minimal drama. When an interpersonal issue arises, they may endure it as they watch how it evolves and then get blunt about the need for improvement. Under stress, or when impatient and frustrated by others' repeated taxing behavior, they may deploy sarcasm, silence, or criticism rather than deal with emotional scrutiny or inner psychological change.

With strengths comes one-sidedness. These individuals tend to discount untried ideas with no clear reason for change, and they may easily be awkward in interpersonal situations that require finesse or psychological understanding. Under stress, they can suddenly come off as shifty or flustered, contrary to their usual straight-up demeanor, and they may deal inappropriately with complex human problems, from a particular leader's really questionable personal life to broad institutional biases.

At mid-life or earlier, these individuals experience a gentle push to develop Intuiting and Feeling. This can show up several ways, such as an interest in a humanitarian cause, cross-cultural appreciation, spiritual practice, or skills counseling. Ideally, the activity taps their nuts-and-bolts style. For example, a humanitarian cause might mean serving on a local council or helping youth stay out of trouble and graduate. An interest in spirituality might mean volunteering at or donating to a religious center or building a business around health retreats. Whatever their path, Sensing-Thinking types must often deal with obstacles to growth such as high costs versus unclear benefits, or simply being too busy.

Intuiting-Thinking (NT) Preferences

People who favor Intuiting and Thinking tend to be logical and ingenious, taking a scientific approach to life's big questions and pressing issues. With Intuiting, they notice abstract patterns, possibilities, and ideas. They absorb numerous philosophical frameworks and scientific concepts. With Thinking, they apply those models to come up with strategies to improve whatever they put their mind to.

Generally, whatever the situation, these people seek an abstract view of what's going on and why. They quickly notice patterns, which they can match with their mental models and theories. They likely have one or two primary interests plus a dozen side interests. Some of these usually relate to technology or the future, even if as a hobby, and hopefully, at least one will be how to effectively deal with others. For example, they might draw on Jungian psychological theory to understand people.

On the job, these individuals bring theoretical and technical understanding and, intended or not, tend to set an organization or discipline on a new path into the future. They seek a working knowledge of how things are organized. They prefer to study a problem in a non-personal way and come up with a strategy to address it long-term. As leaders, they can be visionary, though they may have difficulty with the practicalities and the human elements. They will often drive hard for quality, are open to quantitative data and calculated risks, and tend to tap survey feedback to get insights and outside consultants to promote organizational change. Career wise, they gravitate to science, technology, philosophy, and organizational strategy, though they can work in any field, or blend multiple fields. What's important is that the work galvanizes their minds to explore and master new ideas, to gain expertise.

In relationships, people who prefer Intuiting and Thinking want a stimulating partnership that's like a meeting of minds. They love discussing ideas, learning, and doing creative projects together. When an interpersonal issue arises, they may be oblivious to it, try to solve it logically, and/or seek expert help. When stressed, impatient or confused, they may deploy sarcasm, critiquing, and abstract theorizing rather than deal with emotions or pressing practical daily issues.

With strengths comes one-sidedness. These individuals tend to discount feedback that does not fit their mental model or strategy. Also, they may over-extend their expertise into an area they don't actually know. Under stress, they can suddenly get irrational, contrary to their usual clear thinking, and they can really lose touch with their practical needs, letting health and happiness slip away. When they miss others' humanity, they may be viewed as arrogant or devious.

At mid-life or earlier, these individuals experience a gentle push to develop Sensing and Feeling. This can show up several ways, such as enjoying nature, improving health and fitness, spending more time with family, developing an artistic or musical skill, or delving into psychology. Ideally, the activity taps their scientific mindset and need for life-long learning. For example, they might research and develop their own fitness strategy. Or, time with family might involve museum trips or anything else that is educational and somewhat challenging. Whatever their path, Intuiting-Thinking types must often deal with obstacles to growth such as their innate skepticism, a penchant for turning play into more work, or a sense they can grow simply by thinking about it.

Intuiting-Feeling (NF) Preferences

People who favor Intuiting and Feeling tend to be insightful and enthusiastic, taking a romantic approach to life's big questions and pressing issues. With Intuiting, they notice abstract patterns, possibilities, and ideas. They notice other's behavioral patterns and ways to catalyze growth. With Feeling, they remain in touch with their values and make choices that align with who they are at their core.

Generally, whatever the situation, these people attend to the complex web of human behavior, relationships, and society. They notice patterns, future potential, people's stories, new projects that motivate others to realize their potential, and ways to bring healing and important truths to light. They tend to perceive what's going on psychologically, such as seeing beyond the masks people wear, the scripts they repeat, and the roles they play to the underlying human being. This can be painful, joyful, inspiring, heart-breaking, and everything in between.

On the job, these individuals bring personal warmth and insight into people issues, and they often seek to make procedures and structures more human-centric. They soak up information about people, their values, and the organization, and prefer to use group- and people-oriented techniques to promote change. They tend to be good communicators of possibilities and values, and they rely on stories, metaphors, and imagery to make points. They may ignore numerical evidence, get preachy, talk "pie in the sky", or over-estimate their ability to implement plans. Career wise, they gravitate to counseling, human subject research, media, and the dramatic arts, though they can work in any field. What's important is that the work affords creativity and allows them to positively impact society.

In relationships, people who prefer Intuiting and Feeling want a stimulating partnership that's like being with one's soul mate. True love is like a fairytale story that sweeps them off of their feet, takes them on adventures, and allows them to live happily ever after. When problems arise, they may hold fast to the belief that love conquers all. When stressed—especially when feeling impatient, confused or unheard—they may engage in idle fantasizing rather than address their own deep needs, and may engage self-discovery activities (such as exploring their personality preferences!) over pressing practical daily problems.

With strengths comes one-sidedness. These individuals tend to discount feedback that does not fit their values. Similarly, they may ignore negative outcomes simply because they had good intentions. Under stress, they can suddenly start misreading people, contrary to their usual empathic insights, and they can lose touch with their practical needs such as health and finances. When they over-prioritize others, or put an abstract ideal before themselves, they can lose touch with their core.

At mid-life or earlier, these individuals experience a gentle push to develop Sensing and Thinking. This can up show up several ways, such as starting a business, learning a scientific or technical skill, or turning to a more objective philosophy of life. Ideally, the activity fits their focus on people and desire to improve the human condition. For example, they might earn a degree in medicine to help solve a personal or world health issue. Or they might start a business to personally get aligned with an important cause. Whatever their path, Intuiting-Feeling types must often deal with obstacles to growth such as their innate optimism, poorly thought out strategies, or a lack of inspiration or belief in themselves.

Please take a moment to reflect. Now that you've had a chance to learn how preferences play out in daily life, consider the people you know, and yourself of course. What are their needs, preferences, and behaviors? Very likely, you will know people across the board.

Explore the 16 Types

The upcoming 2-page spread provides a thematic snapshot of each of the 16 types. The columns are organized by the function pairs: first up are the 4 Sensing-Feeling types, then the 4 Sensing-Thinking types, and so on for 16 thematic snapshots total.

Take some time to explore the themes. You might find that the themes of a type adjacent to your own appeal to you in some ways. For example, you might relate to the ENFJ and ENFP snapshots. In that case, check against the type code. Do you have more of a Perceiving preference or more of a Judging preference? Or, you might be torn between ENTP and ENFP. You can sort by comparing the function-pairings (NT vs NF) in the prior section. Often, we relate to some of the themes encouraged strongly by our culture, gender roles, parental role-modeling, and career skills. What's important: Try to look at the whole picture.

After this, feel free to jump to the chapters for types you relate to most. Or, you can continue reading about the 8 cognitive processes and the story behind the 64 subtypes.

The 4 Sensing-Feeling (SF) Types

ESFJ - Facilitator Caretaker™
Extraverting • Sensing • Feeling • Judging
ESFJs easily accept and help others. They are often managing people. They hear out others, voice concerns, and accommodate needs. They easily keep in mind what's personally important, and they have a talent to provide what's needed. ESFJs admire others' success. They strive to keep things pleasant. They keep up a sense of continuity. They account for the human costs. They can surprise others, act as a rebel, or get inventive. They can easily feel let down by entrepreneurial projects.

ISFJ - Protector Supporter™
Introverting • Sensing • Feeling • Judging
ISFJs notice what's needed and valuable. They have a talent for arranging careful support. They enjoy their traditions and work to protect the future. They often listen closely to remember a lot of details. They tend to be agreeable. They are sensitive to the small things, with strong preferences. When appropriate, ISFJs like to volunteer. They like to feel a sense of accomplishment. They can get technical, knowing all of the ins and outs. They get frustrated when people ignore rules and don't get along.

ESFP - Motivator Presenter™
Extraverting • Sensing • Feeling • Perceiving
ESFPs are active and fun. They easily engage others. They have a sense of style and a talent to present things in a useful way. They look for ways to motivate and stimulate action, to take pleasure in life. They enjoy learning about people. ESFPs like their freedom and are open to taking risks. They are adaptable, charming, and enjoy opening others to what they can do. In their heart, they care deeply. Many kinds of tasks come naturally to them. Over-analyzing situations can trouble them.

ISFP - Composer Producer™
Introverting • Sensing • Feeling • Perceiving
ISFPs seek life's pulse to go with its flow. They are patient to take advantage of opportunities as they come up naturally. They stick with what's important, to be their true selves with their own personal style. They have a talent for pulling together what feels just right for an artistic impact. ISFPs attract others' loyalty and build relationships with care. They like to play against expectations and can get really creative at solving a problem. They struggle to nurture their self-esteem.

The 4 Sensing-Thinking (ST) Types

ESTJ - Implementor Supervisor™
Extraverting • Sensing • Thinking • Judging

ESTJs strive to bring order to chaotic situations. They have an industrious, hard-work attitude. They quickly educate themselves and connect the dots. When needed, they step up to supervise. They rely on a philosophy of life and seek the steps to success. ESTJs like to keep up traditions and reflect on life's wealth of experiences. They value being well balanced. To reveal a person's character, they can get sharp. They can feel let down when their standards for economy and quality are not met.

ISTJ - Planner Inspector™
Introverting • Sensing • Thinking • Judging

ISTJs like to be prepared and draw up plans. They take responsibility as best they can. They get work done first, are active in the community, and loyal to their roles. Doing the right thing is important to them. Everyday they strive to cultivate good habits. ISTJs bear life's burdens and cross bridges of adversity. They have a talent to plan, sequence, fill in details, and note what's missing. They have a sense of history and a subtle sense of humor. Learning so much in hindsight pains them at times.

ESTP - Promoter Executor™
Extraverting • Sensing • Thinking • Perceiving

ESTPs smoothly get on top of things. They are tactical and quickly play off of the relevant details. They set a priority while staying open to options. They enjoy exhilaration at the edge. They have a talent for negotiating and can win over people to get a lot done through others. ESTPs want a bottom-line measure of their success. They enjoy acting as a consultant. They have a deep, heart-felt care for their family and friends. They are disappointed when others don't show respect.

ISTP - Analyzer Operator™
Introverting • Sensing • Thinking • Perceiving

ISTPs are hands-on problem solvers. They closely observe how things work. They will carefully take apart or poke at something to understand it. They have a talent for using tools to take the best approach to a problem. ISTPs need to be independent to follow their own paths. They like to test, challenge, and push their own limits to find success. They act on their hunches or intuitions. Making and sharing their own discoveries is satisfying. Powerful emotional experiences can really unsettle them.

The 4 Intuiting-Thinking (NT) Types

ENTJ - Strategist Mobilizer™
Extraverting • iNtuiting • Thinking • Judging
ENTJs easily act as leaders with a vision. They bring in resources of all kinds and maximize talents to make the most progress. They can predict what's coming up in the big picture. They enjoy intuitive explorations and can buck convention. Where they can, ENTJs forge partnerships, mentor, and empower others. Often, they find they are running many projects. They know peace and conflict go together. They have a soft spot. They can get overwhelmed managing a lot of details of time and resources.

INTJ - Conceptualizer Director™
Introverting • iNtuiting • Thinking • Judging
INTJs are abstract, self-directed thinkers. They have a drive for self-mastery to make the most of what they can achieve. They have a talent to calculate far ahead and see deep reasons behind things. They think in terms of concepts, evidence, efficiency, systems, and strategies. INTJs build a vision and take steps to realize progress to their goals. They like to stay independent and be at the leading edge. Their secret is a creative intuition. They can find it hard to let go to interact freely with others.

ENTP - Explorer Inventor™
Extraverting • iNtuiting • Thinking • Perceiving
ENTPs are inventive and life-long learners. They explore lots of ideas. They have a talent to build prototypes and launch projects. They enjoy creative problem solving. They share their insights about life's possibilities. ENTPs are pragmatic as they come up with strategies for success. They enjoy the drama of give and take. They try to be diplomatic, invite others, and host. At some level, they need to feel safe. They are surprised when strategizing a relationship doesn't work.

INTP - Designer Theorizer™
Introverting • iNtuiting • Thinking • Perceiving
INTPs like to explore ideas to deepen their expertise. They notice new patterns and elegant connections. They easily cross boundaries of thought. They play with ideas and detach to analyze. They clarify, reference, and define. INTPs have a talent to design and redesign. They are open to try whatever starts up their imagination. They like to reflect on thinking. They hold to core principles and solid models. Making discoveries brings them joy. They struggle to attend to the physical world.

The 4 Intuiting-Feeling (NF) Types

ENFJ - Envisioner Mentor™

Extraverting • iNtuiting • Feeling • Judging

ENFJs like to communicate and share values. They set goals and seek shared success at relationships. They strive to realize dreams—their own and others. They look for ways to grow together. They heed the call to a life's work or mission. They have a talent for noticing potential in others. ENFJs enjoy being creative, using their intuitive intellect. They try to bridge the past and the future. When needed, they can get very precise or technical. They find it hard to live in the present moment, to feel at peace.

INFJ - Foreseer Developer™

Introverting • iNtuiting • Feeling • Judging

INFJs focus on personal growth. They have a talent for foreseeing. A flash of insight comes and they know what will happen. They can sustain a vision while honoring the gifts of others. They need a sense of purpose and take a creative approach to life. INFJs can get into exploring issues to bridge differences and connect people and ideas. They can get analytical when problem solving. Living an idealistic life often presents them with a great deal of stress and a need to withdraw.

ENFP - Discoverer Advocate™

Extraverting • iNtuiting • Feeling • Perceiving

ENFPs explore perceptions and try out stories. They often see what's hidden and voice what's really meant. They notice others' potential and like to inspire. They ask what-if and fly with creative new ideas. They want goodness and happiness. ENFPs strive to honestly believe in and live with themselves. They have a talent to bring about ideal or magical moments with someone. When needed, they can organize. They often feel restless with a hunger to discover their true direction.

INFP - Harmonizer Clarifier™

Introverting • iNtuiting • Feeling • Perceiving

INFPs need a quest or core meaning. Yet they go with the flow. They have a talent to listen in order to help, noticing what sits behind what is said. They explore moral questions. They enjoy uncovering mysteries. INFPs relate through stories and metaphors, and they have a way of knowing what is believable. They seek to balance opposites. To get to really know oneself again is a beautiful moment. They can manage others pretty well. They struggle with structure and getting their lives in order.

Under the Hood: 8 Cognitive Processes

Dr. Jung took one more step to better describe his clients. He noticed that each of the four functions is used in an extraverted or introverted way, for a total of eight "psychological types" (aka cognitive processes). These are eight ways that people metabolize their experiences as they go through life.

In theory, we might develop and deploy all eight in some optimized way; but in practice, this is not the case. As we learned about handedness and the 4 functions, as we grow up, we necessarily use—develop and prefer—some of these cognitive processes over others.

What are the eight cognitive processes? Let's keep it brief for now. Jung noticed that people have a bias (stronger or weaker) for extraverting or introverting. Roughly, this means being more energized by interacting with people and activities out in the world or by our own company and solitary activities in our inner world. Secondly, he noticed that people gather information (perceive) and make decisions (judge), and they do so in four ways total. They may perceive by Sensing (S) or Intuiting (N), and they may judge by Thinking (T) or Feeling (F). The result is eight "types" or cognitive processes as summarized at right.

Each process gets a code and a name. For example, Thinking in an extraverted way is coded as "Te" and called "Timely Builder", while Sensing in an introverted way is coded as "Si" and called "Cautious Protector". You will see the names with the codes throughout the book. You don't need to memorize the names. They are merely guides to give a feel beyond codes.

The processes are organized into two tables because everyone has two favorite processes, just as they have two hands and two main executive centers in the brain. You will have one favorite from each set.

Now, explore the opposite page, working through the two tables any way you like. You can read and rank each of the four options (1st, 2nd, 3rd, and 4th) with 1st as "most like you" and 4th as "least like you". Or, distribute 10 points among the 4 options in each table to help you decide. You can take the free assessment at www.keys2cognition.com as well, or take a similar pencil-paper questionnaire at the back of this book (page 383). You can read through the chapters ahead to see what resonates. Ideally, take the official MBTI® or a similar assessment and meet face-to-face with a professional profiler.

Summary of the 8 Processes

OPEN-ENDED CEOs: Four ways we gather information and otherwise function in an open-ended way.

"Active Adapting" (Se)
Enjoy the external world using your five senses and take concrete actions based on options before you.

"Cautious Protecting" (Si)
Reference a massive storehouse of rich past experiences as you cultivate familiarity, comfort, and stability.

"Excited Brainstorming" (Ne)
Perceive, pursue, and play with life's many potential possibilities, facilitating the promising ones.

"Keen Foreseeing" (Ni)
Focus on a vision of the future, and on insights and realizations from the inner hidden world of the unconscious.

GOAL-FOCUSED CEOs: Four ways we organize, decide, and otherwise function in a goal-focused way.

"Timely Building" (Te)
Utilize measurable data, tools, resources, and efficient procedures as you organize and make effective decisions.

"Skillful Sleuthing" (Ti)
Analyze and define situations, solve problems, and apply leverage according to universal logical principles.

"Friendly Hosting" (Fe)
Tend relationships, social norms, and people's needs and values as you organize and make thoughtful decisions.

"Quiet Crusading" (Fi)
Listen to your feelings, convictions, and conscience to make choices that align with your identity and beliefs.

Overcoming One-Sidedness

It's great to know and build upon our strengths, and there is more to the story. Your "type" is more than a list of favorite processes. It is the pattern of all the processes together, including your weaknesses.

Dr. Jung's focus on therapy: Helping people overcome biases—useful and inevitable though they may be—in order to grow. A big part of this is observing the opposite of our preferences and finding ways to expose, develop, and integrate them before one-sidedness causes trouble. Here are common examples of when we overdo a function:

Sensing (S)	Intuiting (N)
Materialistic, literal-minded, missing the big picture	Ungrounded, overly abstract, pie in the sky
Thinking (T)	**Feeling (F)**
Critical, stiff and robotic, inhumane	Melodramatic, hopelessly idealistic, needy

In practice, imbalance shows itself in many ways. It might be brief, such as a terrible dream. Or we might shift to an ugly, immature use of our opposite. For example, when a Feeling person gets stressed and one-sided, then Thinking is neglected and erupts in troubling ways. That person is normally quite friendly, then gets overly dramatic, and then is suddenly highly critical. Or imbalance may drag on subtly for a long time. For example, an artist has talent but procrastinates taking steps to success. Or, a tycoon builds a huge business but is cruel with his family. With bias, we can get "beside ourselves" or fall "in the grip" of something unpleasant.

When an imbalance becomes too much—when our heroic side fails us or our inferior side erupts like a fussy toddler, we have a chance and a choice to make a change in our lives. And we do this by bringing opposites together. Dr. Jung called this *alchemy*. He found ways to restore balance to the psyche. Such therapy also balances people's practical affairs and relationships, and improves their life story. As you go through the book, you will find many examples of alchemy in action, namely about the "neurotic zone", energy management, and secret aspirations.

3

The Journey: From 16 Types to 64 Subtypes

The Journey to Subtypes

What are the subtypes? And why use a subtype lens anyway? It has been a bit of a journey to get here. Let's talk about it.

Whether or not you know the 16 types well, you might feel that 16 is ample. It's already a big step up from Jung's initial observation of four mental functions. Yet, when it comes to practical applications, there are many benefits. Whether doing career counseling, bridging cultural differences, or just puzzling out someone's best-fit type, the subtypes are an easy way to name and work with the wide variety around us.

The story begins decades ago. For a long time, practitioners and enthusiasts in the Myers-Briggs community have informally recognized that people of the same type differ. "Every ENFP," as the pithy quote starts, "is like all other ENFPs, like some other ENFPs, and like no other ENFP." This quote acknowledges that every person is unique.

Now, how can we best understand differences? Let's remember that type is a developmental model. So the question becomes, how can we talk about development in an easy and consistent way?

Two Sides: Nature and Nurture

Years ago in my lab, two students both picked INTP preferences. When this came to light, they looked curiously at each other. One student was more verbal, critical, and confident. Let's call that an *analytic* or *yang* style. The other student was more quiet, demure, and hesitant. Let's call that a *holistic* or *yin* style. After they looked into type more carefully, they still identified as INTPs. Really? They were quite different in style, and despite sharing the same 4-letter code, they did not even seem to get along well. And among the other fifteen types around them, they likely found easy allies in different quarters too. What explains this?

Both nature and nurture influence personality. Specifically, we know from the Minnesota study of identical twins raised apart that genetics accounts for 40% to 60% of Myers-Briggs type preferences. Which means career, culture, gender, physiology, and so on are the other half. What can we say about all of these other factors?

One option might be MBTI Step II®, a questionnaire that allows us to describe individuals in terms of specific traits such as being more or less critical or gregarious or such, with 20 traits total. Step II can easily show how three ENFPs vary a little or a lot. It helpfully reminds us that people of the same type vary meaningfully. But it is not a developmental framework. It's merely traits. Moreover, a set of 20 traits is a lot of detail to remember and too much to convey quickly to anyone else.

Three-Plus Calls for Subtypes

Why have specific subtypes? Let's look at three practical reasons.

First, we can better help people find their best-fit type. For example, a person may be struggling between INFJ and INTJ or between INTJ and ISTP. Typically, the options vary by just one or maybe two letters, and practitioners see certain "lookalikes" quite often over others.

Imagine a boxing ring with its four corners. In one corner are INFJs who are more gregarious and look like ENFJs. Likely, they hold a leadership position. In another corner are INFJs who look a bit like INFPs or even ISFPs. Chances are, they are in the arts or work one-on-one with others. Then there are INFJs in a third corner who look like INTJs. They are likely in a technical or academic job. Fourthly, there are those IN-FJs who look like ISFJs. Typically, they work in more conventional jobs, such as teacher, nurse, or clerk. In the center of the arena is the classic INFJ stereotype.

Whichever types a person is debating, the options often make sense in a vague way based on background, career choice, and such. And since there are concrete links to their lives, there are concrete applications as well, such as advising what professional change might suit someone.

Recently, more organizations and individuals have been asking, "Is it possible for us to get more than 16 types?" That's a practical question: Can we deliver reports to people with more specificity, yet also keep it all simple? We might also wonder, can't we get more detailed in this era of computers and AI? That's a fair question. There's a tremendous amount of personal choice today. Perhaps the notion of "just" 16 types is a little bit too 20th century?

Certainly, subtypes can have a big impact. Imagine dealing with a team of individuals who are homogeneous in terms of their type preferences. Perhaps among a team of 10, five have ISTJ preferences—it happens! Among those five, there are surely meaningful differences. Isn't there a way to describe those variations simply and helpfully?

Finally, culture makes an impact. For anyone who does cross-cultural work, or tries to profile others' types in a foreign country, working with subtypes can help us better understand differences. In a more collectivist society, for example, people may relate more to a quieter, more conforming version of their type compared to people in a more individualistic society. If we don't think this way, we risk, for example, typing everyone as an introvert in a country like Japan simply because the baseline of what's considered normal differs from the standard USA Myers-Briggs conception.

Along this line, there's an Eastern European version of the 16 types: Socionics. In many cases, Socionics descriptions of the 16 types match the Myers-Briggs descriptions. However, in other cases, they don't. For example, the Socionics ISFP does not sound much like the Myers-Briggs ISFP. Is the difference really due to some tragic, unbridgeable difference in theory, or is it due to culture differences in how people process events? Or is it something else? It turns out that using a subtypes lens can explain the differences in a friendly, simple, and multicultural way.

What is a Subtype?

Briefly, let's talk about our language. Is "subtype" the best term to use? Why not say variant, facet, lifestyle, or perhaps even edge?

To be frank, the term "variant" is likely the more accurate term. Why? Our foundation is still 16 types, and within each type, there are certain developmental expressions, specific and predictable variations that capture the diverse effects of age, culture, career, education, physiology, gender, and other variables. Whatever the roots of development, we're talking about a variation on an underlying pattern. Thus, the term "variant". That said, unfortunately, this term also conjures other associations for many people. And, while the term "subtype" may suggest a box, the term is easy to grasp. So we mostly use the word subtype here.

Four Inspirations Converge

There are four inspirations for the subtypes. Let's take a look.

The first inspiration is the work of Dr. Victor Gulenko in Ukraine. He comes from the Socionics tradition, is well-aware of the differences between Myers-Briggs and Socionics, and has observed four variations within each type. Long story short, Dr. Gulenko figured out a trick—subtypes—to reconcile the systems. By this trick, for example, one variation of ISFP aligns with Myers-Briggs while another variation aligns with Socionics. Based on his expertise and years of experience, Dr. Gulenko penned 64 descriptions. They differ somewhat from the brain-based descriptions here. But the two are close enough that, with his permission, this book uses his terms.

A second inspiration is Dr. Helen Fisher's work. She does not use the Myers-Briggs framework; rather, she focuses on neurotransmitters. From her data, she discovered four personality types based on behavioral traits and relative hormone levels. We might be tempted to match her types to the Jungian functions or such, but they seem to match best with the subtypes that Dr. Victor Gulenko has described, and that also come out of brain-imaging data.

The third inspiration is the work of Dr. Richard Nisbett, who has focused on cultural differences, and on the work of Dr. Zhihan Cui in China. Dr. Nisbett has not looked at the 16 types, but Dr. Cui has. The differences they describe in terms of cognition across cultures, namely the USA and China, and the biases that people show in mental processing, are strikingly similar to the brain imaging results, and to what Drs. Victor Gulenko and Helen Fisher have found.

Finally, there is my own own neuroscience research. Along with a type code, we can look at demographic differences such as career, sex, ethnicity, and age. The journey started by analyzing the brain-wiring patterns among one type (ENFP), and in looking at all types, it turns out that sorting into four career choices draws consistent, interesting results.

The subtype profiles on the right bring together these various inspirations. Take a look before we head into the second half of the story.

Dominant* (D)

Has an assertive style. Is driven, goal-focused, and confident. Often in a leader or entrepreneur role, or climbing to that. Well-suited to hierarchy and dealing with known tasks and set leaders, and can work independently if needed. Tends to focus on outcomes, is competitive, and knows and plays by the rules of the game. Whether male or female, there is a feeling of a lot of testosterone. May act too quickly or cause damage, and can benefit from being more open-ended and reflective. Brain wiring is densest toward the front and/or in the left hemisphere.

Creative* (C)

Has an enthusiastic style, bringing new ideas and spurring interactions and connections. Is eager to make an impact in a fun or novel way. Often an innovator or trend setter. Enjoys travel whenever possible. Tends to come off as eccentric with diverse interests and tangential responses. Dopamine is the key hormone here—the rush of excitement is the reward. May easily get off task or push the impossible, and can benefit by adhering to some norms. Brain wiring is either a "whole brainstorm" pattern or a set of non-overlapping complex networks.

Normalizing* (N)

Has a linear style. Works in a careful, thorough, detailed way that tends to ensure a particular value or outcome. In organizations, often fills a low-level or specialist role, or at a higher level is striving to make a particular practice the norm. Otherwise, fairly balanced and sociable. Serotonin is the key hormone here. May act too slowly or be stuck in particular ways of behaving. Brain wiring is often distributed evenly over the cortex like a checkered farm field, with maybe one or two dense hubs reflecting specialization. Or has a clear back or left bias.

Harmonizing* (H)

Has a relational, egalitarian style that attends to body language, voice, symbols, emotions, and values. May rely on imagination to fill in gaps and make powerful inferences. Often fills a human relations or social support role such as a psychologist. Tends to be cooperative in a one-on-one way, working with others in their context and capabilities. Whether male or female, there is a feeling of a lot of estrogen. May act too softly or have difficulty pushing or being heard. Brain wiring is densest toward the back and/or in the right hemisphere, or shows diamond patterns.

* Names used with permission from Dr. Victor Gulenko.

Brain Basics

Your brain consists of many small modules, linked in networks. While the brain is very complex, we can look at it, and understand its activity, its modules and networks, in a broad way.

At a basic level, modules assist us to do specific tasks. Some tasks are concrete such as recognizing faces, hearing voice tone, and moving a hand. Other tasks are abstract such as evaluating ethics, adjusting to others' feedback, and mentally rehearsing a future action. There are easily five dozen modules just in the neocortex, which is the brain's outermost, thick layer and seat of educated awareness. The big figure on the next page is a bird's eye view of the neocortex (with ears at the sides and a triangular nose at the top). It highlights key modules. Take a look.

We each prefer some modules over others. We differ by the tasks we enjoy and how well we do them. Similarly, for each of us, modules activate with a different degree of stimulus, competence, motivation, and energy level. Figures 1 and 2 compare the average brain activity of two people over several hours. The figures are almost opposites! Those people's behaviors and self-experience differ greatly too. If you wish, feel free to explore the big figure and circle ten tasks that you enjoy or excel in. In particular, what skills do you use when most creative and productive?

There are whole-brain patterns. For example, the solid blue map in Figure 3 correlates with a state of "flow" where all modules are in sync. There are more patterns, and we are pretty diverse. Situations may prompt everyone's brain differently. Take a moment to reflect, when do you get into "flow", into your high-performance "zone"?

Figure 4 shows an example of brain regions linked together. It's merely one example of one person's brain. Wiring varies greatly from one person to the next, and the wiring results from our habits, and reflects our developed self, how we've come to meet our practical and psychological needs.

To meet our needs, the brain's elements work in concert. As an analogy, if a module is a musical instrument, then the brain is a symphony orchestra that affords complex performances. The coming pages describe typical patterns and their meanings relevant to the subtypes.

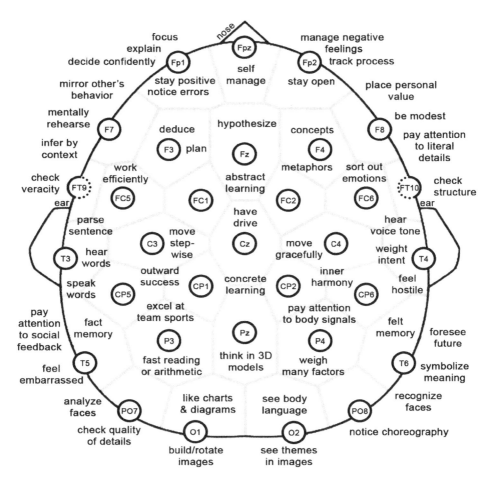

The Big Brain: The map above is a bird's eye view of the neocortex, divvied up into 32 regions with examples of functions. The regions correspond to EEG (electroencephalogram sensors). The map is based on commonly known neuroscience data and hands-on research since 2006. Below are examples of the same map, but showing differences among individuals (Figures 1 and 2), flow (Figure 3), and brain wiring—how various regions fire in sync to work with each other together (Figure 4).

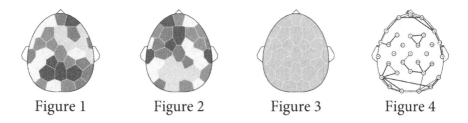

Figure 1   Figure 2   Figure 3   Figure 4

Decoding the Brain Lingo

The subtype profiles are based on brain imaging; fortunately, you don't need to know neuroscience to understand the profiles. Instead, you will notice general references such as, "...more of a left brain bias, indicating analytical skills." That is, brain references are briefly explained. If you are curious, you can use the brain map and the reference sheet below to better understand what's meant. Here are common terms:

Executive skill refers to pre-frontal cortex EEG regions Fp1 and Fp2 while managerial skills refer to strongly linked frontal regions F7-F8. Multiple strong links between Fp1, Fp2, F7, F7, F3 and F4 are hallmarks of a front-brain bias.

For other regions, auditory skills like speaking and listening to refer to EEG regions T3 and T4, while language-based reasoning refers to regions F3, Fz, and F4. Contemplative and reflective thinking involving factual and narrative memory refer to a strong T5-T6 link.

Visual regions refer to regions O1 and O2, but also include links from there to T5, T6, P3, Pz, and P4. Many of these links indicate a back-brain bias. Strong visual-spatial reasoning often means strong P3-Pz-P4 links. A person may be strong there without an overall back-brain bias.

Body or kinesthetic skills, including action and mental routines, refer to regions C3, Cz and C4.

Left bias and right bias refer to the left and right hemispheres, respectively. The left hemisphere is home to more analytical, linear and rule-based skills, including understanding words. In contrast, the right hemisphere is home to more holistic, emotional, and spatial understanding. Each hemisphere is also home to a region that complements the rest of it.

Regarding whole-brain patterns, a starburst refers to all EEG regions firing in sync, which means all 16, 20 or 32 sensor areas, depending on the equipment used.

In contrast, a diamond-shaped network refers to 3+ regions, at least one of which is in a different hemisphere, that fire together. These patterns mix analytic ("left brain") and holistic ("right brain") skills. A zig-zag looks like a diamond but the regions only fire in pairs; thus, it is more linear and less sophisticated thinking.

Finally, an even-field refers to regions linking in squares only to their neighbors in a linear, step-by-step way.

More Analytic vs. More Holistic

There are clear patterns in the brain-imaging data. For example, among individuals with ENFP preferences, we can sort them into two subgroups based upon career, sex, culture, background, age, or so forth. Here are side-by-side figures of ENFP brains sorted into two career areas.

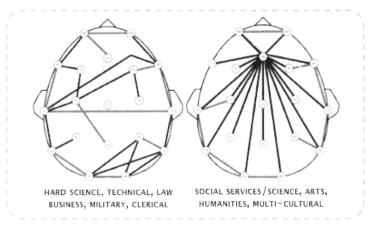

HARD SCIENCE, TECHNICAL, LAW
BUSINESS, MILITARY, CLERICAL

SOCIAL SERVICES/SCIENCE, ARTS,
HUMANITIES, MULTI-CULTURAL

Let's compare. On the left are ENFPs who reported a career in the hard sciences, engineering, business, law, the military, and trade professions. Let's call those individuals more *analytic* or *yang* in style. In contrast, on the right are ENFPs who reported careers as coaches, counselors, psychologists, individuals in the soft sciences, the arts and humanities, or in some kind of relational role or cross-cultural discipline. Let's call those individuals more *holistic* or *yin* in style.

Now, compare the lines in the diagrams, the brain wiring. We see on the right, for example, a strong black starburst pattern that spans across the brain. This is a stylized way to indicate that all of the regions frequently light up and work together simultaneously. In contrast, the ENFPs on the left show a starburst pattern but it's in gray in the background. It's not as strong. In terms of the other colors, normally shown as red, grey and yellow lines, they are similar but vary in strength.

What does this mean? Elements that are in the background on the right are in the foreground on the left. And vice versa. Overall, ENFPs as a whole show a particular pattern, and subtype reflects a bias: What's in the foreground (a top priority) for one subtype is in the backgroun (a secondary priority) for the other subtype. And vice versa.

From Two to Four Variants

Why stop at two variants? With over 600 people in the database, there is sufficient data to go to four. Though there are perhaps two-dozen notable variations in brain wiring, we can sort every person into one of four variants or subtypes. Using Dr. Victor Gulenko's terms, let's call those Dominant, Creative, Normalizing, and Harmonizing.

The matrix below briefly summarizes the four variants with visual examples for ENFPs. The other types vary similarly with their own details.

Dominant	Creative
More confident and driven.	More exploratory and sociable.
More often in leader roles.	More often in rebel roles.
Brain: strong front bias	*Brain*: whole-brain starburst
Normalizing	**Harmonizing**
More conventional and dedicated.	More empathic and reflective.
More often in support roles.	More often in relater roles.
Brain: even-field and back bias	*Brain*: diamond networks

These four link to more than our career choice. Really, they link to the kind of social structure we engage with each day. That includes our roles, how we relate to others and society, and the size of the organizations that we work in. Consider the implications. If you go work in a large company for a number of years, that will likely reshape your brain to be more Normalizing. Your brain will be pushed and honed in a different way than if you are, say, an independent consultant or if you work intimately one-on-one with people. It's all about your daily activities.

The Hidden Link to Berens' Interaction Styles

You might be familiar with Dr. Linda Berens' Interaction Styles model. Dr. Berens describes four styles that occur within each of the four Keirseyian temperaments, for 16 combinations total (the 16 types). She describes In Charge, Get Things Going, Chart the Course, and Behind the Scenes. For example, there are In Charge Improvisers (ESTPs), Get Things Going Improvisers (ESFPs), and so on. The four subtypes presented here look and feel like Dr. Berens' four interaction styles, but they address something different. Berens' interaction styles are essential to each type. In other words, all ESTPs have the In-Charge style. But among those, some are Dominant In Charge, others are Normalizing In Charge, yet others are Creative In Charge, and finally some are Harmonizing In Charge. In short, Berens' interaction styles are intrinsic to the types, whereas the subtypes are developmental.

What about cross-cultural differences, age, romantic relationships, and so forth? In some cases, such as biological sex and gender, there are correlations but mainly for younger people, so it's best to focus on the subtypes themselves, and not make any strong assertions or assumptions. In other cases, there are trends, such as people in the same organization or close friendship circle having similar brain wiring, regardless of their career activities. It's as if the people we spend time with shape who we are—pick your colleagues and friends wisely! Statistically speaking, at least from the data so far, some brain-wiring patterns, and thus subtypes, are more common than others by cultural region. For example, psychologists in Europe tend to differ, statistically, from their counterparts in the USA. However, it is best to approach every person uniquely in the spirit of cognitive and developmental diversity.

What's your likely subtype?

Over the next 4 pages, read and check the lists.
1. Try to set aside what you know about yourself, particular from a model like the 16 types.
2. Focus on what you do in your career and on your overall energy and activities.
3. Some things like brain-wiring, you may not know, and in some cases, others' feedback can be useful.

Dominant Subtypes

Here are typical Dominant traits including strengths, weaknesses, and interpersonal dynamics. Feel free to check what fits.

☐More assertive, confident, driven, goal-focused.

☐Often in a manager, leadership or "alpha" role, or climbing up toward such a role, or work independently such as a corporate consultant or entrepreneur to maintain personal freedom.

☐Have adopted a more "in charge" style.

☐Relatively more testosterone (cf. Dr. Helen Fisher). Act more as leaders, territorial and aggressive, thrive on competition, are direct and okay with confrontation, and like to win. Can be dogmatic. May come off as calculating or pushy.

☐Strive for territory, social status, control, power, might / conquest, being right, and influence over others.

☐Are well-suited to hierarchy, and power structures in general, and dealing with ambitious, big tasks and set leaders. Like opportunities to move upward.

☐Tend to focus on outcomes, are competitive, and know and play along with the rules of the game, while open to taking advantage of loopholes, others' missteps, and similar opportunities.

☐Brain wiring: Front-of-brain bias, and often with some analytical left brain bias as well. Quick to respond to input based on pre-worked out ways of responding. Often have a strong "managerial" link—they can quickly balance the current context against a set of constant principles. And they often sport good language-based reasoning—deduction, linear planning, concepts/categories, and/or metaphor.

☐Often skilled at physical activities, especially those requiring strength, confidence, and competition.

☐Quickly bounce back from injury and difficulties, and can easily ignore most criticism and failure.

☐May act too quickly or cause damage, be crude or demanding, or have a biting humor. Benefit from being more open-ended, open-minded, and reflective, asking questions to connect with others.

☐Often find themselves drawn to individuals with the Harmonizing style, and in general attracts others' interest. Often take advantage of or utilize the skills of people with the Normalizing style. Inspired or confused by people with the Creative style.

Creative Subtypes

Here are typical Creative traits including strengths, weaknesses, and interpersonal dynamics. Feel free to check what fits.

☐More curious, exploratory, open-minded, and sociable.

☐Often in a creative role, whether that's idea generation, or more concrete such as art or music performance. Often good with small to medium-sized groups (e.g. classroom teacher).

☐Have adopted a more "get things going" style.

☐Relatively more dopamine (cf. Dr. Helen Fisher). More travelers and risk-takers, need lots of stimulation, are reward and pleasure seeking, interested in novelty and change, and like many different topics. May come off as disruptive or rebellious.

☐Strive for enjoyment, self-expression, the "rush", social influence, stimulus, adventure, discovery, invention, and innovation.

☐Have an enthusiastic style, bringing new ideas and spurring interactions and connections. Are eager to make an impact in a fun or novel way. Often innovators or trend setters.

☐Enjoy travel whenever possible. Tend to come off as eccentric with diverse interests and tangential responses.

☐Brain wiring: A starburst pattern. This is when all (or most) regions of the brain fire simultaneously in response to stimuli, whether like a flashing Christmas tree or in a more Zen-like synced way. As part of this—or alternatively—may show a right hemisphere bias. Often have just enough executive coordination and conventional or analytical skills to get by.

☐Often skilled at artistic pursuits and dabble in many different areas, especially in whatever is unusual or promises a high payoff.

☐Quickly digest new material. At their best, are inventive and future-oriented rather than focused on pleasures for their own sake.

☐May easily get off task, get into trouble, fail to follow through, fall into addictive behaviors, or fall short of conventional standards of acceptance. Benefit by adhering to some norms, clarifying goals, prioritizing, and raising standards.

☐Often find themselves in conflict with or repelled by individuals with the Normalizing style. Can often fit in with, yet feel inhibited by, people with the Harmonizing style. Can benefit from those with the Dominant style but dislike being pushed or controlled.

Normalizing Subtypes

Here are typical Normalizing traits including strengths, weaknesses, and interpersonal dynamics. Feel free to check what fits.

☐More conventional, methodical, prudent, and compartmentalized.

☐Often in a support role or aiming to implement something as a norm for a group or society. Comfortable in large, conventional institutions where they give and receive wide support.

☐Have adopted a more "chart the course" style.

☐Relatively more serotonin (cf. Dr. Helen Fisher). This helps a person feel comfortable with a group. Are pro-social and concerned with fairness, reciprocity, and others' outcomes. Care to contribute. Averse to harm. Can come off as slow or overly collectivist.

☐Strive for job and home security, material possessions, wealth, social status, and service for others.

☐Have a linear style, and work in a careful, thorough, detailed way that tends to ensure a particular value or outcome.

☐In organizations, often fill a low-level or specialist role; or at a higher level, strive to make a particular practice the norm. Generally, fairly balanced and sociable, at least in customary ways.

☐Brain wiring: Often show a farm-field or grid like pattern where every brain region is linearly linked one-on-one to adjacent neighboring region. This encourages step-by-step thinking. Also, tend to be more left hemisphere (analytical), mid-brain, and more back of the brain (contemplative), but not always. May sport one or two central "hubs" that reflect their specialized day-to-day roles.

☐Among the subtypes, are the most comfortable with conventional everyday social, cultural, and physical activities.

☐Can be uncertain or insecure without group approval or support.

☐May act too slowly or be stuck in particular routine or bad habit. Can take excessive pride in their social status and accomplishments. Benefit from travel, experiencing new cultures, stretching into new roles, and changing their routine.

☐Easily find themselves intrigued but frustrated by individuals with the Creative style. Can fall under the sway of people with the Dominant style, and then feel unappreciated or over-worked. Can benefit from those with the Harmonizing style but are not well-equipped for constant interpersonal contact and reflection.

Harmonizing Subtypes

Here are typical Harmonizing traits including strengths, weaknesses, and interpersonal dynamics. Feel free to check what fits.

☐More empathic, integrative, reflective, and sophisticated.

☐Often in a highly personal role. Good working one-on-one in a personal way such as a therapist or a close adviser. Come to rely on a specialized set of contemplative and helping skills.

☐Have adopted a more "behind the scenes" style.

☐Relatively more estrogen and oxytocin (cf. Dr. Helen Fisher). Thie latter hormone is activated by physical touch for nurturing and pair bonding. Thus, feel closely and warmly connected to a few individuals. Can come off as passive or needy.

☐Strive for contemplation, deep caring, one-on-one connection, healing, inclusion, and personal growth.

☐Have a relational, egalitarian style that attends to body language, voice, symbols, emotions, and values. May rely on imagination to fill in gaps and make powerful inferences.

☐In organizations, often fill a human relations or social support role such as a liaison or customer relations specialist.

☐Tend to be private yet cooperative, easily adjusting to others' needs. Can get on with people from all walks of life, even across cultures.

☐Brain wiring: Often show one or more complex diamond patterns. A diamond is a network that links back and front, left and right sides of the brain, for sophisticated thinking. Alternatively, show zigzag patterns that connect brain regions in unusual ways, giving an odd or intuitive feel. Can be more right hemisphere (holistic) and back of brain (contemplative), but not necessarily.

☐Outside of their familiar environments and ways of doing things, may come off as odd, detached, excessively concerned, or passive.

☐May act too softly, have difficulty standing up for themselves, or being seen or heard. May feel shy, and show odd or limited eye contact with unfamiliar people and situations. Benefit from finding their core, energy and confidence to lean into jobs and step into their power.

☐Easily find themselves drawn to, or repulsed by, individuals with the Dominant style. Can fit in with—yet feel suffocated by— people with the Normalizing style. Can apply and add nuance and quality to the output of people with the Creative style.

Rank Your Results

Now that you've explored the 4 subtype lists, you are invited to complete the matrix below. For each subtype, you may count the number of checkmarks from each list and write the totals into the boxes. The box with the highest score is the first best guess regarding your subtype.

Dominant
More assertive, confident, driven, and goal-focused.

Creative
More curious, exploratory, open-minded, and sociable.

Normalizing
More conventional, methodical, prudent, and compartmented.

Harmonizing
More empathic, integrative, reflective, and sophisticated.

Remember that people come in infinite variety, and the 64 subtypes are simply a way to get a handle on all of that. A subtype represents the fruits of development over a life. It *compresses* many variables such as cultural background and job roles into a single picture. Even when you read in depth about the 4 subtypes for each Myers-Briggs type, you still need to "unpack" those portraits. Also keep in mind, although the protraits are based on brain-imaging, hormone levels, and such, we could arrive at many more "subtypes". Finally, subtype can shift, and thus a great alternate term to use is *variant*.

What Now?

You've learned about the subtypes and can:
1. Read 4 vignettes illustrating how the subtypes play out in everyday life for a sample type (ISFP).
2. Read the chapter for your personality type, such as INFP or ESTJ, to explore your likely subtype.
3. Explore several chapters to help narrow down your likely type and subtype.

4

Subtypes in Action: Four Vignettes

The Subtypes In Action

Spotting personality is not necessarily easy, especially as we go from 16 types to 64 finely-shaded subtypes. Here is your chance to experience the subtypes in a narrative way. You will find four vignettes that illustrate how differences play out among one type: ISFP. These vignettes all follow the characters over a single day.

All four characters share ISFP preferences and central themes. They favor Introverting to recharge and do their best work, gather information to stay grounded using Sensing, make decisions that foremost align with their convictions using Feeling, and stay open-ended using Perceiving. They also share the type's core themes:

Core ISFP Themes

ISFPs seek life's pulse to go with its flow. They are patient to take advantage of opportunities as they come up naturally. They stick with what's important, to be their true selves with their own personal style. They have a talent for pulling together what feels just right for an artistic impact. ISFPs attract others' loyalty and build relationships with care. They like to play against expectations and can get really creative at solving a problem. They struggle to nurture their self-esteem.

The four vignettes show how the preferences and themes can play out in different ways, as a blend of favored role, the kinds of organization they work in, their background, and overall energy. For each vignette, you will find a byline about the subtype and a name such as "Enterprising Lead" for the Dominant ISFP. As you read, ask yourself how these qualities show up. For example, how is James, the Dominant ISFP, particularly assertive, confident, driven, and more in a leader role?

Taken together, the vignettes cover a fair amount of ground, but of course many more vignettes are possible. What about an ISFP politician, travel guide, engineer, or diplomat? (These would be Dominant, Creative, Normaling, and Harmonizing, respectively.)

Now please enjoy. Hopefully, these vignettes will help prepare you to understand the subtypes going forward.

James: The Enterprising Lead
(a Dominant ISFP)

More assertive, confident, and driven.
More often in a leader role.

The sun hadn't yet risen, but James was awake, his mind racing with the day's tasks. As the owner of a thriving import/export business, every day was a new challenge, a new opportunity. The soft glow of his phone illuminated his face as he checked his emails, his fingers swiftly typing responses to overseas clients.

James's office was a testament to his success. Overlooking the bustling city harbor, it was filled with artifacts from around the world, each telling a story of a deal made, a relationship forged. But what set James apart wasn't just his knack for business; it was his confidence, his drive. You would not find him lost in thought or daydreaming.

By 9 am, he was meeting with his team, discussing some issues around a new shipment from Asia. His voice, deep and resonant, kept everyone's attention. But it wasn't just authority that he exuded; it was a genuine passion for his work. He listened intently to his team, asking pointed questions, pushing them to think outside the box.

Today's lunch hour was a chance to network. Today, he was meeting a potential client, a chainstore CEO, at a chic downtown restaurant. As they sat, James's energy was palpable. He leaned in, making direct eye contact, his body language open and assertive. The conversation flowed effortlessly, from business to shared interests. By the end of the meal, they had not only struck a deal but also formed a budding friendship.

However, running a business wasn't without its challenges. In the afternoon, James received news of a delayed shipment due to a strike at a foreign port. For many, this would be a cause for panic. But James approached the situation with a calm determination. He immediately convened his team, aiming to come up with a solution. His ability to remain level-headed, and his innate hands-on problem-solving skills, meant that by the end of the day, an alternative plan was in place. It wasn't much different to him than hockey strategy in high school.

As evening approached, James took time to reflect. He gazed out of his office window, watching as the sun set over the harbor, the ships silhouetted against the fiery sky. It was so nice to enjoy a break by himself and appreciate nature. Despite the day's challenges, he felt a deep satisfaction. He was living out his vision, his convictions.

Of course James wasn't all business. He deeply appreciated aesthetics and beauty. He often found relief in hiking, swimming, and in playing his trombone, letting the melodies transport him to another world, to be himself. Tonight, he was going to meet with friends at a local jazz bar, a place where he could unwind and let his creativity flourish. But inspired by the sunset, he took the harbor ferry home. At the end of today, he enjoyed someone else piloting as he listed to a podcast about the industry. Soon at home, his girlfriend greeted him with a surprise: a fancy dinner! He put on some music and after they ate, they danced. In that moment, he felt a profound connection to her, his life, and the wide, wide world.

In the world of import/export, where unpredictability was a constant, James's blend of confidence, creativity, and compassion made him not just a successful businessman, but a leader in every sense of the word.

Kurt: The Rebel Explorer
(a Creative ISFP)

More exploratory, innovative, and sociable.
More often in a rebel role.

The first rays of dawn painted the city in a soft, golden hue, but for Kurt, the night was just ending. The echoes of the last guitar strum, the final drumbeat, still resonated in his ears. As the lead singer and guitarist of a punk rock band, Take Flight, his life was a whirlwind of sound, color, and many small acts of rebellion.

Kurt's apartment was a riot of art and anarchy. Homages to punk legends adorned the walls, interspersed with his own scribbled lyrics and sketches. He liked to use markers or car paint. Guitars lay scattered around, each telling a story of a gig played, song written, or romance played out. But amidst the chaos, there was a method, a rhythm that only Kurt, in his creative genius, understood.

Today like any other, Kurt wasn't dictated to by schedules or routines. He woke up late, the remnants of last night's gig still fresh. A quick shower, a stronger coffee, and he was off to a local music and record store. He heard that a shipment of titles had come in. For Kurt, music wasn't just a passion; it was an obsession. He'd spend hours sifting through vinyl, searching for that one track, that one sound that would inspire his next song. Or maybe he'd just be playing around, smoking or drinking, and something good would come.

Lunch was a hasty affair at a nearby diner, where he'd often scribble lyrics on napkins, lost in thought. Though today a friend popped in and she joined him. The spirit of punk was about rebellion, about challenging the status quo, and Kurt lived and breathed that ethos. His songs were a reflection of his world view, a mix of anger, hope, and raw emotion.

The afternoon was band practice. The big garage, with its worn-out equipment and graffiti-covered walls, was their sanctuary. As the lead singer, Kurt was the driving force, but he was also the glue that held the band together. Their sessions were intense, filled with creative disagreements, but also moments of pure magic.

Of course, life in a punk rock band posed its challenges. The evening brought with it a gig at a local club, and as they set up, they faced the usual technical glitches and sound issues. Kurt was good at improvising, turning a glitch into a unique sound, a mistake into a memorable moment, a delay into a chance to rile up the audience.

The gig was a roaring success. The crowd, a mix of die-hard fans and curious onlookers, was swept up in the raw energy of the performance. Kurt, with his devil-may-care vibe, knew how to push people's buttons. His voice, raspy yet melodic, conveyed the depth of his emotions, the essence of his convictions.

Post-gig, the band would often hang out at a local bar, sharing stories, laughing, and planning their next move with a few special fans at their sides. For Kurt, these moments were precious, a reminder of the bond they shared, the journey they were on.

As the night turned into dawn, Kurt found himself back in his apartment, guitar in hand, lost in his own world and perhaps feeling a bit sad. Such is life. The challenges, the highs and lows, were all part of the journey. And for Kurt, every day was an adventure, a chance to push boundaries, to create, to be oneself, and be true to the music. No wonder he was a legend in the making.

Lisa: The Dedicated Careerist
(a Normalizing ISFP)

More conventional, dedicated, and thorough. More often in a support role.

The morning sun streamed through the tall windows of the art studio, casting a warm glow on the easels and palettes scattered around. Lisa, an art professor with a penchant for the traditional Greek and Roman forms, stood in the center, her eyes scanning the room, taking in the quiet energy of the space. In a world dominated by technology, Lisa was a beacon for the old school, a champion of feeling and capturing the raw, unfiltered pulse of life.

Her day began with a ritual. A cup of herbal tea, a quick glance through an art history book, and a few moments of solitude to center herself. Dedicated to her career, her approach to art was meticulous, methodical, and deeply rooted in appreciating and adapting the ancient traditions.

By 10 am, her students began to trickle in. They were a diverse group, each with their own style and perspective. But under Lisa's guidance, they were learning the value of patience, of observation, of truly seeing and feeling the world around them. Today's lesson was on still life, and

Lisa had arranged a tableau of fruits, flowers, and fabrics. "Look beyond the obvious," she'd often say, "find the story, the emotion." Indeed, she encouraged them to not convey the whole tableau, but instead select a few partial elements to convey, such as half of a piece of fruit in a half-obscured hand. She found this was a great way to get across the essentials.

Lunch was a quiet affair, often spent in the university's courtyard. Lisa would sit, sketchbook in hand, capturing the fleeting moments around her. Or she might join fellow faculty or a fun student to enjoy the time. The flutter of a bird's wing, the play of light and shadow on the statues, the gentle sway of a tree. For her, art was everywhere, in every moment.

The afternoon brought some challenges. She faced a hill of paperwork, and a meeting with the department head focused on integrating digital tools into the curriculum. She was not entirely opposed to these over-populating machines, but she happily raised some points with a colleague about the relevance of a classic approach in a digital age. Of course, she navigated the conversation with grace. She was not a barbarian. She wasn't opposed to technology; and after all, her university degree was Art, Design, and Computing. She simply believed in the power of the human touch, the magic of handcrafting art.

This term's evening class was her favorite. It was a smaller group with more advanced students who shared her passion for the classics. Today, they were studying the Impressionists, and Lisa's eyes lit up as she spoke of Monet, Renoir, and Degas. She spoke not just of technique, but of the emotion, their lives and times, and the essence behind each brushstroke.

Post-class, Lisa sometimes wandered the university's art gallery, losing herself in the masterpieces. It was her way of unwinding, of reconnecting with her passion. But tonight she felt inspired from within. She found herself back in her silent studio, palette and brush in hand. The world outside was a blur of technology and noise, but in here, time stood still. With each brushstroke, Lisa sought the pulse of life, the beauty of the mundane, the magic of the everyday.

In a world that often overlooked the simple pleasures, Lisa's dedication to her craft, her belief in the power of the classics, made her not just an art professor, but a guardian of the soul of art.

Maria: The Empathic Maestro
(an Harmonizing ISFP)

More empathic, reflective. and particular.
More often in a relater role.

The chirping of birds and the gentle rustling of leaves greeted Maria as she stepped onto her porch, a steaming cup of lavender tea in hand. The early morning sun bathed the world in a soft, golden light, and Maria took a moment to breathe it all in. As a physical therapist with a deep connection to the wilds of the world, she believed in the healing power of nature.

Maria's home, nestled on the edge of a forest, was her sanctuary. The rooms were filled with plants, and the walls adorned with photographs of her hiking and tennis adventures. Her approach to life was simple: enjoy every moment, bring beauty, and help others do the same.

Her day began with a quick game of tennis with a friend. The court, surrounded by tall trees on one side, was her favorite spot. Maria played well, her movements graceful and fluid. Though she's played competitively in the past, it wasn't about winning; it was about the joy of the game, the rhythm of the rally, the feel of the racket in her hand.

By midmorning, she was at her clinic, ready to start her day. As a physical therapist, she had a unique gift, and her clients knew it. She went beyond techniques. She was intuitive, able to pick up on the smallest sensory clues about her patients' conditions. A slight limp, a subtle wince, a change in posture – nothing escaped her keen eye. These clues tipped off where to make adjustments and shift the client's energy.

Her first patient of the day was a young dancer recovering from a knee injury. As Maria guided her through the exercises, she noticed the dancer's hesitation. A fear of reinjury was holding her back. Maria took a moment to connect, to reassure her. "Trust your body's healing power," she whispered, her voice gentle and soothing.

Lunch was a picnic at the park. Maria believed in the power of the outdoors, and she often encouraged her patients to join her. Today, she was joined by an elderly gentleman recovering from a hip replacement. As they sat on the grass, sharing sandwiches and stories, Maria marveled at how well he'd done, and having avoided all those terribly addictive pain meditations as well.

The afternoon brought some challenges. This was a particularly difficult case, a patient struggling with chronic pain. The person kept describing "my pain" as something she "takes care of", as if the pain were a baby or dog or a substitute for a human relationship. Maria approached the situation with patience and compassion. She listened to her patient's fears and frustrations, offering comfort and hope, and gently suggested that she get up the courage to call her children and ask for some help or at least a visit.

Post-work, Maria would often head to the local lake, paddleboard in tow. The gentle lapping of the water, the serenity of the setting sun, was her way of unwinding, of recharging. That evening, the rays of the sun touching down on reeds, the calls of herons and croaks of frogs, and the whispering spirits of the trees, uplifted her heart.

As the day came to a close, Maria found herself back on her porch, the world bathed in the soft glow of twilight. She reflected on the day's challenges, and the lives touched. Her boyfriend would be arriving soon. She smiled thinking of how much fun they had, even though he could be thick-headed. Life was a beautiful journey, and she was determined to make the most of it, with peace in her heart. Such was a healer's path.

What Now?

Now that you've explored these four ISFPs:

1. Even if it is likely not your type, which character and subtype did you relate to most?
2. What sounded enjoyable for your own life? For example, Kurt's creative process, or Maria's peace?
3. What struck you as a minus, something you'd want to avoid in your life?

5

The 64 Life Paths

ESTP
Life Paths

ESTP Essentials
Promoter Executor™
Extraverting • Sensing • Thinking • Perceiving

Core Themes

ESTPs smoothly get on top of things. They are tactical and quickly play off of the relevant details. They set a priority while staying open to options. They enjoy exhilaration at the edge. They have a talent for negotiating and can win over people to get a lot done through others. ESTPs want a bottom-line measure of their success. They enjoy acting as a consultant. They have a deep, heart-felt care for their family and friends. They are disappointed when others don't show respect.

Unpack the Stack: ESTPs...

Lead with "Active Adapting" (Se)
Enjoy the external world using their five senses and take concrete actions based on options before them.

Support by "Skillful Sleuthing" (Ti)
Analyze and define situations, solve problems, and apply leverage according to universal logical principles.

Struggle at "Friendly Hosting" (Fe)
Tend relationships, social norms, and people's needs and values as they organize and make thoughtful decisions.

Aspire to "Keen Foreseeing" (Ni)
Focus on a vision of the future, and on insights and realizations from the inner hidden world of the unconscious.

Let's explore...

this type from various angles including 4 developmental variants. As you read, consider what fits for you (or others), what has remained the same or changed over time, and options for where to go from here.

How ESTPs Lead with Heroism

Energize the Process
Seek out stimuli. Often appear random, emergent,
and enthusiastic. Attend to the here and now.

Active Adapting
Immerse in the present context.
Extraverted Sensing (Se)

Act quickly and smoothly to handle whatever comes up in the moment. Excited by motion, action, and nature. Adept at physical multitasking with a video game-like mind primed for action. Often in touch with body sensations. Trust your senses and gut instincts. Bored when sitting with a mental/rote task. Good memory for relevant details. Tend to be relaxed, varying things a little and scanning the environment, until an urgent situation or exciting option pops up. Then you quickly get "in the zone" and use your whole mind to handle whatever is happening. Tend to test limits and take risks for big rewards. May be impatient to finish.

What flavor of Active Adapting?
ESTPs can express this process in two ways. They likely develop a bias for one way early in life and may develop the other later.

"Mover" Se	"Sensate" Se
Analytic/Yang Style: active, focused, fixed, outward, top down	**Holistic/Yin Style**: receptive, diffuse, flexible, inward, bottom up
Physically active. Move, and move others. Aggressive style. Tackle problems directly. Alert for relevant data. Court danger. Focus on actionable options for tangible, bottom-line results. Impulsive, strong, and can be crude.	Absorb sensory experiences. Enjoy life's pleasures. Trust rich sensory data. Prefer fun, relaxing activities. Attend to others' motion and get in synch with them. Sensual style. Appreciate beauty. Artistic, graceful, and inviting.

How ESTPs Give Flexible Support

Refine Decision Making
Clarify what's universal, true or worthwhile. Often appear quietly receptive. Trust own judgments.

Skillful Sleuthing
Gain leverage using a framework.
Introverted Thinking (Ti)

Study a situation from different angles and fit it to a theory, framework, or principle. This often involves reasoning multiple ways to objectively and accurately analyze problems. Rely on complex/subtle logical reasoning. Adept at deductive thinking, defining and categorizing, weighing odds and risks, and/or naming and navigating. Notice points to apply leverage and subtle influence. Value consistency of thought. Can shut out the senses and "go deep" to think, and separate body from mind to become objective when arguing or analyzing. Tend to backtrack to clarify thoughts, and withhold deciding in favor of thorough examination. May quickly stop listening.

What flavor of Skillful Sleuthing?

ESTPs can express this process in two ways. They likely develop a bias for one way early in life and may develop the other later.

"Critic" Ti	"Systemist" Ti
Analytic/Yang Style: active, focused, fixed, outward, top down	**Holistic/Yin Style**: receptive, diffuse, flexible, inward, bottom up
Stubborn on principles. Stick to a singular, most worthy framework that can explain everything. Define precisely. Provide expert logic and guidance. Bring order to ideas. Correct errors, poor thinking, and wrong approaches.	Take multiple points of view. Find patterns in the chaos. Notice how systems scale, and apply principles in a fluid way. People, art, nature, and technology all interrelate. Understand and find leverage in the messiness of life.

ESTPs In Their Own Words

From Conversations*: *What's it like to be you?*

I make it happen. How I work—I have a picture in my head on how things will be, and I'm totally involved in the here and now. I am go, go, go. And that creates a lot of successes. I just dodge my way through the sparks and problems. I'm very task oriented. I like to do something, get it done, and move to the next thing. I love circumstances where it's a challenge.

I'm a doer. What's the mission and how are we getting there? Let's work together. Let's go. Throw any obstacle, I'll find a way.

New stuff, that's the thrill. I love to learn. I can take a prior experience and lay it right on top of what I'm doing today and carry it all forward, and it's a snap. I do a lot of brainstorming on my feet, organizing the points in my mind mentally. What's to worry? Just adapt. But draw me a picture, get me a list, or put it on my calendar.

Sitting still is hard for me. I am really activity oriented and I don't need lots of supervision. I look for variety in most positions. If it's not there, I tend not to stay. I'd rather go out there and do it, just get on with things, and I can communicate that without having to spend a lot of time explaining. People know that if I have something that needs to be done, I do it. And I ask for help when it's needed.

I am totally a people person. Working through people is the way to get things done. All of my energy, fun, and most uplifting experiences are focused around people. I don't beat around the bush. Sometimes I have to tone it down a little bit—people may read me the wrong way. I'm very comfortable working either together as a team or individually. I like having flexibility, options, negotiating points. Some people need somebody to be very clear, very direct, and very to the point. That's how I operate. And work needs to be mutually enjoyable for all of the parties involved. Celebrate achievements. Recognition or reward runs very high in my value system.

* Reprinted from *16 Personality Types: Descriptions for Self-Discovery*

I love the challenge of creating something pleasing to the eye. I like the order, to walk into a place that's totally chaotic, nothing's happening, and there's a great opportunity to straighten things out. I like to get the job of placing all the stuff, making it right so it works.

I like somebody with a little sizzle. The most important thing in relationships is absolute autonomy and independence. I admit I like to be in control and yet I'm kind of easygoing in that I just want freedom. Freedom to me is leave me alone, let me do it. Anything that constrains me around that I don't like and kind of rebel against. I don't like to be told what to do or what to think. And although I know it's good for me, I don't like feedback either. It takes a lot to rattle me, and even then I just go on. I tend not to dwell on things, but sometimes I have a tendency to imagine worst-case scenarios, especially when I am stressed.

Family is very important. Just getting together and being close with the family, I think that's satisfying. I don't have a whole lot of really deep friendships, but yet I like to think people would describe me as dedicated, determined, and loyal. I sometimes have difficulty concealing what I am thinking or feeling. I don't like the pressure of having to say no. I can be somewhat cool but a genuine friend as a personal relationship evolves. Trustworthiness in personal relationships is very important, that we can disagree and still be friends, and if our backs were ever to the wall, I'm there and I would expect the same.

If I don't respect someone, I avoid them. If I can find another way to do business I will. I surround myself with people that I feel comfortable with, but they're totally my selection.

I like taking on something that I want to do and getting it done and seeing results, keeping things moving along just to see that I have met some goals—a feeling of accomplishment in a day. I'll always take bigger risks if I feel confident enough. Then I'll work with it for a while, and if I see it's not going anywhere, I just move on and go from there. I guess that summarizes how I deal with situations.

"Intrepid Leader" (ESTP-D)
more driven and confident than other ESTPs
(Dominant subtype)

These ESTPs go bravely into challenging ventures, often with a team. They are ambitious, energetic, determined,
decisive yet flexible, and uncommon in their tactics to succeed. They really embrace an in-charge style

In terms of brain-wiring, they sport a frontal bias for strong executive skills. They quickly take in new information, figure out what's needed, and decide with confidence. They balance a goal-focus with being
open-ended. These ESTPs also attend to body language and voice tone
and can really direct and inspire others.

Their slight left-hemisphere bias supports analytical thinking. They
are fast, logical thinkers. In the heat of the moment, they can catego-
rize, deduce, define, hypothesize, and infer—stepping through an idea
or plan, checking and making corrections as they go. Underlying all of
this, their brain usually shows a partial "even field" and/or "halo" typical
of the general population. They fit but they don't quite do what others
expect.

These ESTPs tend to be private business owners or heads of major organizations, maybe with a wide reach—national or international.
They may be in any industry, though they value meeting practical human needs. Their focus might be aid delivery, live entertainment, health
products and services, resort properties, talent promotion, or whatever
else helps people in a fun way. The business might be small, like a gym,
or grow large. These ESTPs prize effective, reliable employees, and high
customer satisfaction. When they face a failure or obstacle, they find a
way to start anew.

They are territorial. They have little patience for disrespect, incompetence, ingratitude, nonsense, or timidity. They trust their own counsel
and gut instincts, at times to a fault. Some may view them as braggarts,
bullies, or coarse. They can get into trouble with their emotions and
when bypassing bureaucratic obstacles.

"Social Influencer" (ESTP-C)
more exploratory and social than other ESTPs
(Creative subtype)

These ESTPs are active, charming, flexible, fun-loving, risk-seeking, and at times all over the place. They love including others in their adventures. They have a get-things-going feel.

Brain-wise, their trademark is a "starburst" pattern. Their senses catch everything going on around them, and their brain quickly analyzes it all at once and comes up with a next move. This in-the-moment tactics is like playing team sports.

Besides the starburst, they have solid executive skills to decide quickly. They also focus on reading body language, facial expressions, and voice tone. No clue passes unnoticed. They enjoy a keen sense of what others want and how they will likely react. Thus, they can be charmers, playful, and maybe misleading. When reasoning, they tend to visualize ideas, weigh pros and cons, look for leverage, and perhaps bring in a favorite principle. They are not academic thinkers and their future plans tend to be vague. When needed, they can craft a colorful speech or striking presentation. They are fairly visual, their stories paint pictures, and they have a eye for beauty and style. However, metaphorically speaking, their eyes can wander a bit.

Career wise, they like to be interacting and moving around with a lot of variety. Consulting, the arts, public speaking, and traveling for sales are appealing. Being so tuned in to human behavior and motives also inclines them towards entertainment, marketing, politics, and psychology. They can talk to a lot of people and quickly pick out the gold nuggets.

These ESTPs are often younger, tend to court danger, and can get into serious trouble. They may easily "forget" obligations when having fun. That said, their creative brain also has easy access to the artistic muses, intuition, and altered states of consciousness. If, and how, they use these is up to them.

"Tactical Adjuster" (ESTP-N)
more conventional and specialized than other ESTPs
(Normalizing subtype)

These ESTPs are the most analytical, conventional, disciplined, organized, and responsible of their type. Their gauge for fun is more tame, they have endurance, and they attend to details and facts with a chart-the-course style.

Their brains show an "even field" pattern and a left-hemisphere bias. An even-field means that every region links to its neighbors like a grid. Like traveling roads, their brains think though things in a sequential way while also attentive to data and options. Thus, while not so speedy, they adapt in the long-run. As for analytical skills, the left hemisphere aids speaking and listening to word content, mental planning and logic, identify and labeling, recalling physical routines, noting other's feedback, and visual precision. Their minds remember a lot of sensory, technical and factual details that are relevant to their work and lives. As a consequence, they to do well in school and in most workplaces, where knowing the standard procedures leads to success. In time, these ESTPs usually develop decent managerial and executive skills.

They may work for themselves or for an organization. Either way, they can put together a package, portfolio, presentation, product or program that meets the personal needs of clients, customers, and teams in a precise way to maximize bottom-line impact. Similarly, they can figure out the best driving route, football play, promotional schedule, sales floor layout, and so on. They will reevaluate as needed. Thus, they are less "designers" and more "adjusters". For example, for a stock portfolio, they look ahead to the coming season and year for the best investments to shift to. In their expertise, they make decent guides and teachers.

They are less physically active and less talkative than most other ESTPs except when it comes to a work topic, a family or community event, or when someone catches their eye. Then their gregariousness comes out. They love family time, and treat friends well. They also tend to have a private, quiet religious side.

"Personable Connector" (ESTP-H)
more empathic and reflective than other ESTPs
(Harmonizing subtype)

These ESTPs are highly attentive to others' behavior, generally caring, deeply insightful yet also practical, and relatively patient. In time, they can be great mentors. They have adopted a behind-the-scenes style.

For brain-wiring, they show multiple diamond-shaped networks. Each network spans the brain's hemispheres and provides a set of diverse skills that are honed to work together in a quick, smooth way. It's as if each brain region is a member of a mental team. A network may aid many situations such as visually sizing up people in an open-ended, holistic way that looks quite intuitive. Or, a network might be specific to a sport or other high-stakes skilled activity. For example, as an actor, they might bring together speaking, personal likes and dislikes, and a set of standard moves to execute, all within a visual-mechanical-spatial framework. Overall, their brains work in a complex way and they are adept at applying multiple models. Invariably, whatever their networks, they are visual-spatial thinkers with solid body awareness. To pull together everything, they quickly shift what network to use when. Otherwise, they tend to lack a common set of socially-expected skills and have unique ways of handling things.

They are masters of subtly with a particular knack for working one-on-one, live and in-person with someone. They can key into a person, adjust their own language and behavior, and energetically guide the situation. This makes them excellent actors, counselors, diplomats, high-end salespersons, poker players, shamans, and such. Often, they have an international or multicultural background. Perspective shifting comes easily, and they tend to keep things feeling light. Of course, there is always some temptation to use these skills in a manipulative way.

Overall, these ESTPs are sophisticated thinkers, with a clear and nuanced intellectual, philosophical, and spiritual side. They also enjoy creature comforts and leisure activities with friends and family.

Mind Your Neurotic Zone*

Like all types, ESTPs have neurotic moments. These erupt when the ego and unconscious clash. While at times uplifting, the result is often anxiety and insecurity. These episodes are also opportunities to learn and grow.

Friendly Hosting
Nurture trust in giving relationships.
Extraverted Feeling (Fe)

- *Basic Use*: Honor others' needs and preferences.
- *Advanced Use*: Connect with people by sharing values and taking on their needs as yours.
- *Neurotic Use*: Prone to blaming others for causing their emotions. Find themselves feeling needy while also meeting others' needs before their own. Tend to self-aggrandize while also being self-critical. Overly nice (or mean) and respectful (or disrespectful), expecting more from others or from themselves. Can find themselves caught up in endless office politics and relationship drama. Can get hyper-focused on societal values and policy issues (for or against those). Tend to over-analyze emotions and interpersonal issues without actually feeling them.

Manage Your Energy**

ESTPs tend to be physically active. They buzz around, handling multiple tasks with ease, and like to be doing something. Besides work, they like playing sports, or at least watching exciting activity, as well as enjoying parties and such. At times, they can be quiet, simply sunbathing, sightseeing, doing crafts or chores or errands, or enjoying a meal, though these moments tend to not last long or are with friends.

They are easily bored by a lack of stimuli. They have a casual, active style that's attentive and ready to engage the environment and jump into "game play", ideally in expert mode—that is, coming off skillfully. What others hear, see or feel in a moderate or even intense way, they can experience as lack-luster. The want to turn up the music, to really hear it, feel

* Similar here to cousin type ENTP.

it and dance, so-to-speak. In the same way, in the workplace or a class-room, they usually have a lot of physical energy and want to act, keep up a quick pace, get results, and have fun while doing so. What's the point of no pay-offs?

Sometimes ESTPs can come across as overly aggressive. That isn't necessarily physical. Usually it means, for example, an "aggressive sales campaign" or "aggressive gym workout". An aggressive stance can cause a bit of stress. ESTPs benefit by cultivating habits that feel good and are also healthy for themselves and others. E.g. Is their gym routine actually healthy and sustainable? Ideally, they come to appreciate the benefits of eating right, exercising with intention, socializing with kindness, and listening to their body's needs. They also benefit when their work has a big-picture meaning, a personal sense of community.

Pursue Your Aspirations**

Like all types, ESTPs trust and prioritize their heroic strengths. At the same time, they also seek ways to express their opposite. This opposite acts as a bridge to the unconscious, a realm where potential and vulnerability reside. Thus, their opposite is a doorway to growth.

Keen Foreseeing
Transform with a meta-perspective.
Introverted Intuiting (Ni)

- *Basic Use*: Receive "ah-ha" insights and realizations.
- *Advanced Use*: Pursue a greater level of awareness to transform who you are and how you think.
- *Aspirational Use*: Yearn to experience the ultimate answer of life. Can quickly take action based on a realization. Like to sell products and services for personal betterment. Enjoy performing using evocative costumes and imagery. Open to body-mind practices like yoga to connect to their inner spirit. Often foresee the next move in a game or venture, but must learn to foresee the wider consequences of their actions, develop long-term strategy, and hold to a purposeful vision. Fascinated by the mystical and supernatural. Can sometimes get wild or feel things are crazy.

** Similar here to cousin type ESFP.

ESTP Reminders*
for Growth and Success

☐ Noticing relevant evidence, to quickly arrive at a reasoned action, is your strength.

☐ When trying to convince or recruit others, you will get the most buy-in when your approach matches their values.

☐ People also respond well to curiosity.

☐ Keep in mind that your talent for negotiating around (or through) problems can be misread as manipulation or rules-breaking.

☐ After you win people over, they want follow-through.

☐ Find ways to move ahead while maintaining the company of those close to you.

☐ Imagine how much impact you can make problem solving with a team.

☐ Remember that others cannot go as fast as you—or have as much confidence to just "jump into" things.

☐ Mind that disagreements are not disrespect, and not everything should be measured or argued.

☐ Trust that the biggest pay-offs can take patience.

☐ Clients do not count as friends.

☐ In relationships, give others generous opportunities to exercise being in charge, too.

☐ Respect is best earned through wisdom.

☐ You don't need to be conventional—your creativity will win in the end.

☐ Exploring the subtleties of life's philosophical questions is its own reward.

* Adapted from *Quick Guide to the 16 Personality Types in Organizations*

What Now?

Now that you've explored ESTP:

1. How do the strengths and challenges of this type show up in your life?

2. What's an insight or goal you can act on today in some way?

3. See the later chapters to leverage your subtype, neurotic zone, energy, and aspirations.

ISTP
Life Paths

ISTP Essentials
Analyzer Operator™
Introverting • Sensing • Thinking • Perceiving

Core Themes

ISTPs are hands-on problem solvers. They closely observe how things work. They will carefully take apart or poke at something to understand it. They have a talent for using tools to take the best approach to a problem. ISTPs need to be independent to follow their own paths. They like to test, challenge, and push their own limits to find success. They act on their hunches or intuitions. Making and sharing their own discoveries is satisfying. Powerful emotional experiences can really unsettle them.

Unpack the Stack: ISTPs...

Lead with "Skillful Sleuthing" (Ti)
Analyze and define situations, solve problems, and apply leverage according to universal logical principles.

Support by "Active Adapting" (Se)
Enjoy the external world using their five senses and take concrete actions based on options before them.

Struggle at "Keen Foreseeing" (Ni)
Focus on a vision of the future, and on insights and realizations from the inner hidden world of the unconscious.

Aspire to "Friendly Hosting" (Fe)
Tend relationships, social norms, and people's needs and values as they organize and make thoughtful decisions.

Let's explore...

this type from various angles including 4 developmental variants. As you read, consider what fits for you (or others), what has remained the same or changed over time, and options for where to go from here.

How ISTPs Lead with Heroism

Refine Decision Making
Clarify what's universal, true or worthwhile. Often appear quietly receptive. Trust own judgments.

Skillful Sleuthing
Gain leverage using a framework.
Introverted Thinking (Ti)

Study a situation from different angles and fit it to a theory, framework, or principle. This often involves reasoning multiple ways to objectively and accurately analyze problems. Rely on complex/subtle logical reasoning. Adept at deductive thinking, defining and categorizing, weighing odds and risks, and/or naming and navigating. Notice points to apply leverage and subtle influence. Value consistency of thought. Can shut out the senses and "go deep" to think, and separate body from mind to become objective when arguing or analyzing. Tend to backtrack to clarify thoughts, and withhold deciding in favor of thorough examination. May quickly stop listening.

What flavor of Skillful Sleuthing?
ISTPs can express this process in two ways. They likely develop a bias for one way early in life and may develop the other later.

"Critic" Ti	"Systemist" Ti
Analytic/Yang Style: active, focused, fixed, outward, top down	**Holistic/Yin Style**: receptive, diffuse, flexible, inward, bottom up
Stubborn on principles. Stick to a singular, most worthy framework that can explain everything. Define precisely. Provide expert logic and guidance. Bring order to ideas. Correct errors, poor thinking, and wrong approaches.	Take multiple points of view. Find patterns in the chaos. Notice how systems scale, and apply principles in a fluid way. People, art, nature, and technology all interrelate. Understand and find leverage in the messiness of life.

How ISTPs Give Flexible Support

Energize the Process

Seek out stimuli. Often appear random, emergent,
and enthusiastic. Attend to the here and now.

Active Adapting
Immerse in the Persent Context.
Extraverted Sensing (Se)

Act quickly and smoothly to handle whatever comes up in the moment. Excited by motion, action, and nature. Adept at physical multitasking with a video game-like mind primed for action. Often in touch with body sensations. Trust your senses and gut instincts. Bored when sitting with a mental/rote task. Good memory for relevant details. Tend to be relaxed, varying things a little and scanning the environment, until an urgent situation or exciting option pops up. Then you quickly get "in the zone" and use your whole mind to handle whatever is happening. Tend to test limits and take risks for big rewards. May be impatient to finish.

What flavor of Active Adapting?

ISTPs can express this process in two ways. They likely develop a bias for one way early in life and may develop the other later.

"Mover" Se	"Sensate" Se
Analytic/Yang Style: active, focused, fixed, outward, top down	*Holistic/Yin Style*: receptive, diffuse, flexible, inward, bottom up
Physically active. Move, and move others. Aggressive style. Tackle problems directly. Alert for relevant data. Court danger. Focus on actionable options for tangible, bottom-line results. Impulsive, strong, and can be crude.	Absorb sensory experiences. Enjoy life's pleasures. Trust rich sensory data. Prefer fun, relaxing activities. Attend to others' motion and get in synch with them. Sensual style. Appreciate beauty. Artistic, graceful, and inviting.

ISTP Self-Portrait

From Conversations*: What's it like to be you?

Inside I am continually reworking an issue. I am constantly open to new directions, always tweaking and bringing in new information. I solve a problem by looking at all the angles, probably whatever side I need to. There is an answer, and I just need to get to the best way to figure it out—to meet my objectives and give it to people how it is without annoying anyone.

To work with difficult situations I become very logical and very analytical, and I look to see where things fit. I always watch and if there's a problem, I go back inside myself to see what may need to be done and how best to approach a situation. I like to find a technique.

The observational part of me is the ability to see when an opportunity exists and to actually act on it to make things a little bit better. I like to choose the timing for when it's appropriate to say or do something. I spend a lot of time considering scenarios before I make decisions. I'll usually go with a hunch, my intuition, what's the most likely cause. I do my best problem solving in my head away from whatever it is. I step back outside of things, think for a while, and make adjustments—could this be better than that, how do these react, and how does the whole system go together? I'm willing to do the upfront work, which makes it expedient because I never have to repeat it.

In my work, I don't want to be just doing stuff for the sake of doing stuff. I like to accomplish things—make a contribution. That's real important. I take a "do it" type of approach. It's very practical. It's very here and now. That does not mean I don't take into consideration the big picture and what's down the road and what's best for the organization, but at the same time my big focus is "let's get this show on the road and let's do it." I do it as well as I can. Then I think very well on my feet. I can be quick with the verbal comeback—I like the impact. I just get in there and do it, and whatever job I go into, I hit the ground running. And I'm very competitive, often with myself. I tie one hand behind my back and see if I can still do it.

* Reprinted from *16 Personality Types: Descriptions for Self-Discovery*

Those times that I have to use my heart, it drives me crazy because I'm looking for things in clear-cut answers. I have a hard time agreeing that other people look at things completely differently. People should think things through. I have a problem with people reading between the lines. They hear words I never say, and I select my words carefully. I can take myself out of it so I usually don't take things personally. And I find I have to make a point to remember that people are part of the equation. I have to work that in.

I rarely work on one thing at a time. I get an idea and chase it down. I'm always studying—not just books but looking at what interests me. I customize everything I touch; people tell me I can't do something, and I say sure I can. And I like time to just sit down and enjoy. But when I have too much time I tend to just pick away at things. I am really much better when there is a deadline.

I look at the world as a place to enjoy. I like things to smell good, taste good, look and feel good. I love exploring the outdoors. The peace and stillness, the little noises and different views. I feel really comfortable out there. I have no desire to be with people when I don't know anybody. It's a delightful sensation when I see an animal.

I don't like the social stuff. It takes too much time, too much energy. I'm bored. I can't figure out how to make myself more relaxed, and I never really know what I'm supposed to be saying. I have only a few close friends that I really see a lot. Yet people have seen me as someone very lively and talkative. That's the part of me that likes life to be an adventure.

I like flexibility in what I do. Fun means something that interests me. Organized things don't come to me easily, but I can do them. I've always found ways to make things fun. It's a game to make sure you can come to the next point where you have freedom again. There's something insincere about doing something just because of somebody or something else. What I do has to make sense, have impact. I cannot stand just busy work. It has to be meaningful. I have an incredible amount of enthusiasm and passion for certain things that I do and want to see done.

"Success Manager" (ISTP-D)
more driven and confident than other ISTPs
(Dominant subtype)

These ISTPs actively make the most of situations, often finding smart ways to be successful. They steer themselves and others to make the most from their capabilities. They've learned how to be in charge.

Brain-wise, they show extra wiring toward the brain's front and left, usually with an "even field" in the background. The front bias supports managerial and leadership skills or it may simply reflect confidence and fast reactions to problems. A left bias signals an analytical bent. The even field means every brain region links to its immediate neighbors, helping these ISTPs tackle a wide variety of situations, though maybe with extra time and mental steps. They typically have good verbal and visual-spatial skills, language-based reasoning, and a strong neural "halo", indicating they are fairly well-socialized. Though confident and active, they still tend to be quiet and contemplative.

Career-wise, they tend toward administration, business, science, and technology. And sooner or later, they get into a managerial, training, or leadership position, especially where there is a larger structure with room to make their own decisions. In a place like the military, they figure out how to best work the system and its rules in order to thrive. If they cannot find a fit in an organization, they work as consultants, bringing in their expertise. Whatever their role, they are persistent realists, speak with certainty, and are difficult to sway. Their methods and views are grounded in facts and first-hand experience, they are independent thinkers, and they focus on putting knowledge into practice for tangible results.

They relish their solo spare time and try to keep up hobbies and activities, ideally athletics, a craft, or immersing in nature. When under a bit of pressure, uncertainty, or interpersonal stress, they can get paranoid, pessimistic, or sarcastic.

"Diverse Designer" (ISTP-C)
more exploratory and social than other ISTPs
(Creative subtype)

These ISTPs are curious with multiple interests, naturals at design in whatever form that may take, and known for their intriguing creations. Around their favorite interests, they can really give off a get-things-going style.

Their brains usually sport a strong "starburst" pattern. As information comes in, the whole brain gets involved, helping them see connections and respond in a holistic, intuitive way.

They often have left and back brain biases well. These support analytical thinking and help them synthesize new information with prior observations using their favorite frameworks. Their creativity is buttressed by categorizing, deducing, labeling, weighing pros and cons, and seeking leverage. They rely on a toolkit of creative tricks that they've worked out. They easily notice visual and behavioral patterns. And they can get goal-focused particularly around visual detail. Although they enjoy simulating conversation, they usually have average auditory skills. When presenting or teaching, they must focus to communicate clearly. They can learn to use metaphor.

These ISTPs are exceptional designers. They bring in artistic, systemic, and visual-spatial thinking. They tinker and experiment to find ways to satisfy multiple parameters at once. This might be in architecture, computer simulation, games, fashion, financial modeling, horticulture, industrial product design, landscaping, or the visual or mechanical arts such as putting together "mutant art cars". All of these require creativity with technical precision. They enjoy imparting their how-to knowledge and insights to others.

Ideally, they can move around in their workspace and travel regularly such as visiting client sites. They enjoy time in nature such as hiking, swimming, and gardening, if they can. When traveling, they like to explore and learn the options for what's around to see, learn, and do.

"Quiet Troubleshooter" (ISTP-N)
more conventional and specialized than other ISTPs
(Normalizing subtype)

These ISTPs fit pretty well into general society. They learn the ins and outs of a specific trade and really develop expertise in it, both out of deep interest and to help out others. They take a strong chart-the-course style.

In terms of brain-wiring, they show a solid bias toward the back of the brain. As input comes in through the five senses, it mostly flows to the back for thorough consideration. They take time and really reflect, matching what they observe against what they know, analyzing things and figuring out the best way to respond with deep understanding. As part of this, they tend to rely on language-based reasoning, such as deductive logic and categorizing, as well as observation and physical skills. Underlying it all is a soft "even field" pattern, which means each brain region links to its neighbors. This helps them tackle pretty much any kind of situation, though mostly they do so in a step-by-step, linear way, checking their thinking as they go at their own pace. Finally, they also tend to sport a halo pattern, which correlates with being socially well-adjusted at least for analytical introverts.

They tend toward conventional service jobs that require technical skills, ideally using their hands or moving around. For example, they might be an accountant, athlete, biologist, computer programmer, garage mechanic, lab technician, nature photographer, or a web marketer. Most often, they work on their own within—or do jobs for—organizations. Beside their specialty, they may keep up side jobs such as accounting during the week and couriering by bicycle on weekends.

They tend to be very private. They like family excursions such as going on to the beach or woods. They may surprise others with their intuitive and humanistic sides. Occasionally, a "starburst" comes up from deep within. When alone and given time, they can receive remarkable insights. These experiences—positive or negative—may impact their work, hobbies, and spirituality.

"Humane Investigator" (ISTP-H)
more empathic and reflective than other ISTPs
(Harmonizing subtype)

These ISTPs are hands on and face-to-face. They focus on applying complex ideas to help individual people solve problems. Given the subtleties of human nature, they take more of a behind-the-scenes style.

Their brain-wiring tends to cluster around one or more central points and spread out across the hemispheres with one or two diamond-shaped patterns. A typical center point toward the back helps them represent complex systems in a visual-spatial way. They take in an observation, then run a mental simulation to learn what solution is needed or how things will play out. This is not verbal, though with effort they may learn how to communicate it. One common diamond network helps them notice body language and other visual patterns. Yet another diamond aids tactical thinking, especially in physical or social situations. They notice cues, diagnose, and adjust their moves as they go. Other diamonds are possible, each reflecting a particular problem solving technique. Overall, these ISTPs think in unusual ways and usually lack the halo of conventional skills most people rely on.

Typical careers have a hands-on human element such as anthropologist, chiropractor, documentary filmmaker, herbalist, massage therapist, nutritionist, psychology researcher, shaman, or hobby club organizer. All of these relate to something physical with holistic awareness. Whatever they do officially, there is a high chance that they also meditate or practice a martial art or explore altered states of consciousness. They like exploring their intuitive side. They can come off as fairly introverted, thoughtful, and a little strange.

More than other ISTPs, it's important they have a daily routine and means for success. They really do things their own way. They like simple pleasures over exertion. And they trust personal trial-and-error over the mainstream. They explore, experiment, and blend ideas to develop their own system. In doing so, they can get off track and miss out on rewards.

Mind Your Neurotic Zone*

Like all types, ISTPs have neurotic moments. These erupt when the ego and unconscious clash. While at times uplifting, the result is often anxiety and insecurity. These episodes are also opportunities to learn and grow.

Keen Foreseeing
Transform with a meta-perspective.
Introverted Intuiting (Ni)

- *Basic Use*: Receive "ah-ha" insights and realizations.
- *Advanced Use*: Pursue a greater level of awareness to transform who you are and how you think.
- *Neurotic Use*: Overly negative theorizing (particularly about everyday situations). Find it hard to perceive their own psychological projections, accusing others of their own faults. View themselves as stupid (or conversely, as super genius). Manic excitement around a vision of an amazing outcome or future but quickly give up on it. Make wild inferences based on one or two data points. Can be incredibly confidently wrong (brash and dismissive based on some deep assumption). Anti-social spirituality. Easily drawn into what most others see as marginal, weird or extreme.

Manage Your Energy*

ISTPs like to ride life's ever-shifting challenges. They tend to be quiet, spontaneous souls that treasure freedom, peace of mind, and room to enjoy life's many small pleasures. They are acutely aware of nature, beauty, plants and animals, and the physical cues and vibes that others give off. They value high quality over raw stimuli, and they like to move around and use their hands, senses, and body with skill and keen attention.

They mind their energy, doing what works best personally. They approach situations in a way that's observant and flexible yet also a little bit wary and self-protective. Their energy can go up and down like the weather or ocean tide. They act when the timing feels right. They are taxed when they feel others are trying to hem them in, rush them, or

* Similar here to cousin type ISFP.

control them, or when they must stick with purely mental activity. Then they feel like they are suffocating.

For ISTP, a big challenge is dealing with other people. Even as they learn social skills, they struggle to understand why most people behave in the illogical, overly dramatic ways that they do. In particular, they can lose people's interest when they engage in nitpicking, negativity, and sarcasm. A second challenge: ISTPs can also waste a bit of energy focusing on excessively negative outlooks and the dark side of things.

They benefit from mental training, to understand and tame their own psyche as part of the physical activities that already come naturally to them. They also benefit when their work gets into building and managing something that helps people in a personal, practical way.

Pursue Your Aspirations**

Like all types, ISTPs trust and prioritize their heroic strengths. At the same time, they also seek ways to express their opposite. This opposite acts as a bridge to the unconscious, a realm where potential and vulnerability reside. Thus, their opposite is a doorway to growth.

Friendly Hosting
Nurture trust in giving relationships.
Extraverted Feeling (Fe)

- *Basic Use*: Honor others' needs and preferences.
- *Advanced Use*: Connect with people by sharing values and taking on their needs as yours.
- *Aspirational Use*: Yearn to be useful to others and society. Will apply a model, philosophy, set of techniques, or a scientific principle to deal with human behavior. Tend to remain calm and independent when most others fall prey to emotions or group-think. Stay informed about and support social policy causes, often from the sidelines. Uncomfortable in the spotlight. At their best, apply their problem solving skills to aid people, or at least fix things that matter to others. Like to be in a network of fellow experts. Can latch on to someone in a sticky way as an idealized companion.

** Similar here to cousin type INTP.

ISTP Reminders*
for Growth and Success

☐ Find a place where you can use your creative problem solving and adaptiveness without rules and regulations.

☐ Find your own path to learning.

☐ Know people who explore alternate ideas and meanings.

☐ Travel to distant lands.

☐ Maintain a comfortable, fun, natural working and living environment.

☐ Build in daily alone time, outdoors time, and tool time.

☐ Find places where people tend to gather, such as for a shared hobby, to meet and interact with new people who share your values.

☐ Spend some time learning about your values.

☐ Successful interpersonal relationships require negotiating to the other person's pace and attitudes.

☐ With others, consider three ways they could perceive the ethics and intentions of your words and actions.

☐ Have a set of tools to activate and use your intuitions, to think outside the box, and to cultivate strategy over mysticism.

☐ Realize that sometimes you can vary things a lot and have a powerful impact.

☐ Notice that not everything or everyone responds to a problem -solving approach.

☐ Sometimes, the uncertainty of tomorrow is a clear reason to play it smart today.

☐ Trust your hunches. Just know, you can't outsmart god or the devil.

* Adapted from *Quick Guide to the 16 Personality Types in Organizations*

What Now?

Now that you've explored ISTP:

1. How do the strengths and challenges of this type show up in your life?

2. What's an insight or goal you can act on today in some way?

3. See the later chapters to leverage your subtype, neurotic zone, energy, and aspirations.

ESFP
Life Paths

ESFP Essentials
Motivator Presenter™
Extraverting • Sensing • Feeling • Perceiving

Core Themes

ESFPs are active and fun. They easily engage others. They have a sense of style and a talent to present things in a useful way. They look for ways to motivate and stimulate action, to take pleasure in life. They enjoy learning about people. ESFPs like their freedom and are open to taking risks. They are adaptable, charming, and enjoy opening others to what they can do. In their heart, they care deeply. Many kinds of tasks come naturally to them. Over-analyzing situations can trouble them.

Unpack the Stack: ESFPs...

Lead with "Active Adapting" (Se)
Enjoy the external world using their five senses and take concrete actions based on options before them.

Support by "Quiet Crusading" (Fi)
Listen to their feelings, convictions, and conscience to make choices that align with their identity and beliefs.

Struggle at "Timely Building" (Te)
Utilize measurable data, tools, resources, and efficient procedures as they organize and make effective decisions.

Aspire to "Keen Foreseeing" (Ni)
Focus on a vision of the future, and on insights and realizations from the inner hidden world of the unconscious..

Let's explore...

this type from various angles including 4 developmental variants. As you read, consider what fits for you (or others), what has remained the same or changed over time, and options for where to go from here.

How ESFPs Lead with Heroism

Energize the Process
Seek out stimuli. Often appear random, emergent, and enthusiastic. Attend to the here and now.

Active Adapting
Immerse in the present context.
Extraverted Sensing (Se)

Act quickly and smoothly to handle whatever comes up in the moment. Excited by motion, action, and nature. Adept at physical multitasking with a video game-like mind primed for action. Often in touch with body sensations. Trust your senses and gut instincts. Bored when sitting with a mental/rote task. Good memory for relevant details. Tend to be relaxed, varying things a little and scanning the environment, until an urgent situation or exciting option pops up. Then you quickly get "in the zone" and use your whole mind to handle whatever is happening. Tend to test limits and take risks for big rewards. May be impatient to finish.

What flavor of Active Adapting?
ESFPs can express this process in two ways. They likely develop a bias for one way early in life and may develop the other later.

"Mover" Se	"Sensate" Se
Analytic/Yang Style: active, focused, fixed, outward, top down	*Holistic/Yin Style*: receptive, diffuse, flexible, inward, bottom up
Physically active. Move, and move others. Aggressive style. Tackle problems directly. Alert for relevant data. Court danger. Focus on actionable options for tangible, bottom-line results. Impulsive, strong, and can be crude.	Absorb sensory experiences. Enjoy life's pleasures. Trust rich sensory data. Prefer fun, relaxing activities. Attend to others' motion and get in synch with them. Sensual style. Appreciate beauty. Artistic, graceful, and inviting.

How ESFPs Give Flexible Support

Refine Decision Making
Clarify what's universal, true or worthwhile. Often appear quietly receptive. Trust own judgments.

Quiet Crusading
Stay true to who you really are.
Introverted Feeling (Fi)

Listen with your whole self to locate and support what's important. Often evaluate importance along a spectrum from love/like to dislike/hate. Patient and good at listening for identity, values, and what resonates, though may tune out when "done" listening. Value loyalty and belief in oneself and others. Attentive and curious for what is not said. Focus on word choice, voice tone, and facial expressions to detect intent. Check with your conscience before acting. Choose behavior congruent with what's important, your personal identity, and beliefs. Hard to embarrass. Can respond strongly to specific, high-value words or false data. May not utilize feedback.

What flavor of Quiet Crusading?
ESFPs can express this process in two ways. They likely develop a bias for one way early in life and may develop the other later.

"Quester" Fi	"Romantic" Fi
Analytic/Yang Style: *active, focused, fixed, outward, top down*	***Holistic/Yin Style***: *receptive, diffuse, flexible, inward, bottom up*
Pursue a singular life quest or truth. Aim for moral clarity. Dedicated to a congruent set of beliefs. Align quest and core personal identity. Listen to a select voice like one's own conscience. Contain your feelings.	Live a life of deep quiet feeling. Listen to and harmonize with many voices. Pursue multiple soft quests. Allow room for inner and outer conflicts. Identity is subtle, diffuse, and varies in the context of each relationship.

ESFP Self-Portrait

From Conversations*: *What's it like to be you?*

I like variety. I like people. I am whatever is happening at the moment. I accomplish as much as I can to keep from getting bored—I find something I like and can tolerate, that I can see myself good at down the road. And I'm almost always up and positive. I always have a compliment and look for the good in a situation. I love the simple things in life, and I'm also interested in people and a lot of different things. I look at life's possibilities: the excitement of what might come out of a situation and what I might learn about a person and how I can help.

Freedom is the most important thing. If I don't have freedom, then what do I have?

I love talking to people. Making and having friends is gratifying, and I value my friendships. People see me as someone they can tell something to and not just as boring or average. Somehow I charm people, and I am very genuine in my interest. I observe the game of life, and a lot of times it's about being open and observant on my part. Whenever I find things getting heavy, I say something light to make everyone laugh again. I am offended when things are impersonal and harsh. Some people are so serious and many people feel guilty about having fun. Fun is important because I can get more work done in a few hours than most people do in a whole day. My biggest contribution is in just listening to what people are trying to do, probing and pushing and mirroring back to them what I hear they're saying.

I love not having to practice and still being good at something. I don't like having to do a lot of planning. I want to accomplish something and move on to the next thing. I am really good at pulling things off, especially if there is a last-minute crisis. It's just a matter of trying to keep things together, doing what you have to do in the moment. Being outside, getting physical, is also something I have a need for. Everyone always wants me on their team. People say I'm lucky.

I want to be of value. And I want there to be an equal exchange. I will give a lot but not so people use me—that limit is a very fine line. Sometimes I don't have a clue what the person needs, but given enough pieces I can help them solve their problems.

Don't let me sit down and have to do a repetitive task. I want to be efficient and fast. I'm able to simplify things and say whether it's going to work or not. I have fairly grounded views and can see things fairly quickly. I don't get mired down. I believe in moderation and balance. I only want to do something once, and any structure I put on is for a short time only, to be sure we're all heading in the same direction. People don't expect me to be organized, but I am.

I believe that if there's a problem, until somebody actually does something about it, then it's all just talk. It's not real. If there's no real progress, then eventually I'm out of there. I like people to know that they have a real place in the world, that they can do something, that they can actually physically act and that will make a difference. Everyone is unique and has a contribution to society, and maybe they don't have a plan, but I feel great when I can help someone realize they are special.

When the moment that I am living in becomes difficult, then I close up physically. I just move through life and react as things come up. I can get worried about the future and go down this long road of awful possibilities or thinking about the past, especially if others will be affected.

I am an individual. I can't imagine following others, and it's a waste of time if someone's not going to do their best. I want freedom for being able to do what I want to do when I want to do it. Don't tell me I can't do something. Rules and regulations infuriate me. Doing something by the book isn't always logical or reasonable. What makes a difference is if you do a good job or not. Do a good job and I respect you. I want to do my best.

"Charismatic Leader" (ESFP-D)
more driven and confident than other ESFPs
(Dominant subtype)

These ESFPs are energetic, optimistic, outgoing, and confident. Their charisma can quickly energize a room and win over difficult people. They take a more in-charge style.

In the brain, they have a clear frontal bias. The front of the brain supports executive skills to gather information and make decisions in a quick, effective way. The front is also home to managerial skills—balancing one's values against the demands of specific situations. And, this area supports mental planning, logical reasoning, and the use of metaphor. From all these frontal regions, strong links go out to support body motion and sensation as well as speaking and listening. Thus, they have a strong physical presence, are active hands-on learners, and are tactful, friendly communicators with fairly good self-control. Finally, there is often an undergirding "even field". When something new needs addressing, they can move through the problem step-by-step to figure it out.

These ESFPs lead active lives as they pursue their ambitions. They do well academically so long as study time is balanced with social and physical activities. They tend to be popular, and given their sensitivity to others' telltale cues, can be practical counselors, particularly to those who resist help. They tend to excel at marketing, media production, outdoor adventure, politics, recruiting, and talent scouting. They are interested in creative and analytical topics, but in practice they sit between such people and the public or executives. For example, they gather resources to make a film rather than hold a camera. At times, they can get competitive or territorial, though usually quietly so.

They must have spice in their life to keep it enjoyable. Maybe they ride a motorcycle or do an extreme sport. They are not adverse to helping people in bad situations. Of course, there are their own inner dark corners, and they do their best to avoid stumbling into those.

"Energizing Entertainer" (ESFP-C)
more exploratory and social than other ESFPs
(Creative subtype)

These ESFPs are adventurous, bold, entertaining, ex-pressive and curious, especially about people. They live for the moment, ideally with friends and loved-ones. They epitomize a get-things-going style.

In terms of brain-wiring, they show a "starburst" pattern. They take in a lot of information at once with extra attention to facts, people, and the physical environment, and they act on all of that really quickly, easily improvising. Imagine a rap artist in a duet or duel who comes up with rhyming lines on the fly. They have decent managerial and communication skills, but they tend to focus more on themselves than others. In fact, they usually show just enough of a "halo" and executive skills to keep things together and be presentable to society. Their main strengths: they are in touch with their convictions, deeply appreciative of style and beauty—with an eye for artistic details and patterns—and can memorize efficient steps to do things.

These ESFPs have strong artistic potential, from acting, comedy, dance, DJing and fashion design to modeling, music, singing, sports, and video blogging. They rapidly pick up how-to skills, sometimes looking like an expert on a first try, especially if it involves the whole body. They like travel to explore places and people. Routine bores them. They may have a technical side such as advertising, banking or marketing, but their passion will be working with an audience or group. They value self-improvement and like to turn on light-bulbs for others. Thus, they may find a home in business or human development.

They can turn on the charm and make for fun and genuine friends. When present, they are like the sun. Then they are gone. Keeping up connections and commitments takes effort. They lack discipline and often struggle in school. They are uninhibited and get carried away at times, especially in youth. They enjoy the hit of a reward and then get tunnel vision around an activity. Their talent to notice patterns in others' behavior can also stir up trouble.

"Lively Participant" (ESFP-N)
more conventional and specialized than other ESFPs
(Normalizing subtype)

These ESFPs are the most detailed, organized, and sub-
dued of their type. They do a lot to help their group and
those they care about. Don't underestimate them! They
take a more chart-the-course style.

Their brain-wiring shows an "even field" pattern and consistent
"halo". An even-field means every region links to its neighbors like a
quilt. Whatever comes to their attention, they process it step-by-step
from A to B to C and so on—though going all the way to Z is usually
more than they like or need. A halo provides the skills that society expects for the workplace, classroom and community. So overall, they have
a balance of skills. They can get to know a discipline or career in a fair
amount of depth. But overall, they are good-to-go, a jack-of-all-trades,
in just about any of life's many small situations. They are also moderately
contemplative with good observational skills. While they can multi-task
as well as other ESFPs, they tend to stick to straight-forward tasks and
everyday amusements.

They prefer professions that are hands-on and offer some problem
solving with concrete results. They have a knack for business, marketing, office administration, and goods trading. Just as easily, they might
be a chef, hair stylist or make-up artist. They might be in the theater or
the military. Even if their day job is dull, they will take up a fun hobby.
In fact, they might engage in quite a stimulating, detailed hobby, even a
secret long-term project such as a book that they put a lot of heart and
thought into. Overall, they are down to earth and avoid abstraction.

These ESFPs take the time to make things comfortable and tasteful.
They make good buddies, they are often involved with community, and
like family outings and little adventures such as a day at an amusement
park. They may take more rides than the kids do! They may splurge.
They try to be discrete. Usually, they have a lot of energy; sometimes,
they burn out and need to rest and reorient.

"Soulful Uplifter" (ESFP-H)
more empathic and reflective than other ESFPs
(Harmonizing subtype)

These ESFPs are capable of great emotional, interpersonal and spiritual depths, both within and to lift up others. They take on a more behind-the-scenes style.

For brain-wiring, they show multiple diamond-shaped networks. Each network handles a different kind of situation. And the networks tend to be disconnected. So, which to tap when? They may let the situation decide. If they have strong executive function, then they can really thrive. Or, if they lack the ability to stay focused and active with foresight, they can get lazy or lost, fall into an unhealthy lifestyle, or come off as aloof or skittish. They also tend to lack the "halo" of skills that society expects to be well-adjusted. But, one-on-one or in small groups, they excel. They have fine listening and speaking skills, clarity and depth around values, and awareness of how to "work" complex interpersonal situations, with the best steps to take. Overall, their brain map is a bit like a modernist painting. They can carry a lot of life wisdom, but at a personal cost if they cannot quite figure out their own mind.

Whatever their work, these ESFPs look past common assumptions and conventions. They accept others as unique individuals and do not want to let ethnicity, social class or race complicate an interaction. They are great for international trade, aid missions to foreign countries, cultural ambassadorships, and so forth. Of course, psychology is a draw. If one of their diamond networks supports athletics or music, they are exceptional there too. A great role for them is to assist a few quality people who can, in turn, help many more. They also shine in a healing role such as doctor, massage therapist, yoga teacher, or even as a shaman.

Depending on their environment, luck, and an ability to make smart decisions, their lives can turn out very differently, from turbulent struggle with themselves and others, to incredible heights of care-giving and success.

Mind Your Neurotic Zone*

Like all types, ESFPs have neurotic moments. These erupt when the ego and unconscious clash. While at times uplifting, the result is often anxiety and insecurity. These episodes are also opportunities to learn and grow.

Timely Building
Measure and construct for progress.
Extraverted Thinking (Te)

- *Basic Use*: Follow steps, points, and time tables.
- *Advanced Use*: Create structure, reason by measures and evidence, and implement complex plans.
- *Neurotic Use*: Tend to under- or over-manage. Easily frustrated or feel lost in logistical and technical details such as paperwork. Can panic at deadlines. Under or over explain, either losing others when they think they're clear, or fear they're confusing when it's clear. Reject hierarchy/authority figures and rules, yet also easily buy into or ignore institutional failures. Confuse being blunt—or making up reasons—for actual reasoning with evidence. Troubleshooting (under-do or over-do). Easily take a "consequences be damned" attitude. Struggle to stay detached or objective.

Manage Your Energy**

ESFPs tend to be physically active. They buzz around, handling multiple tasks with ease, and like to be doing something. Besides work, they like playing sports, or at least watching exciting activity, as well as enjoying parties and such. At times, they can be quiet, simply sunbathing, sightseeing, doing crafts or chores or errands, or enjoying a meal, though these moments tend to not last long or are with friends.

They are easily bored by a lack of stimuli. They have a casual, active style that's attentive and ready to engage the environment and jump into "game play", ideally in expert mode—that is, coming off skillfully. What others hear, see or feel in a moderate or even intense way, they can experience as lack-luster. The want to turn up the music, to really hear it

* Similar here to cousin type ENFP.

and feel it and dance, so-to-speak. In the same way, in the workplace or a classroom, they usually have a lot of physical energy and want to act, keep up a quick pace, get results, and have fun while doing so. What's the point of no pay-offs?

A big challenge for ESFPs tends to be around over-indulgence. A life of outings and parties, eating and drinking, over-work, dating and sports can catch up with them health-wise. They benefit by cultivating habits that feel good and are also good for them. For example, is their gym routine, diet, or study routine actually healthy and sustainable? Ideally, they find true freedom that comes with eating right, exercising with intention, socializing with love, and listening to their body's needs. They also benefit when their work has a big-picture meaning, a personal sense of community.

Pursue Your Aspirations**

Like all types, ESFPs trust and prioritize their heroic strengths. At the same time, they also seek ways to express their opposite. This opposite acts as a bridge to the unconscious, a realm where potential and vulnerability reside. Thus, their opposite is a doorway to growth.

Keen Foreseeing
Transform with a meta-perspective.
Introverted Intuiting (Ni)

- **_Basic Use_**: Receive "ah-ha" insights and realizations.
- **_Advanced Use_**: Pursue a greater level of awareness to transform who you are and how you think.
- **_Aspirational Use_**: Yearn to experience the ultimate answer of life. Can quickly take action based on a realization. Like to sell products and services for personal betterment. Enjoy performing using evocative costumes and imagery. Open to body-mind practices like yoga to connect to their inner spirit. Often foresee the next move in a game or venture, but must learn to foresee the wider consequences of their actions, develop long-term strategy, and hold to a purposeful vision. Fascinated by the mystical and supernatural. Can sometimes get wild or feel things are crazy.

** Similar here to cousin type ESTP.

ESFP Reminders*
for Growth and Success

☐ Your ability to do basically anything in life moderately well is among your most impressive abilities.

☐ Do something good with your gift of genuine feeling by taking actions to help people.

☐ Always keep exploring, expanding your horizons, and trying out ideas to act on.

☐ Throwing yourself into work to meet a clear goal can bring rewards large and small.

☐ If you are unhappy, then your life lacks balance.

☐ Cultivate three friends who are different from you, because the people you have fun with can't help you grow.

☐ Sometimes it is best to let sleeping dogs lie.

☐ When people are avoiding or delaying an action, try to understand why before giving suggestions or helping them make a change.

☐ Let go of past injustices by keeping and sharing what you have learned.

☐ Remember to care deeply about your own well-being and happiness—as well as the desires of other people.

☐ Part of being selfish is not seeing the selfishness.

☐ It is important to check your imagination and perceptions by thinking about others' perspectives.

☐ Notice that real sophistication and substance are often complex, quiet, and hidden.

* Adapted from *Quick Guide to the 16 Personality Types in Organizations*

What Now?

Now that you've explored ESFP:

1. How do the strengths and challenges of this type show up in your life?

2. What's an insight or goal you can act on today in some way?

3. See the later chapters to leverage your subtype, neurotic zone, energy, and aspirations.

ISFP
Life Paths

ISFP Essentials
Composer Producer™
Introverting • Sensing • Feeling • Perceiving

Core Themes

ISFPs seek life's pulse to go with its flow. They are patient to take advantage of opportunities as they come up naturally. They stick with what's important, to be their true selves with their own personal style. They have a talent for pulling together what feels just right for an artistic impact. ISFPs attract others' loyalty and build relationships with care. They like to play against expectations and can get really creative at solving a problem. They struggle to nurture their self-esteem.

Unpack the Stack: ISFPs...

Lead with "Quiet Crusading" (Fi)
Listen to their feelings, convictions, and conscience to make choices that align with their identity and beliefs.

Support by "Active Adapting" (Se)
Enjoy the external world using their five senses and take concrete actions based on options before them.

Struggle at "Keen Foreseeing" (Ni)
Focus on a vision of the future, and on insights and realizations from the inner hidden world of the unconscious.

Aspire to "Timely Building" (Te)
Utilize measurable data, tools, resources, and efficient procedures as they organize and make effective decisions.

Let's explore...

this type from various angles including 4 developmental variants. As you read, consider what fits for you (or others), what has remained the same or changed over time, and options for where to go from here.

How ISFPs Lead with Heroism

Refine Decision Making
Clarify what's universal, true or worthwhile. Often appear quietly receptive. Trust own judgments.

Quiet Crusading
Stay true to who you really are.
Introverted Feeling (Fi)

Listen with your whole self to locate and support what's important. Often evaluate importance along a spectrum from love/like to dislike/hate. Patient and good at listening for identity, values, and what resonates, though may tune out when "done" listening. Value loyalty and belief in oneself and others. Attentive and curious for what is not said. Focus on word choice, voice tone, and facial expressions to detect intent. Check with your conscience before acting. Choose behavior congruent with what's important, your personal identity, and beliefs. Hard to embarrass. Can respond strongly to specific, high-value words or false data. May not utilize feedback.

What flavor of Quiet Crusading?
ISFPs can express this process in two ways. They likely develop a bias for one way early in life and may develop the other later.

"Quester" Fi	"Romantic" Fi
Analytic/Yang Style: active, focused, fixed, outward, top down	**Holistic/Yin Style**: receptive, diffuse, flexible, inward, bottom up
Pursue a singular life quest or truth. Aim for moral clarity. Dedicated to a congruent set of beliefs. Align quest and core personal identity. Listen to a select voice like one's own conscience. Contain your feelings.	Live a life of deep quiet feeling. Listen to and harmonize with many voices. Pursue multiple soft quests. Allow room for inner and outer conflicts. Identity is subtle, diffuse, and varies in the context of each relationship.

How ISFPs Give Flexible Support

Energize the Process
Seek out stimuli. Often appear random, emergent, and enthusiastic. Attend to the here and now.

Active Adapting
Immerse in the Persent Context.
Extraverted Sensing (Se)

Act quickly and smoothly to handle whatever comes up in the moment. Excited by motion, action, and nature. Adept at physical multitasking with a video game-like mind primed for action. Often in touch with body sensations. Trust your senses and gut instincts. Bored when sitting with a mental/rote task. Good memory for relevant details. Tend to be relaxed, varying things a little and scanning the environment, until an urgent situation or exciting option pops up. Then you quickly get "in the zone" and use your whole mind to handle whatever is happening. Tend to test limits and take risks for big rewards. May be impatient to finish.

What flavor of Active Adapting?
ISFPs can express this process in two ways. They likely develop a bias for one way early in life and may develop the other later.

"Mover" Se	"Sensate" Se
Analytic/Yang Style: active, focused, fixed, outward, top down	**Holistic/Yin Style**: receptive, diffuse, flexible, inward, bottom up
Physically active. Move, and move others. Aggressive style. Tackle problems directly. Alert for relevant data. Court danger. Focus on actionable options for tangible, bottom-line results. Impulsive, strong, and can be crude.	Absorb sensory experiences. Enjoy life's pleasures. Trust rich sensory data. Prefer fun, relaxing activities. Attend to others' motion and get in synch with them. Sensual style. Appreciate beauty. Artistic, graceful, and inviting.

ISFP Self-Portrait

From Conversations*: *What's it like to be you?*

Probably I'm the happiest when things are just a little different everyday. I don't want to commit to any particular way to be. I want to be able to be a lot of ways. In my mind, I am peacefully assimilating myself to a lot of different situations, flowing easily between them all. Most people don't understand there's a lot going on inside. It's always different, and if it's not always different, it's no fun.

When I'm someplace, doing something, I'm really there. The whole experience is related to that time and place. And people only see the part of me that is with them that day. That's who I am for that day, but little do they know that tomorrow I might be different.

I'm reserved when I first meet people, but I am friendly, warm, and outgoing once I've gotten to know someone. I really enjoy listening to people, hearing other people's stories and learning about them. I remember a lot of the details. I ask a lot of questions and like the challenge of recognizing where people are coming from and why they might be coming from that perspective. I love the give and take of conversations. I really feel thrilled and excited learning from that intellectual energy combined with that emotional energy. It gives me a sense of the person. In any situation, I love the give and take, the playfulness and energy, the excitement and a little bit of competition, a little bit of one-upsmanship. But when it becomes abrasive and people personally attack others, I'm offended.

I have a lot of interests and I can get interested in one thing, and then something else comes along and that looks fascinating. I enjoy using the skills that I do have, and they're varied. I'm always on the lookout for something that uses my skills and abilities, that will give me variety and still be stimulating and let me have a mission with people. In my best jobs, I was connecting with people and problem solving and often using tools, adapting equipment or techniques.

* Reprinted from *16 Personality Types: Descriptions for Self-Discovery*

My nature is when things get to a crunch, I'll make something happen that will make it all right. I just know that I can do that and will do that. I love solving people problems.

But part of me shivers if someone tells me their expectations of me, even if they're expectations I have for myself. I need the freedom to be able to change my mind or direction. I like to get a feel for what they're looking for and then just make it happen and hope they enjoy it. And don't ask me how I did it because I have a difficult time communicating that. It's whatever moves me at the time. I probably don't even remember half of what I've done. I can spin around doing nothing and then spend two minutes and get something done. It's a whole process that I can't communicate, because it's not something that can always be written down on paper—because when I'm doing it, I'm enjoying it. It's like I'm in a different world. It's not a task to me—it's a creative outlet.

I enjoy family and friends. I enjoy being with them and doing things with them—developing that relationship, bonding with them. I carry through with my commitments and I'm a very responsible person. Deep friendships are important to me, but not too many.

When I am angry I get quiet. Others don't know though, that's the problem. Because it's not an external, visible reaction—it's more passive, turned inward. I'm trying to think it through to figure a way to get my point across so they understand because I wouldn't want to attack somebody. That's something about me, that noncommunication, or withdrawal.

I like recognition. It's very important to get complimented soon after an accomplishment. If something goes unnoticed or unrewarded, it doesn't have the immediate impact that I want. I've been learning my own positive self-talk. I tend to be a workaholic at whatever it is I am doing. You might say I'm a perfectionist. I want people to be impressed with my performance. I don't want anyone to be unhappy with my performance so I continue to perform, and that is kind of a driving force. It has been a constant struggle to not overdo it. I need a positive environment to work in and I need the people I'm working with to support me.

"Enterprising Lead" (ISFP-D)
more driven and confident than other ISFPs
(Dominant subtype)

These ISFPs are ambitious, active, friendly, practical, and willing to put in time and energy to succeed at their goals. They have developed an "in charge" style and are drawn to leadership roles or at least being their own boss.

Brain wise, these ISFPs have dense wiring toward the front of the brain. Their strong executive functioning helps them quickly act on new information. They have managerial skills. They are particularly skilled at aligning their open-ended approach to situations with their bigger goals and deep-values. They are adept with planning and conceptualizing, and have good visual and kinesthetic awareness. They also self-manage well, keeping themselves together. In contrast to these many strengths, they are not as creative, as good listeners, or quite as reflective as other ISFPs.

They often work with others, leading a team or acting as part of a team as they assist clients, customers, students, patients, etc. They have clear goals and are entrepreneurial and even business-minded. They tend to enjoy a good grasp of technical elements, whatever their area. That may be software coding, a scientific research process, business strategy, or methods in education, policy making, or health care. If in the arts, they have solid hands-on technical skills. For example, they really know the ins and outs of lighting, sound, visual design, and so on for film-making. Importantly, they tend to do well academically. And they are the most hard-working of all ISFPs. They are riding a vision or passion that energize them to get to their goals.

For their aspirations, they know they need to stay open to meeting new people and making connections, including new friendships. However, they can also be particularly stubborn and "confidently wrong" in their methods. Or they may be correct now, but long-term with blinders on, they miss out on new avenues to take. Occasionally, they may enjoy a philosophical or mystical discussion.

"Rebel Explorer" (ISFP-C)
more exploratory and social than other ISFPs
(Creative subtype)

These ISFPs are explorers, mavericks, and wanderers. They are open-minded as they explore and develop their creative spirit, whatever it is. They can stir the pot to energize relationships, teams, and society.

In terms of brain-wiring, they usually show a soft "starburst" pattern. That is, they easily call on their intuitive side to brainstorm or get creative insights, though it can take time to get into and then it feels like a whirlpool. Otherwise, they usually have decent self-management and rapport building skills, with high perceptiveness of voice tone and body language. They can have a bit of difficulty setting or sticking to goals, and most lack a full suite of "everyday" brain skills. That is, they can get so immerse themselves in an artistic endeavor or their creative process that they neglect other things like writing clearly or paying bills.

These ISFPs really enjoy a free-flowing life. They may be talented and still getting established, or they may be re-developing themselves. This can look like a lack of balance, direction or commitment. Often, they are open to discover what everything will come to. As part of that, they are perceptive, sociable, imaginative, and can "put themselves out there" to enjoy exciting activities, especially for travel and with friends. They tend to have a daring or rebellious style in their look, attitude or ideas, while also being egalitarian. They can handle the good, the bad, the beautiful, and the ugly. They have a lot of creative potential and are open to entertain ideas, even highly abstract ones, from almost anywhere. They will try something new in hopes of discovering what works. However, they may not easily process what they take in. For example, they can ask a question yet struggle to do something with the answer they get.

These ISFPs may pay for their "random" style. Their brain's creative starburst tends to lift them away from the concrete reality they normally trust. The result can be episodes of emotional and mental turmoil. Those can feed their inspiration or set them back.

"Dedicated Careerist" (ISFP-N)
more conventional and specialized than other ISFPs
(Normalizing subtype)

These ISFPs are serious, private, and focused on balance. They are steady, perfectionistic, and can be anywhere in society, as their brains are closer to the norm. They have adopted a more chart-the-course style.

For brain-wiring, they show an "even field" where every part of the brain is linked in pairs to every other, like a quilt. Thus, their thinking tends to be linear and concrete. They take in data through their senses and process it carefully, slowing determining what needs to be done with each nuance or cue. They don't like to "wing it". Rather, they want to really hone every aspect of their discipline or specialty. Ultimately, they can perform in their sleep, so to speak, and deliver with amazing impact.

These ISFPs typically have a small bias for the left or right hemisphere reflecting their artistic, physical, social or technical specialty. That said, they all tend to show extra strength around auditory skills and more wiring in the back of the brain to contemplate input in terms of what they know. They are well-rounded enough to get by in institutions, and they can be patient assistants and managers (past whom nothing goes unnoticed). They prefer to work alone or in a small group of equals such as an acting troupe or office clerical pool. They value balance and privacy, and they deal well with routine demands such as paying bills. Where they tend to shine, however, is how they connect language with feeling and body motion. This often shows as a blend of skills in design, media, and performing arts. Education and social work are also favorite areas. They can be compensated quite well for their skill.

They tend to keep work and play separate. They like free time alone but are also talkative and active with friends and family. Recharging is important, ideally in nature or with music. They tend to self-educate, listening to podcasts, reading books, or so on. They have strong boundaries about what does or does not fit in their daily life. Where they run into trouble is "connecting the dots", seeing patterns where none exist.

"Empathic Maestro" (ISFP-H)
more empathic and reflective than other ISFPs
(Harmonizing subtype)

These ISFPs come off as caring, mystical, and peaceful. They are among the most spiritual of all types. Often, they work in the background for their family, community or society in a capacity as a creator, counselor, healer, or teacher.

For brain-wiring, they tend to show a right brain bias, remarkable emotional intelligence, and one or two specialized networks that cross the hemispheres to bring together a unique set of skills. The network (or two) plays out as a special "mode" that these ISFPs can enter as a key part of what they do. This might be artistic, a meditative state, or to fill a therapeutic role. This is in addition to an overall skillset that is sufficient to get by in society (a "halo" pattern), though they are not excited to do so. They may also have some zigzag connections that similarly lead to unusual insights and unconventional ways of thinking and living life.

One common special network helps them work tactically with people. They approach a situation with a person in an open-ended way. As they go, they notice practical visual and auditory indicators to work off of, to assist the person in terms of energy and emotions. A second common network helps them work with abstract patterns, feeling and seeing what's going on. Whichever network, their visceral process feels really intuitive to them. They can connect with animals and all of nature in the same way.

These ISFPs tend to be further along in their career and/or older or more mature than other ISFPs. They have a balance of artistic and technical skills plus their own unique creative style for working with others, whether those are colleagues, clients, sponsors, or so on. They bring a particularly peaceful strength of character. This comes at the cost of fitting into a lot of what general society considers "normal" or necessary. While very grounded, they are perhaps more at home in some other world.

Mind Your Neurotic Zone*

Like all types, ISFPs have neurotic moments. These erupt when the ego and unconscious clash. While at times uplifting, the result is often anxiety and insecurity. These episodes are also opportunities to learn and grow.

Keen Foreseeing
Transform with a meta-perspective.
Introverted Intuiting (Ni)

- *Basic Use*: Receive "ah-ha" insights and realizations.
- *Advanced Use*: Pursue a greater level of awareness to transform who you are and how you think.
- *Neurotic Use*: Overly negative theorizing (particularly about everyday situations). Find it hard to perceive their own psychological projections, and accuse others of their own faults. View themselves as stupid (or conversely, as super genius). Manic excitement around a vision of an amazing outcome or future but quickly give up on it. Make wild inferences based on one or two data points. Can be incredibly confidently wrong (brash and dismissive based on some deep assumption). Anti-social spirituality. Easily drawn into what most others see as marginal, weird or extreme.

Manage Your Energy*

ISFPs like to ride life's ever-shifting challenges. They tend to be quiet, spontaneous souls that treasure freedom, peace of mind, and room to enjoy life's many small pleasures. They are acutely aware of nature, beauty, plants and animals, and the physical cues and vibes that others give off. They value high quality over raw stimuli, and they like to move around and use their hands, senses, and body with skill and keen attention.

They mind their energy, doing what works best personally. They approach situations in a way that's observant and flexible yet also a little bit wary and self-protective. Their energy can go up and down like the weather or ocean tide. They act when the timing feels right. They are taxed when they feel others are trying to hem them in, rush them, or control them, or when they must stick with purely mental activity. Then

* Similar here to cousin type ISTP.

they feel like they are suffocating.

For ISFPs, a big challenge is their own inner moods. Their emotional life fluxes in unpredictable ways, maybe sunny with joy and optimism one day, then miserable and judgmental the next, and indifferent or lazy inbetween as they wait for life to magically carry them along. A second challenge: ISFPs can also waste a bit of energy focusing on paranoid thinking, connecting dots in ways that don't actually add up.

They benefit from mental training, namely meditation and mindfulness, to step away from judgments, to understand and tame their own psyche, along with the physical activities that already come naturally to them. They also benefit when their work gets into building and managing something that helps people in a personal, practical way.

Pursue Your Aspirations**

Like all types, ISFPs trust and prioritize their heroic strengths. At the same time, they also seek ways to express their opposite. This opposite acts as a bridge to the unconscious, a realm where potential and vulnerability reside. Thus, their opposite is a doorway to growth.

Timely Building
Measure and construct for progress.
Extraverted Thinking (Te)

- **_Basic Use_**: Follow steps, points, and time tables.
- **_Advanced Use_**: Create structure, reason by measures and evidence, and implement complex plans.
- **_Aspirational Use_**: Yearn to channel their deeply felt emotions and convictions into a productive life. Establish a nonprofit, design a set of tools or methods or a platform, follow a strict training regime, or manage an effective business venture—aims that align with their values. Enjoy producing creative compositions (art, music, etc.) to put out in the world. Love to see objective validation, such as scientific measures. Harbor a hidden drive for effective organization, objective structure, and impactful execution. Can occasionally become overly critical, fixated on success metrics, or subtly controlling.

** Similar here to cousin type INFP.

ISFP Reminders*
for Growth and Success

☐ Surround yourself with people who recognize and support your talents and your originality.

☐ Be captain of your own ship and explore places beyond your sphere of life.

☐ Give yourself permission to follow the educational path best for you.

☐ Be careful people don't get the wrong idea when you behave like their friend.

☐ When giving suggestions, let people know whether or not you can really be involved.

☐ You will be happier and freer if you address some of the problems in your environment instead of living with them.

☐ So you made a mistake; you can address it, ignore it or try again.

☐ Notice that silence doesn't count as communication.

☐ If you're not doing something with your life, then what are you doing? Do until your heart is content.

☐ Find ways to be rewarded without losing your ethics—imagine who you can help with your success!

☐ Use all of your natural skills.

☐ Continually push your limits through new knowledge.

☐ Build up a tolerance to people who annoy you.

☐ Step outside to change your mind.

☐ Too simple a life stifles opportunities.

☐ Find three ways to experience the freedom that a structure can provide.

* Adapted from *Quick Guide to the
16 Personality Types in Organizations*

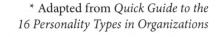

What Now?

Now that you've explored ISFP:

1. How do the strengths and challenges of this type show up in your life?

2. What's an insight or goal you can act on today in some way?

3. See the later chapters to leverage your subtype, neurotic zone, energy, and aspirations.

ESTJ
Life Paths

ESTJ Essentials
Implementor Supervisor™
Extraverting • Sensing • Thinking • Judging

Core Themes

ESTJs strive to bring order to chaotic situations. They have an industrious, hard-work attitude. They quickly educate themselves and connect the dots. When needed, they step up to supervise. They rely on a philosophy of life and seek the steps to success. ESTJs like to keep up traditions and reflect on life's wealth of experiences. They value being well balanced. To reveal a person's character, they can get sharp. They can feel let down when their standards for economy and quality are not met.

Unpack the Stack: ESTJs...

Lead with "Timely Building" (Te)
Utilize measurable data, tools, resources, and efficient procedures as they organize and make effective decisions.

Support by "Cautious Protecting" (Si)
Reference a massive storehouse of rich past experiences as they cultivate familiarity, comfort, and stability.

Struggle at "Excited Brainstorming" (Ne)
Perceive, pursue, and play with life's many potential possibilities, facilitating the promising ones.

Aspire to "Quiet Crusading" (Fi)
Listen to their feelings, convictions, and conscience to make choices that align with their identity and beliefs.

Let's explore...

this type from various angles including 4 developmental variants. As you read, consider what fits for you (or others), what has remained the same or changed over time, and options for where to go from here.

How ESTJs Lead with Heroism

Expedite Decision Making
Proactively meet goals. Often appear sure and confident.
Organize and fix to get positive results soon.

Timely Building
Measure and construct for progress.
Extraverted Thinking (Te)

Make decisions objectively based on measures and the evidence before you. Focus on word content, figures, clock units, and visual data. Find that "facts speak for themselves". Tend to check whether things are functioning properly. Can usually provide convincing, decisive explanations. Value time, and highly efficient at managing resources. Tend to utilize mental resources only when extra thinking is truly demanded. Otherwise, use what's at hand for a "good enough" result that works. Easily compartmentalize problems. Like to apply procedures to control events and achieve goals. May display high confidence even when wrong.

What flavor of Timely Building?
ESTJs can express this process in two ways. They likely develop a bias for one way early in life and may develop the other later.

"Manager" Te	"Builder" Te
Analytic/Yang Style: active, focused, fixed, outward, top down	*Holistic/Yin Style*: receptive, diffuse, flexible, inward, bottom up
Eyes success at a few ambitious goals. Speak logically and confidently. Apply a business mindset to affairs. Manage and drive others as resources to get things done. May put speed and profit above usefulness or accuracy.	Helpful hard worker. Efficient, frugal, economical, and timely. Focus on doing work right. Avoid distractions. Perfect details and optimize functionality. Comfortable with different forms of complexity and multiple projects.

How ESTJs Give Flexible Support

Chart the Process
Reflect on data and perceptions. Often appear focused
and preoccupied. Attend to reference points.

Cautious Protecting
Stabilize with a predictable standard.
Introverted Sensing (Si)

Review and practice to specialize and meet group needs. Constant practice "burns in" how-to knowledge and helps build your storehouse. Specialization helps you reliably fill roles and tasks. Improve when following a role-model or example. Easily track where you are in a task. Often review the past and can relive events as if you are there again. Carefully compare a situation to the customary ways you've come to rely. In touch with body sensations. Strong memory for kinship and details. Rely on repetition. Check what's familiar, comforting, and useful. Tend to stabilize a situation and invest for future security. May over-rely on authority for guidance.

What flavor of Cautious Protecting?
ESTJs can express this process in two ways. They likely develop a bias for one way early in life and may develop the other later.

"Defender" Si	"Hearth" Si
Analytic/Yang Style: active, focused, fixed, outward, top down	*Holistic/Yin Style*: receptive, diffuse, flexible, inward, bottom up
Act as an anchor. On guard, and guard others. A firm sense of culture and history. Stick with the strongest impressions from your upbringing. Prefer convenience and familiarity. Block big changes. Traditional. Aim to civilize.	Maintain home and traditions. Draw on a big memory bank of sense impressions. Feel grounded. Adapt to the group's changes and flex to others' will. Prefer comfort and safety. Sensitive to subtle sensory variations.

ESTJ Self-Portrait

From Conversations*: *What's it like to be you?*

I like for things to be organized, and when they are not, I'm great at getting them organized.

I am very strong on work ethic and expect that from others. I cannot just sit around and do nothing for very long, especially if I have a lot to do and I don't have a plan. I am extremely organized when I work and I can work on four or five things through the course of the day. I think about what I have to do on the way to work or the way home or the night before. It's very gratifying to work extremely hard and sacrifice in order to take care of people, and I like when people appreciate that I have given of myself for them. I feel a lot of responsibility for what goes on when I have put time and effort into something and want to see that continue.

Things have to make sense to me. They have to be reasonable, logical, and simple and when they are not, that's frustrating. I think a lot of my life is tied up in responsibility and structure and organization. That's key—to have a frame around which to build everything else. It's satisfying to see something that was not working start working with tangible results. Once the structure is in place, then it fades into the background and allows the other, relational elements to bloom. You've got to have that backbone and structure or the rest of it falls apart. I can't relax when things aren't done right.

I have a sense of order and I like making sure things run smoothly, the practical nuts and bolts, on a day-to-day basis. Planning is challenging and exciting. I make sure others have what they need, not just what they want. I am pretty fast paced and want things done, and I get aggravated when people are late. I want to keep ahead of things to be ready to move on to the next thing. I am always trying to find the best way to save money, but I have very high expectations and I take the extra steps that need to be done. I take pride in my accuracy and detail, and I take pride in my accomplishments.

I have a very strong family commitment. I enjoy good neighbors and loyal friends. Values and traditions are important because I think a

* Reprinted from *16 Personality Types: Descriptions for Self-Discovery*

lot can be gained from those. And celebrating is fun. I think it's import-ant to teach responsibility and encourage talent, shaping and molding and moving people in the right direction. Sharing my experiences in life is satisfying. I enjoy the simple things—walking, good food, looking at flowers, home life and my family. I love to put something together for fun to see what makes it tick.

I have always been very confident about the choices I make. I am fairly forward with how I think and I am not always particularly tactful. I have to think about how to be appropriate, to have some grace and em-pathy sometimes. But when I feel like I'm not in control, when someone is trying to take advantage of me, I very much let someone know about it. I'd prefer to research things very hard to make sure I'm not walking into something bad. Security is very important. I'm always trying to be effi-cient.

I'm not the type of person that can see a different future before it is actually there. I plan for the future by looking at the present facts. I see what's in front of me in the current situation and weigh the pros and cons of the alternatives. Until that happens, I don't really see all the coming changes in advance or how the future is affected. So I never really understand why people are doing the things they do. But once things happen, it's clear and my desired goals for the future are gener-ally a driving force.

I hate when things fall apart because of disorganization and lack of leadership. I hate fraud, inefficiency and waste, cheating and stealing, lack of loyalty and integrity, and people who don't play by the rules or are only going after their own good. When people take the easy quick way out that really irritates me. And I resent it when other people don't respect my time. I need people I can depend on, and I get rid of people I can't depend on.

I have a lot of common sense. I believe you can build leadership by giving people genuine responsibility and genuine recognition, and I'm someone who can get things done. Sometimes people think I am too structured, but I feel best when I accomplish a lot. I relax when my work is done.

"Fortifying Commander" (ESTJ-D)
more driven and confident than other ESTJs
(Dominant subtype)

These ESTJs are active, ambitious, decisive, outgoing, and practical. They work hard as they make their way into roles of responsibility—and maybe, power—where they can get a lot done, even in quickly changing environments. They have poise. They epitomize an in-charge style.

Brain-wise, they show a strong frontward bias with quick executive function. Their language-based reasoning combined with body awareness translate as putting ideas into action. They talk and work on the go. Nearby regions support quick efficiency and awareness of group dynamics. They communicate with a goal focus, attending to visual and factual details, and to social feedback. As part of this, they can deal with people in a tactical way, asking a question and adjusting accordingly. Often, but not always, they show the telltale wiring for managerial skills to balance firm values against the shifting challenges of specific situations.

These ESTJs usually act as leaders, business owners, independent consultants, and public speakers. Whatever their role, they are comfortable dealing with full rooms and organizations. They gravitate to business or community work. Their background may easily include accounting, human resources, marketing, medicine, or statistics. But they are not analysts or technicians and lack patience for bureaucracy and solo detailed work. A typical favorite role is as a branch manager where they enjoy autonomy to set rules, assign tasks, instruct, and so on—they have a personal sense of the best ways to fulfill responsibilities. They have the confidence to walk into almost any place and do what they need to.

Their weak side: sensitivity to feelings and dealing with their shadowy depths, which requires quiet, relaxation, contemplation, and acceptance. When they have their inner and outer life in balance, they can be really inspiring.

"Inventive Coordinator" (ESTJ-C)
more exploratory and social than other ESTJs
(Creative subtype)

These ESTJs are astute, engaging, expressive, inclusive, inventive in everyday challenges, and interested in learning and new ideas. They give off a get-things-going style.

For brain-wiring, they show a moderate "starburst" pattern. That is, when information or a prompt to act comes, the brain considers all it knows at once to come up with a novel or best-fit response. For ESTJs, that's often a witty remark or a surprise out-of-the-box idea. It also signals adaptability. The more of a learning environment they are in, the stronger the starburst.

They sport decent executive skills and are goal-focused, just more short-term than other ESTJs. They can surprise people with their drive and quick ideas. Also, they lack the "halo" of social skills that many others have. Thus, they can be insensitive or act as a rebel (or counter-revolutionary) if even in small ways. They are strong conversationalists and can gab, explore and debate for hours. They tend to have a few favorite regions in both hemispheres, left and right—these diverse skills show as art appreciation, cultural exchange, people watching, and similar pastimes.

These ESTJs tend to take on careers and roles that task them to constantly self-educate and keep up with advances, changes, and competition. Whatever their role, they can get creative, such as manufacturing products or crafting artistic presentations. They like something tangible and can coordinate many disparate pieces. They like some daily variety. In an entertainment career, they stick to classic favorites and a business mindset. They bring ingenuity and a can-do spirit to face new situations, get familiar with things, overcome failures, and build to success.

They may be somewhat scattered, such as jumping between jobs. They notice social trends. They can be rabble-rousers for a worthy cause. They have a pointed sense of humor and capacity to "play" with people. Their insights can be as blunt or tricky as they are accurate.

"Administrative Chief" (ESTJ-N)
more conventional and specialized than other ESTJs
(Normalizing subtype)

These ESTJs are conscientious, detail-oriented, dutiful, objective, practical, and strict. They work hard, follow procedures, and aim to set a good example. They take a more chart-the-course style.

In terms of brain-wiring, they have an "even field" pattern with a back and/or left bias. The even-field is like an expanse of square farm fields, neatly linked to each other by local roads. Thus, they tend to think in a sequential way, connecting a few dots at a time to build up a picture. They can be quite thorough as they check off boxes. The left bias supports accurate speech, mental planning, operating procedures, social rules, and visual details. The back bias gives them a more introverted feel and a bit of reflective depth. Typically, as new input comes in, they thoroughly vet it against their huge storehouse of knowledge and past experiences to be sure their response will be the best possible, and align with norms and values. Finally, they may develop managerial skills.

These ESTJs tend to fill jobs in large organizations that require a mix of administrative and technical work. They are often interested in economics, finance, history, law and law enforcement, medicine and health services, the military, and so on. They may have laboratory or research experience. They can be extremely versed in logistical and technical elements, knowing all the ins-and-outs of supplies, tools, and how-to methods in order to make decisions and carry out plans in the most efficient, effective ways. They can focus academically. And they strive to be highly objective as they "work the problem", ideally one problem at a time.

They like being a part of something larger than themselves. They strive to give the most to their family, coworkers, and community, keeping up values, standards, and traditions. They can hold strong religious or philosophical sentiments. They care about their heritage. Others may view them as unexpressive, bottled-up, officious, and unimaginative.

"Measured Humanist" (ESTJ-H)
more empathic and reflective than other ESTJs
(Harmonizing subtype)

These ESTJs are especially personable with a thoughtful, sophisticated, and multi-faceted way of thinking and acting. They have charm and create room for others while encouraging growth. They have adopted a more behind-the-scenes style.

For brain-wiring, these ESTJs usually show two or three diamond-shaped networks. Each network spans the brain hemispheres in a specific way, bringing together a variety of "soft" and "hard" skills into one package. Each diamond is like a rich, sophisticated how-to procedure. Thus, in what they know, they are multi-faceted with a balance of technical, artistic, and people-oriented skills. Unlike many other types with these diamond networks, they have decent executive skills for Decision Making. They also have a reflective side that grounds them in their memories and knowledge more than many others of their type. Finally, brain-wise, they tend to have strong visual skills, both in terms of aesthetics and accurate details.

Generally, they focus on others as unique individuals with practical needs and the potential for improvement. Typical roles include adult educator, customer relations officer, diplomat, media producer, skills coach, teen counselor, salesperson, social worker, or talent manager. In more technical areas such as information technology they take a systems view and factor in people. They can comfortably interact with persons of different ages, social classes, and cultural backgrounds. Often, they have a cross-cultural or multi-cultural outlook. This ultimately makes them more discerning with an ability to shift perspective and see deep value. More than other ESTJs, they recognize quality in products, people, and experiences.

They don't take life too seriously beyond the essentials. They have a sophisticated way of thinking about things with a philosophical or spiritual streak. They give and take advice. They are willing to sacrifice. And they are open to new ideas and habits so long as those are functional, and ideally, harmonious.

Mind Your Neurotic Zone*

Like all types, ESTJs have neurotic moments. These erupt when the ego and unconscious clash. While at times uplifting, the result is often anxiety and insecurity. These episodes are also opportunities to learn and grow.

Excited Brainstorming
Explore numerous emerging patterns.
Extraverted Intuiting (Ne)

- *Basic Use*: Notice abstract patterns as they emerge.
- *Advanced Use*: Shift a situation's dynamics and explore imaginative potential possibilities.
- *Neurotic Use*: Deliver nasty humor (e.g. hurtful zingers). Quickly reject or even belittle creative, unfamiliar, and outside-the-box thinking. Drawn to meddle in other people's affairs, often leading to unpleasant surprises. Can get inventive with details to help (but also limit) others. Or similarly, strive to keep things light and safe (but rigid) no matter what. Struggle to bring diverse data points into a cohesive focus. Engage in conversational "trolling" (to reveal others' character, make a point, feel superior, etc). Can easily role-play spirituality as mere rituals.

Manage Your Energy*

ESTJs is among the most common types in most societies. They are the proverbial administrator of every community and workplace. They spend a lot of energy fulfilling responsibilities, meeting their own goals, and taking care of others, often from a young age.

They easily see what needs to be done, especially the practical, concrete needs like who makes dinner or earns enough to pay bills. Their activity is measured: They like the feeling of moving, keeping busy, and checking off accomplishments. They also tend to be social, or at least view social events as necessary. Their community and workplace tend to look to them, and they notice what needs addressing to sustain society. To get everything done, they may skip sleep, exercise, healthy food, and

132

* Similar here to cousin type ESFJ.

other essentials for themselves.

ESTJs tend to suppress their emotions. They "put up and shut up" until they can't any longer. And, they are particularly stressed by others' shenanigans—when the people they are responsible for keep getting into trouble or making things harder than needed for themselves and others.

They need exercise and relaxation time, ideally alone. That might be a consistent morning run or an afternoon nap or whatever else works. Diet is also key; not just calorie counting but also quality. It's important that they listen to their bodies and take time to find what works for them personally. Some variety on weekends is also good energy-wise. They also benefit when their work exposes them to a variety of view points, interests, and options.

Pursue Your Aspirations**

Like all types, ESTJs trust and prioritize their heroic strengths. At the same time, they also seek ways to express their opposite. This opposite acts as a bridge to the unconscious, a realm where potential and vulnerability reside. Thus, their opposite is a doorway to growth.

Quiet Crusading
Staying true to who you really are.
Introverted Feeling (Fi)

- **Basic Use**: Adhere to personal beliefs about what's important.
- **Advanced Use**: Evaluate situations and choose what you believe is congruent with your personal identity.
- **Aspirational Use**: Yearn to improve the human condition on a mass scale by the power of efficient organization. Will quickly gather facts, present logical arguments, and organize people and resources for a good cause. Can lead a moral crusade. Secretly really enjoy quiet relaxation. Benefit from self-reflection such as journaling. Want to help people get to know their unique potential and develop into exemplary individuals. Must practice patience. Find that hardship breeds character. Need a good cry in private on rare occasion. Can be childish emotionally, or hold simplistic black-or-white judgments.

** Similar here to cousin type ENTJ.

ESTJ Reminders*
for Growth and Success

☐Remember that navigating "the system" for others' success is one of your greatest strengths.

☐Accept that the only constant is change.

☐You can be a responsible adult in many ways—not all of them are traditional; it's okay that not all of them will work for you.

☐Remind yourself to give people privacy.

☐Relationships will be better if you refrain from saying, "I told you so" when the consequences you predicted come to pass.

☐When the values of others or society disturb you, consider the broader enduring principles that you share.

☐When something is irregular, pointedly ask if (or how) the situation is an exception.

☐It's okay to be a little cheesy and have fun.

☐If you want people to support you, then take the time to get to know and support them as the unique human beings that they are.

☐Different is not crazy, but nor are people so rational.

☐In important situations, check three times to make sure you are following in the spirit, as well as the letter, of your beliefs.

☐An official personal guide in life can be a good thing, so choose wisely.

☐Notice what you did that you did not intend, and what door to learning it opened.

* Adapted from *Quick Guide to the 16 Personality Types in Organizations*

What Now?

Now that you've explored ESTJ:

1. How do the strengths and challenges of this type show up in your life?
2. What's an insight or goal you can act on today in some way?
3. See the later chapters to leverage your subtype, neurotic zone, energy, and aspirations.

ISTJ
Life Paths

ISTJ Essentials
Planner Inspector™
Introverting • Sensing • Thinking • Judging

Core Themes

ISTJs like to be prepared and draw up plans. They take responsibility as best they can. They get work done first, are active in the community, and loyal to their roles. Doing the right thing is important to them. Every day they strive to cultivate good habits. ISTJs bear life's burdens and cross bridges of adversity. They have a talent to plan, sequence, fill in details, and note what's missing. They have a sense of history and a subtle sense of humor. Learning so much in hindsight pains them at times.

Unpack the Stack: ISTJs...

Lead with "Cautious Protecting" (Si)
Reference a massive storehouse of rich past experiences as they cultivate familiarity, comfort, and stability.

Support with "Timely Building" (Te)
Utilize measurable data, tools, resources, and efficient procedures as they organize and make effective decisions.

Struggle at "Quiet Crusading" (Fi)
Listen to their feelings, convictions, and conscience to make choices that align with their identity and beliefs.

Aspire to "Excited Brainstorming" (Ne)
Perceive, pursue, and play with life's many potential possibilities, facilitating the promising ones.

Let's explore...

this type from various angles including 4 developmental variants. As you read, consider what fits for you (or others), what has remained the same or changed over time, and options for where to go from here.

How ISTJs Lead with Heroism

Chart the Process

Reflect on data and perceptions. Often appear focused and preoccupied. Attend to reference points.

Cautious Protecting

Stabilize with a predictable standard.

Introverted Sensing (Si)

Review and practice to specialize and meet group needs. Constant practice "burns in" how-to knowledge and helps build your storehouse. Specialization helps you reliably fill roles and tasks. Improve when following a role-model or example. Easily track where you are in a task. Often review the past and can relive events as if you are there again. Carefully compare a situation to the customary ways you've come to rely. In touch with body sensations. Strong memory for kinship and details. Rely on repetition. Check what's familiar, comforting, and useful. Tend to stabilize a situation and invest for future security. May over-rely on authority for guidance.

What flavor of Cautious Protecting?

ISTJs can express this process in two ways. They likely develop a bias for one way early in life and may develop the other later.

"Defender" Si	"Hearth" Si
Analytic/Yang Style: active, focused, fixed, outward, top down	**Holistic/Yin Style**: receptive, diffuse, flexible, inward, bottom up
Act as an anchor. On guard, and guard others. A firm sense of culture and history. Stick with the strongest impressions from your upbringing. Prefer convenience and familiarity. Block big changes. Traditional. Aim to civilize.	Maintain home and traditions. Draw on a big memory bank of sense impressions. Feel grounded. Adapt to the group's changes and flex to others' will. Prefer comfort and safety. Sensitive to subtle sensory variations.

How ISTJs Give Flexible Support

Expedite Decision Making
Proactively meet goals. Often appear sure and confident.
Organize and fix to get positive results soon.

Timely Building
Measure and construct for progress.
Extraverted Thinking (Te)

Make decisions objectively based on measures and the evidence before you. Focus on word content, figures, clock units, and visual data. Find that "facts speak for themselves". Tend to check whether things are functioning properly. Can usually provide convincing, decisive explanations. Value time, and highly efficient at managing resources. Tend to utilize mental resources only when extra thinking is truly demanded. Otherwise, use what's at hand for a "good enough" result that works. Easily compartmentalize problems. Like to apply procedures to control events and achieve goals. May display high confidence even when wrong.

What flavor of Timely Building?
ISTJs can express this process in two ways. They likely develop a bias for one way early in life and may develop the other later.

"Manager" Te	"Builder" Te
Analytic/Yang Style: active, focused, fixed, outward, top down	**Holistic/Yin Style**: receptive, diffuse, flexible, inward, bottom up
Eyes success at a few ambitious goals. Speak logically and confidently. Apply a business mindset to affairs. Manage and drive others as resources to get things done. May put speed and profit above usefulness or accuracy.	Helpful hard worker. Efficient, frugal, economical, and timely. Focus on doing work right. Avoid distractions. Perfect details and optimize functionality. Comfortable with different forms of complexity and multiple projects.

ISTJ Self-Portrait

From Conversations*: *What's it like to be you?*

I think for the most part I try to make my life pretty structured, and one thing that other people can depend on is that I have a very strong sense of duty.

I'm a team player but I work best with some time alone. I like it when everything is laid out and I can just concentrate on doing the job. I hate it when I don't know where I am going, and I like feedback so I know I'm on the right track. If part of the job entails ambiguity, that's fine just as long as the goal is to reduce ambiguity. I like being financially secure with the bills paid on time so my family can enjoy the things that we like to do. I like to have a fallback plan. I do like to laugh and have fun too, but work is more important to me, and then I make my little jokes. I always think I have to get my work done before I can go out or go home, when I can just sit down and relax without anything hanging over my head. I take responsibility seriously, and if I'm going to put my name on something, my desire is to insure it's as good as it can be.

A sense of right and wrong is extremely important, and I will not just stand by and watch people doing things wrong. It really tears me apart. I tend to want things in order and people doing the right things. I want to have some rules. I always wanted to please people, and a safe environment to me is where I don't have to compete with anyone else's wishes. If I get into a situation where I feel very strongly and can't articulate the words or can't win, I just don't say anything. I tend to put up with conflict rather than deal with it. I try to deal with stress, but I am not necessarily a good confronter. I would like to be more of a stress avoider.

I find myself duty bound sometimes and find that I do things because of what's expected of me. People can trust and count on me, and I am very dependable, almost to a fault. I strive to keep balance between work and home, and if I'm going to provide for my family I'm going to have to swallow some things at work. When I see families that really want to be together, that's a relationship that those people worked at for many years to achieve. Being a friend means caring enough about an

* Reprinted from *16 Personality Types: Descriptions for Self-Discovery*

individual to call them to see how they are doing, and if I can see some-one has held true to their word, then they've probably gained my trust. If you were to ask me to define the word *love*, you would get responses like *caring, responsibility,* and *loyalty.*

I am a very private person and I don't like a lot of attention. Although I enjoy being with people, observing them, and just being a part of the group, I really like some solitude. People who don't know me perceive me as pretty formal and rigid, and then I'll get out of character and people don't know how to deal with that. They misinterpret my subtle sense of humor. I do have some ability to improvise every once in a while. I take a lot of pleasure in the simple things.

With a problem, I will try to look at all the parts and line them up to insure I don't miss something. I have to force myself to look at the big picture and solve it before I can say, "Yes, this is going to work." I'm not the idea person, but if I have experience I will give my opinion about how I think it should be done. If it's new, I am very much apt to sit back and take it all in and sit on it and think about it. I try to catch myself, but it's so unnatural for me to see the good side of things, and turning around my perspective takes a lot out of me. I want a rock-solid case for why I feel the way I do. A lot of my ideas are very practical, not theoretical—the down-to-earth stuff people really need to know. Sometimes when people don't see my point, I tend to withdraw or stand back.

I can't stand people who don't care for others, who are irresponsible or rude, who shoot their mouth off without knowing what they are talking about or who don't do what they are supposed to do and want something for nothing. I especially can't tolerate people who don't take other people's time or privacy into consideration.

I get up in the morning and do my routine. And I take time at the end of each day to try to plan what's happening the next day, what I'm going to be working on first, second, third, and so on through out the day, to eliminate the unexpected. Sometimes I might carry a book or something in case I have to wait somewhere. That makes life easy and full. Stability is important to me and change may not be that easy, but variety is good too. I seek advice when I need to change.

"Dedicated Captain" (ISTJ-D)
more driven and confident than other ISTJs
(Dominant subtype)

These ISTJs are often in managerial and leadership positions. They faithfully others move toward goals large and small, and they possess an understated charisma with deep-seated values. They've developed an in-charge style.

They show dense wiring right up front around the executive regions with a clear "even field" over the brain's front half. This supports quick, organized reactions to inputs, especially familiar ones, though given time, they can chart a step-by-step response to most problems. They also tend to show wiring to support speaking and listening, language-based reasoning, and impulse control. They are adept at mental planning, logic and conceptual thinking, and analogies and metaphors. Importantly, they usually have strong managerial skills. They weigh their values and what they know as "hard lines" against the demands of specific "here and now" concerns. They detect voice tone and, when speaking, can inspire others emotionally as they highlight values. Finally, they often sport a very quiet "starburst" pattern that contributes occasionally in the background. When all brain regions fire in synch, they can "connect the dots" or contribute some subtle humor or a new idea.

In terms of careers, these ISTJs often gravitate towards business or technical activities that involve working with others. They usually rise to a managerial or administrative role, mastering whatever technical skills are needed. Along the way, they may also engage in coaching, counseling, instructional design, nursing, teaching, and tech-support. As leaders, they tend to speak and make decisions as moral exemplars, and they may also be surprised or disappointed by complacency and curruption that takes root in the layers below them.

To better know these ISTJs, look closely. The back of the brain is often sparely and oddly wired. Who knows what's down there! Although they are reflective introverts, emotion and introspection are not an orderly affair for them.

"Enthusiastic Prospector" (ISTJ-C)
more exploratory and social than other ISTJs
(Creative subtype)

These ISTJs are affable, enthusiastic, expressive, and friendly. They tend to be congratulatory and convey an excitement about upcoming prospects. They involve others. They have a more "get things going" style.

At first glance, in terms of brain-wiring, they favor the front-left and back-right of the brain. The front-left correlates with analytical Decision Making skills, mental planning, attention to details, and clear speech. This is how they keep themselves organized and focused. Meanwhile, the back-right bias correlates with awareness of others' body language and voice tone as well as noticing visual patterns and recalling personal memories. Overall, they also show most of a halo pattern, which supports a variety of skills to be socially well-adjusted.

At the same time, just as important brain-wise, they sport a soft "starburst". Their whole brain can get involved as they process a lot of information. This is not instant. There's a lag of a few extra seconds, or minutes, as they absorb what's going on. But it's sufficiently quick in most situations. They pair whatever comes their way with their rich, varied storehouse of knowledge, skills, and memories. This give them a fluid, casual, engaged style—they can look like extroverts—though they will be out of their element when something really comes out of left field or links to an unhappy past experience or other negative element. At such times, they can give a little bit of an emotional outburst.

Career wise, they are often interested in the arts, history, psychology and travel, though their practical side may win out with business or engineering. Everything may come together in one career such as industrial psychology. Just as often, they become actors, journalists, painters, or such, running against ISTJ stereotypes. Whatever they do, their mix of interests, openness, and zest to meet interesting people and visit interesting places, results in having rich, memorable lives.

"Dutiful Rolekeeper" (ISTJ-N)
more conventional and specialized than other ISTJs
(Normalizing subtype)

These ISTJs are diligent, loyal, meticulous, and serious. They strive to carefully fulfill their community, family, and work roles. They tend to work a lot under the umbrella of a big organization. They epitomize a chart-the-course style.

Their brains show a left or back bias, or both, as well as an "even field" and "halo". Sometimes their whole brain-wiring is simply very even like an expanse of farmland with neat square fields, where every region links to its local neighbors for a step-by-step, steady way of thinking about everything. Just as often, they have a strong analytical bent—the stereotype of a "left-brained" person who is a linear, literal thinker. Meanwhile, a back bias indicates a particularly measured, stoic, and thoughtful approach to life. Every input goes to the brain's back and memory centers for comparison and contemplation. Finally, they sport a clear "halo" pattern that correlates with the set of skills that society expects from people.

Career-wise, they gravitate to the classic, practical, technical professions such as accountant, computer programmer, doctor, engineer, lab scientist, lawyer, nurse, teacher or technician. Compared to others of their type, they more likely come from a communal culture or work in a large company or institution such as a well-established accounting firm, church or hospital, the military, a school system, or any governmental organization. A large, stable entity gives them a sense of comfort, meaning, and security. They are generally not ambitious and don't strive to high positions. They work at an even, comfortable pace and prefer to keep up energy to give to their family and community.

These ISTJs have a quirky side that only comes out with close friends, a loved one, or—in the right situation, maybe—a total stranger. They are suddenly extravagant or imaginative in a child-like way and may stubbornly make spur-of-the-moment (even rash) decisions.

These ISTJs have really put to heart training to help people, especially at an interpersonal level, and as a result, they have a sophisticated way of thinking and working that requires a behind-the-scenes style.

Brain wise, they usually rely on one or two diamond-shaped networks. Each diamond connects left and right halves of the brain in a specific way to support a particular role or situation. This helps them attend to technical elements such as rules or plans as well as human dynamics and creative possibilities. It's all done according to a specific, learned methodology. For example, in the role of a coach, they patiently pay attention to what a person is showing on their face, how they are speaking and what they're doing; they then see where these behaviors fall into known categories and thus what rule can apply. When they really get into using a favorite network, they look pretty rational and theoretical, and they can feel socially awkward at times, especially in new situations. More often, they sport a moderate "halo" of brain-wiring that supports conventional social skills. They also tend to have a slight bias to the brain's front-left, giving some needed weight to goal-focused Decision Making.

These ISTJs are well-suited to supportive interpersonal work. They advise management, work in marketing, attend to product quality and customer satisfaction, conduct trainings, act as a liaison between organizational layers, or coach students or employees. Whatever the specifics, they keep a large storehouse of past situations to draw on. They listen, observe, and are well-suited to bridge multiple groups or departments, and they are relatively open to change and will flex and search for ways to comfortably implement new ideas and policies.

At work and at home, they enjoy comfort, safety, and convenience. They are particularly sensitive to subtle sensory variations, and their personal philosophy often has a spiritual element.

Mind Your Neurotic Zone*

Like all types, ISTJs have neurotic moments. These erupt when the ego and unconscious clash. While at times uplifting, the result is often anxiety and insecurity. These episodes are also opportunities to learn and grow.

Quiet Crusading
Staying true to who you really are.
Introverted Feeling (Fi)

- *Basic Use*: Adhere to personal beliefs about what's important.
- *Advanced Use*: Evaluate situations and choose what you believe is congruent with your personal identity.
- *Neurotic Use*: Feel extreme loyalty and condemn disloyalty. Tend to be self-righteous or moralistic (especially about hypocrisy) with stubborn black-or-white judgment. Easily repress emotions and pretend they don't care, then have an outburst. Fail to fully hear others' input (notably feelings) and then hurt by the backlash. Endless inner emotional sorting without peace. Easily moody or tense, or suffer chronic low-level depression or anger. Tend to be serious and orderly while pining for joy and freedom. Selfish focus on their own personal wants, goals, values, etc.

Manage Your Energy**

ISTJ is a steady, careful, and conservative type. Here, "conservative" means keeping with daily routines, family and cultural traditions, and the lessons of past experiences. They tend to shepherd their energy by minimizing surprises and crises and maintaining a predictable, smooth way of working and living. They can make big sacrifices to keep life even and orderly.

Like the body itself, they like familiar patterns. They like to eat, work, play, and sleep at predictable times. They aim to damp down changes and extreme reactions. In theory, this leads to a comfortable life with consistent energy. In practice, others around them may push needs and plans onto them, and they may over-extend themselves with too many respon-

* Similar here to cousin type INTJ.

sibilities such that they work themselves to exhaustion. They can skimp on healthy eating, especially if they focus on economy or were raised with poor habits. Other people's dramatics also stress them. For ISTJ, a big challenge is tending to work while giving enough time to the rest of life. They want to be graded as loyal and effective, and when taken advantage of, they easily bottle up their emotions. They tend to internalize stress, especially if they feel it's not their place to complain.

What really helps: simplifying their lives with fewer responsibilities, knowing that it's okay to ask for and receive help, and building in good eating and exercise habits into their days. They also benefit when their work allows plenty of room for their family and community. They hold a "work first, play later" motto and have a habit of scheduling even the details of their "play" time. That's fine if it actually relaxes them.

Pursue Your Aspirations**

Like all types, ISTJs trust and prioritize their heroic strengths. At the same time, they also seek ways to express their opposite. This opposite acts as a bridge to the unconscious, a realm where potential and vulnerability reside. Thus, their opposite is a doorway to growth.

Excited Brainstorming
Explore numerous emerging patterns.
Extraverted Intuiting (Ne)

- *Basic Use*: Notice abstract patterns as they emerge.
- *Advanced Use*: Shift a situation's dynamics and explore imaginative potential possibilities.
- *Aspirational Use*: Yearn for an exciting life of adventure. Enjoy "risk taking" or letting loose in a safe, set environment such as an amusement park or casino. Willing to try a new idea if it links to the past, an authority figure, or the need is pressing. Can connect the dots and come up with a surprising solution given time to do thorough research. Enjoy cute arts and crafts and small-time entrepreneurial ventures (e.g. lemonade stand). Will lighten the moment with PG humor. Can worry excessively about "what if...", and on rare occasions, may make a big rash decision that's far out of character.

147   ** Similar here to cousin type ISFJ.

ISTJ Reminders*
for Growth and Success

☐ Find a place that appreciates your attention to responsibility while letting you care for yourself.

☐ You don't have to always please everyone.

☐ Remember that what you have found in your life is not what many others find in theirs.

☐ It is safer to take small incremental risks rather than a huge impulsive one; to do your homework and really use others' advice in making big decisions.

☐ Live with people who get you out in the world to have fun.

☐ Remember to kick off your shoes when it's time to relax.

☐ Remember, not everything needs a checklist.

☐ Practice naming and expressing your feelings.

☐ Seek volunteer experiences that engage your personal side and expand your identity.

☐ Try to learn three lessons from your children's successes, or from the younger generation.

☐ Sometimes your head will have to swim before your hard work can assure security.

☐ Stay well connected to friends.

☐ You can learn from conflict.

☐ Ask yourself what it takes to soften your heart.

☐ Allow others to do things their own way or they will walk out of your life.

☐ Past a certain point, repetition does not count as experience.

* Adapted from *Quick Guide to the 16 Personality Types in Organizations*

What Now?

Now that you've explored ISTJ:

1. How do the strengths and challenges of this type show up in your life?

2. What's an insight or goal you can act on today in some way?

3. See the later chapters to leverage your subtype, neurotic zone, energy, and aspirations.

ESFJ
Life Paths

ESFJ Essentials
Facilitator Caretaker™
Extraverting • Sensing • Feeling • Judging

Core Themes

ESFJs easily accept and help others. They are often managing people. They hear out others, voice concerns, and accommodate needs. They easily keep in mind what's personally important, and they have a talent to provide what's needed. ESFJs admire others' success. They strive to keep things pleasant. They keep up a sense of continuity. They account for the human costs. They can surprise others, act as a rebel, or get inventive. They can easily feel let down by entrepreneurial projects.

Unpack the Stack: ESFJs...

Lead with "Friendly Hosting" (Fe)
Tend relationships, social norms, and people's needs and values as they organize and make thoughtful decisions.

Support by "Cautious Protecting" (Si)
Reference a massive storehouse of rich past experiences as they cultivate familiarity, comfort, and stability.

Struggle at "Excited Brainstorming" (Ne)
Perceive, pursue, and play with life's many potential possibilities, facilitating the promising ones.

Aspire to "Skillful Sleuthing" (Ti)
Analyze and define situations, solve problems, and apply leverage according to universal logical principles.

Let's explore...

this type from various angles including 4 developmental variants. As you read, consider what fits for you (or others), what has remained the same or changed over time, and options for where to go from here.

How ESFJs Lead with Heroism

Expedite Decision Making
Proactively meet goals. Often appear sure and confident.
Organize and fix to get positive results soon.

Friendly Hosting
Nurture trust in giving relationships.
Extraverted Feeling (Fe)

Evaluate and communicate values to build trust and enhance relationships. Like to promote social/interpersonal cohesion. Attend keenly to how others judge you. Quickly adjust your behavior for social harmony. Often rely on a favorite way to reason, with an emphasis on words. Prefer to stay positive, supportive, and optimistic. Empathically respond to others' needs and feelings, and may take on others' needs as your own. Need respect and trust. Easily embarrassed. Like using adjectives to convey values. Enjoy hosting. May hold back the true degree of your emotional response about morals/ethics, regarding talk as more effective. May try too hard to please.

What flavor of Friendly Hosting?
ESFJs can express this process in two ways. They likely develop a bias for one way early in life and may develop the other later.

"Shepherd" Fe	"Host" Fe
Analytic/Yang Style: active, focused, fixed, outward, top down	*Holistic/Yin Style*: receptive, diffuse, flexible, inward, bottom up
Announce values and prescribe best behaviors. Corral outliers and encourage them to join the group. Actively work to fix relationships. Inspire as an orator. Make sacrifices, and ask others to sacrifice, in a push to meet needs.	Enjoy supporting your community, family, and friends. Value harmony with others over being right. Sensitive to negative feedback. Accommodate people's many differences. Can be self-sacrificing as you even help foes.

How ESFJs Give Flexible Support

Chart the Process
Reflect on data and perceptions. Often appear focused and preoccupied. Attend to reference points.

Cautious Protecting
Stabilize with a predictable standard.
Introverted Sensing (Si)

Review and practice to specialize and meet group needs. Constant practice "burns in" how-to knowledge and helps build your storehouse. Specialization helps you reliably fill roles and tasks. Improve when following a role-model or example. Easily track where you are in a task. Often review the past and can relive events as if you are there again. Carefully compare a situation to the customary ways you've come to rely. In touch with body sensations. Strong memory for kinship and details. Rely on repetition. Check what's familiar, comforting, and useful. Tend to stabilize a situation and invest for future security. May over-rely on authority for guidance.

What flavor of Cautious Protecting?
ESFJs can express this process in two ways. They likely develop a bias for one way early in life and may develop the other later.

"Defender" Si	"Hearth" Si
Analytic/Yang Style: active, focused, fixed, outward, top down	**Holistic/Yin Style**: receptive, diffuse, flexible, inward, bottom up
Act as an anchor. On guard, and guard others. A firm sense of culture and history. Stick with the strongest impressions from your upbringing. Prefer convenience and familiarity. Block big changes. Traditional. Aim to civilize.	Maintain home and traditions. Draw on a big memory bank of sense impressions. Feel grounded. Adapt to the group's changes and flex to others' will. Prefer comfort and safety. Sensitive to subtle sensory variations.

ESFJ Self-Portrait

From Conversations*: *What's it like to be you?*

I like to be involved and doing something. Much of my day is keeping contact with a lot of people. That's an important part of my life.

I enjoy communicating with people, talking, going places and doing things, watching people and learning from watching. Bringing people together is a real pleasure. Sharing and time spent with friends and family, a special person, is very satisfying. I like to think about other people, and find I feel tremendous pleasure in reading them. When I see someone who just doesn't talk, sometimes I feel maybe they're missing something. I don't have trouble revealing what is very close to me, even with a complete stranger if I feel safe. Sharing confidences is a gift. I will anticipate others' needs.

A perfect day is feeling I've made a difference to someone. No tension, no conflicts, just something I've solved in a way that feels good to the best of the standards I've set for myself.

In my personal life, friends are important, and being a good friend and having good friends I can depend on makes life a pleasure and a joy. Long-lasting friendships or new ones—I generally care about others and they sense that. Maybe I care too much sometimes, but I want to listen to their background and rationale of why they did something. Part of me wants to tell them the answer right away, but sometimes people just want someone to listen. When I have a problem I bounce it off of people I respect and take into account how others involved will be affected. It can be difficult to take a hard line when people are going to be slighted, but sometimes I have to go through a lot of conflict, do what I must, and step on some toes. But I don't like conflict.

It's hard for me to be confrontational, even to the point where I can leave myself in a bad place because I really don't have the nerve to confront someone and say really what I think needs to be said. I tend to skirt the issue, put it off, because I am very aware of hurting people's feel-

* Reprinted from *16 Personality Types: Descriptions for Self-Discovery*

ings. But I am not afraid to face a challenge. I will stand up for the rights of others in spite of many obstacles because I believe in justice and helping people. Intolerance and prejudice, people who don't stand by their word or lie to cover up hurting someone else—these raise the hair on the back of my neck. It turns my stomach when people intentionally take advantage of and hurt others. It's not what the person says so much as how it's being said, to the point where I don't hear the message. I want to hear where the person is coming from.

Routine for me is actually something that can be comforting. I think the rhythm of it helps center me. I am good at organizing things. And you've got to have some fun out of your work in order to get up every morning and go. I like doing something just for fun, a random act of kindness. Appreciation and meaningful support can come in a variety of packages—when people intuitively know what I need or a hug or a day off. I've done a lot of the civic-type thing over the years in the community, volunteering part time. That's very rewarding. It's important to raise my kids to be good citizens, to be compassionate in their relationships, to work hard and stick with it through the hard times. Generally what goes around comes around if you wait long enough.

At times, even though by nature I want to be understanding, I can find myself torn between going by the rules and understanding. Often I'm frustrated with decisions because I'm caught between different values, and I have a reputation for expecting others to set goals for themselves and then try to obtain those goals. I tend to be a little too sensitive. I take criticism to heart. Please know that I may not respond right now but I heard you and I will respond.

I follow through on my commitments and obligations and believe in honest relationships and honest communication. I admire people who are not afraid to show affection, who are not embarrassed to try things even though they may not be good at them or are willing to make a change in their life, and who stand up for the rights of others and are not afraid to speak out when they feel someone is out of line. Personal growth means listening to myself and thinking about things, putting my priorities in order, and understanding that setbacks are only for today and that I can go on.

"Societal Advocate" (ESFJ-D)
more driven and confident than other ESFJs
(Dominant subtype)

These ESFJs strive to be of benefit to society and they put themselves out front to do that in an appealing way. They present a more in-charge style.

For brain-wiring, they tend to have denser connections toward the front and in auditory regions. This means they are outgoing and can listen, decide quickly, and speak with confidence even as they take in new information. They also have strong managerial skills to balance their values and preferences against particular needs of the moment. Often, they show a slight left brain bias. That helps them mentally plan, attend closely to the specifics of what people say, build rapport, get detailed, word-smith, and respond to feedback. They also tend to have solid impulse control. As for "right brain" skills, they tend to express ideas and emotions through touch and movement. They can get into metaphor, jokes, and abstract concepts. That said, they are still linear thinkers. They consider one or two pieces of data at a time. Finally, they also sport a "halo" of connections around the brain's perimeter, which indicates a solid set of socially-expected skills.

Fostering people's health and wellbeing is a passion. These ESFJs often have technical training, whether that's acting techniques, applied math, genetics, music theory, or voice training. That said, they quickly put those skills to use for the betterment of those in need and for society as a whole. They may start a company, act as a consultant, or take on an administrative, managerial, or executive role. They become community advocates, health coaches, HR directors, marketing managers, and politicians. Whatever their role, they like to help people form good habits.

They have a reflective side. At times, ideally when alone, they can bring together facts, feedback, memories, and other data, collating and contemplating the bigger meaning of things.

"Flowing Compatriot" (ESFJ-C)
more exploratory and social than other ESFJs
(Creative subtype)

These ESFJs are charming, attentive to others, adaptable, and often diverse in their interests and skills. They involve and inspire others. They epitomize a fun, welcoming get-things-going style.

Brain-wise, these ESFJs show a moderate or strong "starburst" pattern. A starburst means all brain regions fire at the same time in response to an input. They take what comes in—someone's words, an observation or new idea, or a memory, painting or song—and they make various associations, maybe in an amusing way. For example, they might quickly infer what would be a perfect, lovely surprise gift to meet someone's need. A starburst also means they tend to be distractible, and they like their days filled with pleasant, interesting diversions. At the same time, they are still fairly good at setting and following through on plans.

They have varied interests. They might study biology, business or economics. Often, they go into counseling, entertainment, fashion, hosting , media, music, retail, theater, travel, or weddings. They may launch or manage a small business venture or two. They particularly like travel and exploring cultural and historic sites, ideally with time to relax with lovely company. They enjoy being in the lime-light. On the minus side, they can be somewhat careless and may find they have a penchant, at times, for creating a flurry of "surprise drama" around them.

They like to communicate with a casual style. They observe body language, facial expressions, and voice tone. They easily attend to others in an open-ended and supportive way, adjusting to the other person. And when needed, they are skilled at articulating their likes and values. They also tend to have a solid body-based awareness. They learn and repeat procedures, routines, and steps, or they can just dance the night away with energy and style.

"Caring Specialist" (ESFJ-N)
more conventional and specialized than other ESFJs
(Normalizing subtype)

These ESFJs are careful, concerned, friendly, and professional. They fit well in society as they fill familiar roles.
They take a more chart-the-course style.

Their brains show a clear "even field". That is, every
brain region connects with its neighbors like a giant quilt. The result is
step-by-step thinking. To get from A to Z, they check multiple, predictable points along the way. Also, they are grounded in their senses with
keen body awareness. That said, they are more auditory and are mindful
listeners and speakers. Besides the even-field, their brain sports a solid
"halo" that helps deliver what society expects of people. In particular,
they are attuned to others' feedback—the words and facial expressions
that guide human relations. Although they are not sophisticated thinkers, they are thoughtful and contemplative. Whatever comes up in life,
they can dig into their giant database of knowledge and memories to
compare and contrast, to try to understand. If something can fire up
their brain, it is a buzz-worthy new idea.

In terms of careers, they tend to train for and stick to a role and
workplace. Typical jobs include academic counselor, customer specialist, dental hygienist, nurse, or secretary. They are not so ambitious and
need time for community and family. Thus, they might work to become
a doctor and apply to a large, reliable clinic or hospital. As administrators, they can be "friendly enforcers" of norms and values, which may
lead to discontent behind their back. Otherwise, they are personable and
bring daily cheer with an occasional side-helping of dark humor. They
prefer stabilize environments, large or small—at times, large can be too
impersonal.

These ESFJs enjoy quiet time, though ideally a loved one is close by.
They like a beautiful, cozy home and appreciate animals, craftwork, music, and nature. Although they cultivate a calm demeanor, they can produce a dramatic outburst or rebellious surprise to relieve stress.

"Attentive Facilitator" (ESFJ-H)
more empathic and reflective than other ESFJs
(Harmonizing subtype)

These ESFJs are deeply caring feelers. They bring a sophisticated expertise to quietly help others, often face-to-face. They take a more behind-the-scenes style.

For brain-wiring, they tend to show one or more "diamond" networks that stretch across the brain's hemispheres. Or, they may have a lot of "zigzag" connections that look like networks. Either way, they think in a sophisticated and even surprising ways. A diamond network consists of several diverse brain regions that work together harmoniously. For example, as a counselor, they might hear words and voice tone, make inferences from those to fit the client into a conceptual model, and then weigh options to locate a helpful next question to facilitate the client's growth. Similarly, a zigzag links distant regions that don't often go together. This allows them to "connect the dots" for dramatic and intuitive results.

Besides these primary patterns, they have good listening skills and attend to factual details. On the other hand, they often come up short when sticking to plans and making decisions. And, they lack the full "halo" of everyday skills that society expects. Overall, they are observant, sensitive, and empathic yet also a little bit of odd birds with unusual habits and quirks.

These ESFJs are often in a one-on-one role with clients or customers. These roles require a bit of "reading", adapting to, and working with the other person, ideally in a practical way though they are comfortable using complex conceptual models, at least in their specialty. They might be a business aide, counselor, diplomat, executive coach, project manager, psychologist, or social scientist. They often have a multi-cultural or international outlook, or at least are quite comfortable interacting with people from different social classes or cultures.

In their personal life, they enjoy a relaxed, comforting environment. Yet, they also enjoy some novelty to keep life interesting. Most of all, they really value their close relationships.

Mind Your Neurotic Zone*

Like all types, ESFJs have neurotic moments. These erupt when the ego and unconscious clash. While at times uplifting, the result is often anxiety and insecurity. These episodes are also opportunities to learn and grow.

Excited Brainstorming
Explore numerous emerging patterns.
Extraverted Intuiting (Ne)

- **Basic Use**: Notice abstract patterns as they emerge.
- *Advanced Use*: Shift a situation's dynamics and explore imaginative potential possibilities.
- *Neurotic Use*: Deliver nasty humor (e.g. hurtful zingers). Quickly reject or even belittle creative, unfamiliar, and outside-the-box thinking. Drawn to meddle in other people's affairs, often leading to unpleasant surprises. Can get inventive with details to help (but also limit) others. Or similarly, strive to keep things light and safe (but rigid) no matter what. Struggle to bring diverse data points into a cohesive focus. Engage in conversational "trolling" (to reveal others' character, make a point, feel superior, etc). Can easily role-play spirituality as mere rituals.

Manage Your Energy*

ESFJs is among the most common types in most societies. They are the proverbial mother hen of every community and workplace. They spend a lot of energy fulfilling responsibilities, meeting their goals, and taking care of others, often from a young age.

They easily see what needs to be done, especially the practical, concrete needs like who makes dinner or earns enough to pay bills. Their activity is measured: They like the feeling of moving, keeping busy, and checking off accomplishments. They also tend to be social, or at least view social events as necessary. Their community and workplace tend to look to them, and they notice what needs addressing to sustain society. To get everything done, they may skip sleep, exercise, healthy food, and

* Similar here to cousin type ESTJ.

other essentials for themselves.

ESFJs tend to spend a lot of energy tending to other people's needs. They like things to be done "just right" and enjoyable for all. And, they are particularly stressed by others' shenanigans—when the people they are responsible for keep getting into trouble or making things harder than needed for themselves and others.

They need exercise and relaxation, ideally alone. That might be a consistent morning run or an afternoon nap. Diet is also key; not just calorie counting but also quality. It's important that they listen to their bodies and take time to find what works for them personally. Some variety on weekends is also good energy-wise. They also benefit when their work exposes them to a variety of view points, interests, and options.

Pursue Your Aspirations**

Like all types, ESFJs trust and prioritize their heroic strengths. At the same time, they also seek ways to express their opposite. This opposite acts as a bridge to the unconscious, a realm where potential and vulnerability reside. Thus, their opposite is a doorway to growth.

Skillful Sleuthing
Gain leverage using a framework.
Introverted Thinking (Ti)

- **Basic Use**: Adhere to definitions and philosophical principles.
- **Advanced Use**: Analyze a problem using a framework, and find an angle or leverage by which to solve it.
- **Aspirational Use**: Yearn for a consistent, universal philosophy underlying life's squabbles and troubles. Try to see an issue from multiple angles and from voices of all involved in order to find equitable solutions. Drawn to use analytical rigor and a logical framework that can help people live better. Willing to specialize deeply to do that. Generally, seek to analyze situations logically, draw boundaries, and balance their empathy and caregiving with objective outcomes. Tend to admire intellect, scholarship, and deep thinking. May over-apply leverage to move themselves up in social systems.

** Similar here to cousin type ENFJ.

ESFJ Reminders*
for Growth and Success

☐ Your gift of caring for other's needs is surpassed only by your gift for knowing their needs.

☐ Keep in mind that people are diverse, and it's okay if they feel a little odd.

☐ Consider that sometimes leaving people alone is the best way to help them mature.

☐ Interpersonal drama is not a good substitute for genuine love.

☐ Keep in mind that most other people simply cannot be as "up-front" emotionally as you because they are concerned about the meaning of what they are doing.

☐ It's okay to be more independent—you'll survive.

☐ It's okay to say no, or, "Why don't you try first?" in response to others' demands—everyone will survive.

☐ Help people cultivate courage.

☐ Before committing, consider how grateful someone can be.

☐ Try to replace "I deserve it" with "how can I step up and earn it?"

☐ Consider that occasionally, helping hands hurt the most.

☐ Not everyone is at home with tradition.

☐ The group is only one source of answers and identity.

☐ Overcoming adversity can be the highest measure of character.

☐ Try to leave room for people to pursue bright ideas that help others in new ways.

☐ Remind people that love "is" as love "does".

*Adapted from *Quick Guide to the 16 Personality Types in Organizations*

What Now?

Now that you've explored ESFJ:

1. How do the strengths and challenges of this type show up in your life?

2. What's an insight or goal you can act on today in some way?

3. See the later chapters to leverage your subtype, neurotic zone, energy, and aspirations.

ISFJ
Life Paths

ISFJ Essentials
Protector Supporter™
Introverting • Sensing • Feeling • Judging

Core Themes

ISFJs notice what's needed and valuable. They have a talent for arranging careful support. They enjoy their traditions and work to protect the future. They often listen closely to remember a lot of details. They tend to be agreeable. They are sensitive to the small things, with strong preferences. When appropriate, ISFJs like to volunteer. They like to feel a sense of accomplishment. They can get technical, knowing all of the ins and outs. They get frustrated when people ignore rules and don't get along.

Unpack the Stack: ISFJs...

Lead with "Cautious Protecting" (Si)
Reference a massive storehouse of rich past experiences as they cultivate familiarity, comfort, and stability.

Support by "Friendly Hosting" (Fe)
Tend relationships, social norms, and people's needs and values as they organize and make thoughtful decisions.

Struggle at "Skillful Sleuthing" (Ti)
Analyze and define situations, solve problems, and apply leverage according to universal logical principles.

Aspire to "Excited Brainstorming" (Ne)
Perceive, pursue, and play with life's many potential possibilities, facilitating the promising ones.

Let's explore...

this type from various angles including 4 developmental variants. As you read, consider what fits for you (or others), what has remained the same or changed over time, and options for where to go from here.

How ISFJs Lead with Heroism

Chart the Process
Reflect on data and perceptions. Often appear focused and preoccupied. Attend to reference points.

Cautious Protecting
Stabilize with a predictable standard.
Introverted Sensing (Si)

Review and practice to specialize and meet group needs. Constant practice "burns in" how-to knowledge and helps build your storehouse. Specialization helps you reliably fill roles and tasks. Improve when following a role-model or example. Easily track where you are in a task. Often review the past and can relive events as if you are there again. Carefully compare a situation to the customary ways you've come to rely. In touch with body sensations. Strong memory for kinship and details. Rely on repetition. Check what's familiar, comforting, and useful. Tend to stabilize a situation and invest for future security. May over-rely on authority for guidance.

What flavor of Cautious Protecting?
ISFJs can express this process in two ways. They likely develop a bias for one way early in life and may develop the other later.

"Defender" Si	"Hearth" Si
Analytic/Yang Style: active, focused, fixed, outward, top down	**Holistic/Yin Style**: receptive, diffuse, flexible, inward, bottom up
Act as an anchor. On guard, and guard others. A firm sense of culture and history. Stick with the strongest impressions from your upbringing. Prefer convenience and familiarity. Block big changes. Traditional. Aim to civilize.	Maintain home and traditions. Draw on a big memory bank of sense impressions. Feel grounded. Adapt to the group's changes and flex to others' will. Prefer comfort and safety. Sensitive to subtle sensory variations.

How ISFJs Give Flexible Support

Expedite Decision Making

Proactively meet goals. Often appear sure and confident.
Organize and fix to get positive results soon.

Friendly Hosting
Nurture trust in giving relationships.
Extraverted Feeling (Fe)

Evaluate and communicate values to build trust and enhance relationships. Like to promote social/interpersonal cohesion. Attend keenly to how others judge you. Quickly adjust your behavior for social harmony. Often rely on a favorite way to reason, with an emphasis on words. Prefer to stay positive, supportive, and optimistic. Empathically respond to others' needs and feelings, and may take on others' needs as your own. Need respect and trust. Easily embarrassed. Like using adjectives to convey values. Enjoy hosting. May hold back the true degree of your emotional response about morals/ethics, regarding talk as more effective. May try too hard to please.

What flavor of Friendly Hosting?

ISFJs can express this process in two ways. They likely develop a bias for one way early in life and may develop the other later.

"Shepherd" Fe	"Host" Fe
Analytic/Yang Style: active, focused, fixed, outward, top down	**Holistic/Yin Style**: receptive, diffuse, flexible, inward, bottom up
Announce values and prescribe best behaviors. Corral outliers and encourage them to join the group. Actively work to fix relationships. Inspire as an orator. Make sacrifices, and ask others to sacrifice, in a push to meet needs.	Enjoy supporting your community, family, and friends. Value harmony with others over being right. Sensitive to negative feedback. Accommodate people's many differences. Can be self-sacrificing as you even help foes.

ISFJ Self-Portrait

From Conversations*: *What's it like to be you?*

I like feeling I have helped someone with a concern, helping them figure out, deal with, and resolve the problem, knowing that what I recommended or advised really did help that person.

I am fairly quiet with an easygoing attitude and am modest to some extent. I do not mind being alone, although I do like to be with people too. I like having friends, and family is the most important thing in my life. I am a reluctant leader—I like to have some say in things and I am glad I am doing it, but if things go well with someone else as leader, then that doesn't bother me. Privacy is important, though it's nice to be thought of well by others. I like to have some independence; to be able to come and go as I please is nice.

I am dependable and conscientious. I have a big sense of obligation with work. Doing a good job is really important to me. Give me specifics and a plan on how you want me to do it. Brainstorming is generally harder—it's a skill to acquire. I prefer to work by myself without distractions because I like things done a certain way. It's taken me a while to learn that my work is much better quality when I'm drawing from those who see things differently. They help keep up my enthusiasm. And I get upset when work backs up—and it probably takes me longer than most people to do something because I am so thorough. But when I have learned a lot about what I do, I think I get the job done much faster and I can make difficult work look easy. I cannot stand people not doing their best job. I do what I say I'm going to do and stick with it until it's done. And I can find myself overcommitted. It's important to me to be able to say "Okay, this is enough responsibility for now, I don't have to climb that ladder at any cost."

Organization has always been a real strength. I do it all internally, in my head. I am fairly detail oriented and a very structured person. I have to have things in a certain place, with a plan and things prioritized, so I can leave things and pick up the next day where I left off. Being structured is a natural thing with me, to want to have things set.

* Reprinted from *16 Personality Types: Descriptions for Self-Discovery*

I dislike conflict. I really care about treating people with a lot of respect. It's an emotional drain when I have to deal with different opinions and reconcile everyone. I give an opinion based on what I think is fair and what's been done in the past. What's decided for one person shouldn't be really any different than for another. I respect that people are certainly entitled to feel the way they feel, but in working or living together, decisions have to be made and things have to go a certain way. I need positive feedback that I'm doing a good job and that my opinions are similar to the opinions of others, to hear, "Yes, I think that same thing." I worry when there's disagreement. I question myself. I've learned to challenge what I don't feel is right, especially if someone does something to me that I don't feel I would have done to that person.

Anything really major in life can take forever to decide. I look to what matters to people, talk to them and get their ideas, then put it all together into something that satisfies everyone. I am more comfortable preparing first and then starting something, after I've pictured it in my mind, rehearsed it, and perfected it. I feel I do a good job expressing myself when I have a chance to prepare, although I do better in reflection. Answering questions on the spur of the moment can be hard too. I will take something minor and get all freaked out when it's nothing to get upset about. I'm very methodical and prefer things to be laid out. If it's a problem with me and another person, I can analyze the situation endlessly until I talk to the person again and straighten it out.

I consider myself adaptable to anyone. I feel that a lot of people think I am a nice person, and because I was always there for them in the past and willing to help, they try to take advantage of me. But as long as you are doing something okay with your life, then you are okay with me.

I need acknowledgment from people who I really care about. Compliments can be embarrassing face to face, though. A paycheck is a nice recognition too. I like a day when everything works really well, when I get a lot done, people respond very positively and there is a lot of laughter. I have an unusual sense of humor, and I like laughter.

"Group Mediator" (ISFJ-D)
more driven and confident than other ISFJs
(Dominant subtype)

These ISFJs are often in a leadership position or on their way to one. They are adept at shepherding people in organizations and playing a humanistic role in society. They have an in-charge look and feel.

Brain-wise, these ISFJs have a front bias, a strong halo of connections around the perimeter, and skills suited to their roles. The front bias means fast executive function. They gather information and make decisions in a relatively quick way, with care but also a fair degree of confidence. As part of this, they easily build rapport, mentally plan, think conceptually, and trust values. They also have strong managerial skills to balance the unique demands of situations against their values. Behind all of this, an "even field" and "halo" support linear thinking, attentive senses, and essentials expected by society. There are also often a few zig-zag connections for dramatic flair. If their role is public-facing, they are adept communicators and reason using language. Or, if in a more artistic, physical, or technical role, they have good body awareness. Finally, a few sport a hidden "starburst" that produces smart ideas when they relax and entertain questions.

They enjoy improving lives and helping others to get along. A typical career path includes many accomplishments and experiences to draw on. They might run—or help run—a charity organization, human resources department, medical center, school, or professional network. Often they are trained in complementary disciplines. They prize getting the training and status needed to play their role with confidence. Whatever their role, they easily view themselves in a patient yet tough motherly or fatherly way.

Overall, they have honed diplomatic skills and aim to minimize conflict and maximize harmony to get things done. They also have a reflective side. They like quiet moments to review current events against their inner storehouse to ensure they're doing their best.

"Artistic Composer" (ISFJ-C)
more exploratory and social than other ISFJs
(Creative subtype)

These ISFJs are the most artistically inclined, especially with music. They like to feel sufficiently secure to take an open, flowing, inspired approach to their work and life. They give off a get-things-going style.

The most prominent brain-wiring is a "starburst" pattern. A starburst means all brain regions fire in sync. When a new prompt comes, they tap all of their brain's resources—their storehouse of knowledge—to offer a creative response. That might be a what-if idea or off-the-wall joke. Or, what it's usually about for them is crafting a cohesive result, something harmonious with a lot of elements in play. For example, for music, they are suited to jazz and are good composers and band-mates. Whatever they do, they are really adroit at weaving together different pieces.

They are still planful. Besides the starburst, they tend to have a couple of grounding strengths. They often have good auditory skills. They also tend to have a large set of routines akin to knowing a large set of chords to play almost any song. They are in touch with their body, feelings, and sensations. And they easily catch people's expressions, moods, and meanings, particularly in light of shared history. Where they tend to lack is executive skill and are slow to make decisions. They have a quirky side: despite their own sensitivities, desire to be accepted, and worldliness, they generally lack the halo of skills that society expects of "good workers". In this sense, they are independent thinkers, often working solo and approached as experts.

Besides creative work, they enjoy socializing, hosting cozy gatherings, and tending their home so it inspires them. They avoid people and places that are aggressive or draining. Their brains are like a sponge, and the same sensitivity that can inspire can also really hamper them.

"Conscientious Supporter" (ISFJ-N)
more conventional and specialized than other ISFJs
(Normalizing subtype)

These ISFJs are particularly careful, caring, conservative, and responsible protectors. Their brain-wiring is common in the general population. They take a more chart-the-course style.

The clearest brain-wiring pattern is an "even field" with a few favored spots. An even-field means every region neatly links to every other adjacent region like a quilt. Thinking tends to be linear. To get from A to Z requires stepping through multiple points in between. Yet they also can address almost anything, eventually, at least in a familiar way. As part of this, they sport a "halo" of skills expected by society. They use all of their senses, have keen body awareness, and are usually good at reasoning using language. That includes making smart inferences. Where they lack is out-of-the box thinking. Novelty is not in their wheelhouse.

They tend to have a slight right-hemisphere and back-brain bias. While attentive to details and facts, they lean toward registering the artistic merits and emotional tenor of situations. And, extra processing in the back of the brain gives them a strong reflective side. New data goes to the back of the brain for extra processing, making comparisons to their huge database of factual and personal memories to figure out what fits well and doesn't.

They tend toward specialized careers in accounting, charity, editing, fine arts, library science, nursing, psychology, and secretarial work. Whatever it is, they bring a close, detailed attention to the practical human needs—emotional and physical—of the people they're helping. They are particularly comfortable in large institutions and they know how to deliver what the institution can, and cannot, offer.

Home is where the heart is. While a reliable worker, their devotion to family, closest friends, and community comes naturally. They tend to enjoy cooking and handicrafts. Also, they have a quirky side that they only show to those close to them, though they are wary of anything that "flies over their head".

"Gifted Conciliator" (ISFJ-H)
more empathic and reflective than other ISFJs
(Harmonizing subtype)

These ISFJs are gifted, humanistic, and notably sensitive. They have a deep concern for the human dimension,
and they work well one-on-one with others and at complex
endeavors. They embrace a behind-the-scenes style.

For brain-wiring, they sport several diamond-shaped networks.
Each network stretches across the hemispheres, offering a finely-tuned
blend of artistic and technical know-how for a specific activity. Each diamond represents an area of expertise. One typical network supports an
open-ended, adaptable way to process social feedback, such as needed
with clients. Another network helps them to really attend—in a holistic
way—to people's body language and facial expressions. This also links
to remarkable visual artistic skills. A third typical network builds off
of a set of routines that they can select from and combine to assem-
ble a quick, sophisticated response. Underlying these networks is often
a soft "starburst" pattern that helps them to select what's needed when
and keep things together. It ties together everything. Overall, they have
keen minds and are comfortable with complexity. On the down side,
they struggle with being forceful and making decisions, and they can
feel awkward and exposed, particularly in unfamiliar situations.

A typical career such as counseling allows them to work face-to-face
with someone. However, they might be a film editor, media interviewer,
portrait painter, or such; those also deal closely with individuals, each
in their own way that requires a sophisticated patience and appreciation
for nuance. There is a good chance they have a more international or
multi-cultural background. They easily come off as their own unique,
really interesting person.

Among ISFJs, they are the most philosophical, sensitive, and vulnerable to conflict. They have fine preferences and tastes, and anything
falling outside their favorite networks catches them off-guard. They have
a great capacity for concern and love with high standards on themselves
and others.

Mind Your Neurotic Zone*

Like all types, ISFJs have neurotic moments. These erupt when the ego and unconscious clash. While at times uplifting, the result is often anxiety and insecurity. These episodes are also opportunities to learn and grow.

Skillful Sleuthing
Gain leverage using a framework.
Introverted Thinking (Ti)

- **_Basic Use_**: Adhere to definitions and philosophical principles.
- **_Advanced Use_**: Analyze a problem using a framework, and find an angle or leverage by which to solve it.
- **_Neurotic Use_**: Can get hypercritical yet are also personally quite sensitive (even to small slights). Tend to get stuck in analysis paralysis. Constantly grapple with vague big ideas without getting clarity. Prefer simple mental models except a specialty to endlessly tweak and elaborate (word smithing, etc). Strongly favor (or reject) intellectual or cultural elitism (e.g. fetishize scholarship/education). Easily define personal or local experiences as part of some global/grand drama. Feel a strong inner/outer split (e.g. warm on the outside while cold inside, or vice versa).

Manage Your Energy**

ISFJ is a steady, careful, and conservative type. Here, "conservative" means keeping with daily routines, family and cultural traditions, and the lessons of past experiences. They tend to shepherd their energy by minimizing surprises and crises, and maintaining a predictable, smooth way of working and living. They can make big sacrifices to keep life even and orderly.

Like the body itself, they like familiar patterns. They like to eat, work, play, and sleep at predictable times. They aim to damp down changes and extreme reactions. In theory, this leads to a comfortable life with consistent energy. In practice, others around them may push needs and plans onto them, and they may over-extend themselves with too many respon-

* Similar here to cousin type INFJ.

sibilities such that they work themselves to exhaustion. They can skimp on healthy eating, especially if they focus on economy or were raised with poor habits. Other people's dramatics also stress them. For ISFJ, they are hyper-alert to social signals and can struggle to deal with others' feedback and demands. They can easily feel insulted. And, they want to be cooperative and friendly, but then how do they say no? They easily end up venting their frustrations in small, annoying ways.

What really helps: simplifying their lives with fewer responsibilities, knowing that it's okay to ask for and receive help, and building in good eating and exercise habits into their days. They also benefit when their work allows plenty of room for their family and community. Keeping up a scheduler to manage time and responsibilities can also help, otherwise they can feel overwhelmed by too many things to do.

Pursue Your Aspirations**

Like all types, ISFJs trust and prioritize their heroic strengths. At the same time, they also seek ways to express their opposite. This opposite acts as a bridge to the unconscious, a realm where potential and vulnerability reside. Thus, their opposite is a doorway to growth.

Excited Brainstorming
Explore numerous emerging patterns.
Extraverted Intuiting (Ne)

- *Basic Use*: Notice abstract patterns as they emerge.
- *Advanced Use*: Shift a situation's dynamics and explore imaginative potential possibilities.
- *Aspirational Use*: Yearn for an exciting life of adventure. Enjoy "risk taking" or letting loose in a safe, set environment such as an amusement park or casino. Willing to try a new idea if it links to the past, an authority figure, or the need is pressing. Can connect the dots and come up with a surprising solution given time to do thorough research. Enjoy cute arts and crafts and small-time entrepreneurial ventures (e.g. lemonade stand). Will lighten the moment with PG humor. Can worry excessively about "what if...", and on rare occasions, may make a big rash decision that's far out of character.

** Similar here to cousin type ISTJ.

ISFJ Reminders*
for Growth and Success

☐ Your ability to hear and support others—even at the cost of your own interests—is among your greatest gifts—and greatest burdens.

☐ It's okay to take pride in your accomplishments.

☐ Take comfort in the fact that most of history's greatest individuals succeeded quietly through patience, wisdom, and humility.

☐ Keep in mind that three minor commitments can often become more demanding than one major commitment.

☐ Join the philosophical conversation of life—that is, keep asking questions and you will discover a new quality to living.

☐ There is no place like home, but cultivate those who help you go out and travel the road of life on your own.

☐ Beware fancy degrees, big promises, smooth talkers, and empty titles.

☐ Practice saying what is important for you—and for you alone.

☐ You do not need to be perfect to be lovable.

☐ Drowning your sorrows in all work or all play pains the ones who really love you the most.

☐ Go on an adventure now and then.

☐ Most times, people need more challenging and more appropriate responsibilities to succeed.

☐ There's no harm in bending the rules a little every so often.

*Adapted from *Quick Guide to the 16 Personality Types in Organizations*

What Now?

Now that you've explored ISFJ:

1. How do the strengths and challenges of this type show up in your life?

2. What's an insight or goal you can act on today in some way?

3. See the later chapters to leverage your subtype, neurotic zone, energy, and aspirations.

* Similar here to cousin type INFJ.

ENTJ
Life Paths

ENTJ Essentials
Strategist Mobilizer™
Extraverting • iNtuiting • Thinking • Judging

Core Themes

ENTJs easily act as leaders with a vision. They bring in resources of all kinds and maximize talents to make the most progress. They can predict what's coming up in the big picture. They enjoy intuitive explorations and can buck convention. Where they can, ENTJs forge partnerships, mentor, and empower others. Often, they find they are running many projects. They know peace and conflict go together. They have a soft spot. They can get overwhelmed managing a lot of details of time and resources.

Unpack the Stack: ENTJs...

Lead with "Timely Building" (Te)
Utilize measurable data, tools, resources, and efficient procedures as they organize and make effective decisions.

Support by "Keen Foreseeing" (Ni)
Focus on a vision of the future, and on insights and realizations from the inner hidden world of the unconscious.

Struggle at "Active Adapting" (Se)
Enjoy the external world using their five senses and take concrete actions based on options before them.

Aspire to "Quiet Crusading" (Fi)
Listen to their feelings, convictions, and conscience to make choices that align with their identity and beliefs.

Let's explore...

this type from various angles including 4 developmental variants. As you read, consider what fits for you (or others), what has remained the same or changed over time, and options for where to go from here.

How ENTJs Lead with Heroism

Expedite Decision Making
Proactively meet goals. Often appear sure and confident.
Organize and fix to get positive results soon.

Timely Building
Measure and construct for progress.
Extraverted Thinking (Te)

Make decisions objectively based on measures and the evidence before you. Focus on word content, figures, clock units, and visual data. Find that "facts speak for themselves". Tend to check whether things are functioning properly. Can usually provide convincing, decisive explanations. Value time, and highly efficient at managing resources. Tend to utilize mental resources only when extra thinking is truly demanded. Otherwise, use what's at hand for a "good enough" result that works. Easily compartmentalize problems. Like to apply procedures to control events and achieve goals. May display high confidence even when wrong.

What flavor of Timely Building?
ENTJs can express this process in two ways. They likely develop a bias for one way early in life and may develop the other later.

"Manager" Te	"Builder" Te
Analytic/Yang Style: active, focused, fixed, outward, top down	**Holistic/Yin Style**: receptive, diffuse, flexible, inward, bottom up
Eyes success at a few ambitious goals. Speak logically and confidently. Apply a business mindset to affairs. Manage and drive others as resources to get things done. May put speed and profit above usefulness or accuracy.	Helpful hard worker. Efficient, frugal, economical, and timely. Focus on doing work right. Avoid distractions. Perfect details and optimize functionality. Comfortable with different forms of complexity and multiple projects.

How ENTJs Give Flexible Support

Chart the Process
Reflect on data and perceptions. Often appear focused and preoccupied. Attend to reference points.

Keen Foreseeing
Transform with a meta-perspective.
Introverted Intuiting (Ni)

Withdraw from the world and tap your whole mind to receive an insight. Can enter a brief trance to respond to a challenge, foresee the future, or answer a philosophical issue. Avoid specializing and rely instead on timely "ah-ha" moments or a holistic "zen state" to tackle novel tasks, which may look like creative expertise. Manage your own mental processes and stay aware of where you are in an open-ended task. May use an action or symbol to focus. Sensitive to the unknown. Ruminate on ways to improve. Look for synergy. Might try out a realization to transform yourself or how you think. May over-rely on the unconscious.

What flavor of Keen Foreseeing?
ENTJs can express this process in two ways. They likely develop a bias for one way early in life and may develop the other later.

"Visionary" Ni	"Oracle" Ni
Analytic/Yang Style: active, focused, fixed, outward, top down	**Holistic/Yin Style**: receptive, diffuse, flexible, inward, bottom up
Stick to a singular vision of the future to improve self and society. Be certain of a few compelling insights. Don't let go or water down. Turn realizations into principles. Apply many complex concepts. Act as a guiding spirit.	Hold lightly many interrelated insights. Connect to the many facets of the archetypal world. Open to transformation. Respond to others' questions, and innovate for the group. Cultivate an aesthetic or spiritual practice.

ENTJ Self-Portrait

From Conversations*: *What's it like to be you?*

Not organizing and not problem solving is hard for me. I am most comfortable in the idea development stage—the push for putting things together, new solutions, and improvements to take us to the next step. I have several dimensions I work in.

My focus has always been on finding what's preventing us from doing what we need to do. If it's lack of confidence or motivation, the solution is building that. If it's lack of skills, it's building skills. If it's rules or other inhibitors, I work to eliminate those. I value people, but I am quick to judge their value to the system and quick to judge my personal desire to be involved with them. I stand off if they don't meet my standards quickly, which can make me hard to know, and I think I am unwilling to get into other people's motivations.

My response to making a mistake is, "Did you learn anything? If so, great, it was worth it, and don't make the same mistake again." This kind of critiquing is easy for me, and I admire—and like to have around me—people who have a real, genuine concern for others and who see the positives. But then there is a time when I sit back and say people have to get on board with the way I see things because it's the right way to go. It took me a while to learn the value of cutting people some slack. Although I appear to dominate, when people get to know me, I really don't. I let them do their own thing. With people I judge as friendly or want to get to know, I open up quickly, although I don't actually go out and do things to make others like me.

I respect wisdom and kindness and competent, knowledgeable people who are willing to share with others. I won't buy into anything just because the person who says it is the leader. It has to make sense to me—consistent and free of contradictions. If it's a plan, I have to believe it's doable. If it's a philosophy, it must match mine from the outset. I think integrity means keeping one's word and sticking to my espoused principles even when it's easier not to. Honesty is important.
I really value progress, learning, and knowledge and have an in-

* Reprinted from *16 Personality Types: Descriptions for Self-Discovery*

tense need to know things. Probably this is where I get myself into a lot of projects because it is the opportunity to try something new. I tend to over research, and I have an innate ability to handle a great number of diverse things almost simultaneously. I can watch TV and finish a project and read a magazine all at the same time. I think I don't know how to relax. I can sit down and actually go through and identify the problem and gather alternatives and do a mental brainstorm by myself to come up with different alternatives. I force myself to see if I am not looking at something disjointedly or parochially before I come to a conclusion. And I try to look at the small things in order to look at the big picture, just using plain logic and connecting the dots to prognosticate what the likely outcomes are. Often the first conclusion was the right one anyway.

I actually believe you can do anything if you set your mind to it and are willing to pay the price. I will ask myself if I am willing to pay the price.

I tend to push to get the job done, sometimes without regard to others' feelings, and I hate repeating myself. Listening is a problem for me because I have probably already thought out things thoroughly, done my homework, and reached an answer before I even get to the stage of presenting it to other people. Similarly, I may get upset with others' behavior, but it is almost never personalized, which can be a drawback because then I haven't considered what caused the behavior and if I should make some kind of reconciliation.

I am my own worst critic. I want perfect achievement of myself, and sometimes I have a fear of suddenly waking up and being known as someone who doesn't really know anything.

I love to discover new approaches and really prefer creating and beginning things, organizing projects and programs, and then teaching someone else how to do them and handing them off. Although if someone has a better idea, then let's go with it, and if the system's values and mechanisms line up for me, whoever the leader is, then I guess I am probably one of the most loyal. Probably my goals are patience, wisdom, and discipline—wisdom to focus on the right priorities and correct decisions and patience to take the time to listen.

"Visionary General" (ENTJ-D)
more driven and confident than other ENTJs
(Dominant subtype)

These ENTJs are particularly ambitious, commanding, and confident. They can potentially rise to become institutional directors, political leaders, or tycoons of industry. They enjoy leading others to advance a traditional domain (e.g. healthcare, media, politics, transport) to its next evolutionary step. They exemplify an in-charge style.

In terms of brain-wiring, these ENTJs show a clear front and left bias—they are outgoing, tough, analytical, and generally rely on a preset way to rapidly act on anything that comes up. Their brain tends to be efficient, tapping a few favorite regions, akin to sticking to only a few critical rooms in a mansion. Turning on some lights in other, less practiced or expected regions may come slowly for them. Thus, they can be slow to adjust to surprises.

Most favor left-hemisphere regions for word content, facts, and social rules. Others are more well-rounded with a "halo" of brain links. Either way, they aim to excel in whatever endeavors to which they apply their willpower. They may sport strong managerial and communication skills, although not necessarily—a passion for leadership may not translate to finesse.

Their interest is usually business management. Favored domains include advertising, cognitive science, economics, education, games, health care, media, and sales. They like the idea of advancing the public good and society in general. At the same time, they will push for maximum profits and rapid, controlled growth. They rely on impersonal metrics to automate the human elements; others may view them as heartless, even villainous. Even when they fall short of goals, their revolutionary impact can shift an organization, industry, or even society for years to come.

"Renaissance Explorer" (ENTJ-C)
more exploratory and social than other ENTJs
(Creative subtype)

These ENTJs are notably curious, idealistic, and fun-loving. They exude a magnetic energy that tends to attract others' interest and get other people involved in their projects. They have a get-things-going energy.

Neural wiring tends to show a light or medium brainstorm pattern. This pattern is associated with creative, out-of-the-box thinking. Sometimes, they may show mediocre pre-frontal executive wiring and can berate themselves as distractible, indecisive or lazy even when they look active and goal-driven to others.

This variant are adventurers who travel and act with purpose. They dig into diverse topics and are open to new places and new activities, while usually retaining strong technical and business skills. They can come off as a prodigy as they quickly pass peers, particularly in adolescence, excelling in academic, athletic and social skills. Their intuition is not relegated to private time or just for business strategizing. They like to play with a lot of data and ideas at once, believing an optimal result and practical order can be drawn from that. They easily hold an international outlook with ambitions to make a cultural impact on a wide stage, even globally. They have a restless drive for remarkable experiences, be those physical, romantic or mystical such as climbing the tallest mountain with a famous guru and beautiful companion at their side. They tend to be pretty independent, but really need an executive assistant or small team to help manage daily details and implement all of their activities and ideas. Ultimately, they tend to settle into a profession that requires a blend of business, creative, social, and technical skills.

These ENTJs have a peppy demeanor, a natural charisma, and perhaps even a playboy or playgirl flair that draws in others. They may cultivate a celebrity-like following by playing up excitement and opportunity. They can easily be overly idealistic about relationships. They like technical tools and services such as dating-apps and meet-up groups to navigate social goals. This variant is most common among younger ENTJs.

"Change Administrator" (ENTJ-N)
more conventional and specialized than other ENTJs
(Normalizing subtype)

These ENTJs blend well culturally with brain-wiring that is more the norm of the general population. They usually enjoy settled, traditional lives with families, steady jobs, and community activities. They take a more chart-the-course style to be a positive force for change.

Their brain often shows an "even field" pattern—neural wiring is relatively even across the cortex, and every region is connected to its nearest neighbors horizontally or vertically like neat farm fields. This disposes them to a more linear, logical, step-by-step approach to tasks. That said, many also have a right-hemisphere bias—maybe quite strong—supporting a quiet reliance on intuition and creativity with a genuine concern for moral and ethical standards and human welfare. Generally they have mediocre executive coordination. That is, they do not just integrate new information on the spot, but prefer quiet time at their desk to collate and integrate ideas into a coherent understanding and master plan.

These ENTJs tend to be settled and prefer a calm, steady partner and home-life. Often, they work in the technical arts (e.g. electronics, mechanics, music) or the social sciences (e.g. anthropology, psychology). They easily hold a traditional job role, aspiring to general manager or department director, in a large institution such as banking, education, energy, or medicine—areas that require a lot of patience and maneuvering through regulations, working with details and the human political elements to get things done. They have a penchant for focusing and practicing for high performance that other tend to ENTJs lack.

They believe in learning as a major path to improving just about anything. This can include data analysis, mentorships, research projects, teamwork, and automated systems. Often, they will enjoy a side-interest in the arts, philosophy, or psychology. This knowledge helps them better motivate and work with others, and it sheds light on the existential big-picture of the human condition and their own place in it.

"Mystical Practitioner" (ENTJ-H)
more empathic and reflective than other ENTJs
(Harmonizing subtype)

These ENTJs are eccentric, even mystical, highly observant of what's going on, and can act as superb consultants and
counselors. They can restructure and rebuild people. To this
end, they have adopted a more behind-the-scenes style.

Often, these ENTJs show a distinct set of diamond -shaped networks, each acting as a distinct mode of thinking and acting, having
trained and tweaked themselves over time through their own studies.
While sophisticated, they also often show weak executive integration
and perhaps a back-brain bias. Thus, they tend to reflect on observations
and plot strategy rather than take rapid action. Or, they show an array
of unusual connections between brain regions and an overall knack for
holistic thinking.

This variant has an uncanny, intuitive power that they can call up to
analyze an individual, group or situation to instantly understand what is
secretly "out of whack", and they then work the target like a conductor to
move and restructure things to get a desired outcome. Imagine a healer,
educator, hypnotist or even shaman who addresses both physical and
psychological elements in a unified way. To do this, they may easily draw
from ancient practices or disparate cultural traditions, as contemporary
ones often strike them as limited. They are open to complex frameworks,
acting outside the mainstream, and can achieve miraculous results that
others puzzle over or wish to ignore. Like a crafty wizard, they themselves
can be difficult to understand or predict. They can feel like a person out
of place, wondering how they got here though still very focused on their
mission. Perhaps their understanding and tough-love style is born of a
unique realization or their own physical and personal challenges.

This variant can easily be mistaken for some other type altogether.
But one should not mistake their rapport-building and aligning skills
with anything less than a pragmatic power, hopefully to help others.

Mind Your Neurotic Zone*

Like all types, ENTJs have neurotic moments. These erupt when the ego and unconscious clash. While at times uplifting, the result is often anxiety and insecurity. These episodes are also opportunities to learn and grow.

Active Adapting
Immerse in the present context.
Extraverted Sensing (Se)

- *Basic Use*: Notice sensory data in the environment.
- *Advanced Use*: Trust your instincts and take action relevant to the moment and current context.
- *Neurotic Use*: Put health/body in danger. (e.g. skip sleep or meals). Judge something or try to control it rather than experience it. Easily give in to impulses to quickly take actions (even if it's the wrong action). Tend to view all outcomes of their actions as reversible or fixable. Set unrealistic/grandiose plans, yet easily distracted and drawn into adolescent fun. Feel exempt from life's rules due to secret short-cuts. (e.g. "The Secret" style thinking). Get a genius insight while resisting feedback, viewing it as the final answer with no more questions or ideas needed.

Manage Your Energy*

ENTJs tend to set lofty goals and map out big plans for themselves and other people. As part of this, they tend to live in their head, in a realm of high ideals. At the same time, they can get easily side-tracked by fun physical and social activities. While juggling all of this, they can abuse their health. They may repeatedly injure themselves during risky adventures. They may skimp on diet and, especially, sleep. Quality sleep is absolutely essential for sustainable energy and a clear head!

Another challenge: They tend to try to control or judge experiences rather than be open to the beauty or possibilities of a moment. They have clear goals with ideas for how to fill them, and they can feel impatient with a lot of energy to simply actualize those. This leads to tension when

Similar here to cousin type ENFJ.

others resist their expectation or plan, and also they may miss opportunities to genuinely relax. For ENTJ, a big challenge is their tendency to keep pushing to progress faster, make more money, and so on without let up, but then feeling lazy. As part of this, they can decide too quickly on an option that is lower quality than what they need.

They benefit by getting out in nature, ideally with friends, in a way that they must leave work and technology behind. Ideally, a physical activity so absorbs their attention that they entirely forget about their problems and goals. They also benefit from keeping up several body- and health-practices rather than relying on one, since they can easily get stuck in a favorite way of thinking. Finally, they benefit when their work is grounding, when they can experience life "on the front lines" and get a lot of practical feedback to balance the big dreams.

Pursue Your Aspirations**

Like all types, ENTJs trust and prioritize their heroic strengths. At the same time, they also seek ways to express their opposite. This opposite acts as a bridge to the unconscious, a realm where potential and vulnerability reside. Thus, their opposite is a doorway to growth.

Quiet Crusading
Staying true to who you really are.
Introverted Feeling (Fi)

- **Basic Use**: Adhere to personal beliefs about what's important.
- **Advanced Use**: Evaluate situations and choose what you believe is congruent with your personal identity.
- **Aspirational Use**: Yearn to improve the human condition on a mass scale by the power of efficient organization. Will quickly gather facts, present logical arguments, and organize people and resources for a good cause. Can lead a moral crusade. Secretly really enjoy quiet relaxation. Benefit from self-reflection such as journaling. Want to help people get to know their unique potential and develop into exemplary individuals. Must practice patience. Find that hardship breeds character. Need a good cry in private on rare occasion. Can be childish emotionally, or hold simplistic black-or-white judgments.

189 ** Similar here to cousin type ESTJ.

ENTJ Reminders*
for Growth and Success

☐ Mentoring and promoting promising people is one of your greatest abilities.

☐ Trust, develop, and share your intuitions—but don't scare away too many people.

☐ When people seem disinterested in maximizing their potential, consider what strong beliefs are motivating them toward something else.

☐ Even if you rise to the top of something conventional, it's still conventional—and convention can be the source of many of life's demanding details.

☐ Do not underestimate your ability to handle the status quo when it strikes back against change.

☐ Consider that your objective style might leave others confident in you, but wanting something more personal.

☐ Take the initiative to get close to those who interest you.

☐ Develop and check your moral compass early and often.

☐ Reason with principles, not words.

☐ Aim for quality above speed.

☐ Allow yourself and others some time to just play with ideas.

☐ Time off does not mean extra time for more work.

☐ Try three things to maintain your health and build in time for family and friends.

☐ Notice that without a quiet space for yourself, you will feel like all weather and no sunshine.

*Adapted from *Quick Guide to the 16 Personality Types in Organizations*

What Now?

Now that you've explored ENTJ:

1. How do the strengths and challenges of this type show up in your life?
2. What's an insight or goal you can act on today in some way?
3. See the later chapters to leverage your subtype, neurotic zone, energy, and aspirations.

* Similar here to cousin type ENFJ.

INTJ
Life Paths

INTJ Essentials
Conceptualizer Director™
Introverting • iNtuiting • Thinking • Judging

Core Themes

INTJs are abstract, self-directed thinkers. They have a drive for self-mastery to make the most of what they can achieve. They have a talent to calculate far ahead and see deep reasons behind things. They think in terms of concepts, evidence, efficiency, systems, and strategies. INTJs build a vision and take steps to realize progress to their goals. They like to stay independent and are invariably at the leading edge. Their secret is creative flow. They can find it hard to let go to interact freely with others.

Unpack the Stack: INTJs...

Lead with "Keen Foreseeing" (Ni)
Focus on a vision of the future, and on insights and realizations from the inner hidden world of the unconscious.

Support by "Timely Building" (Te)
Utilize measurable data, tools, resources, and efficient procedures as they organize and make effective decisions.

Struggle at "Quiet Crusading" (Fi)
Listen to their feelings, convictions, and conscience to make choices that align with their identity and beliefs.

Aspire to "Active Adapting" (Se)
Enjoy the external world using their five senses and take concrete actions based on options before them.

Let's explore...

this type from various angles including 4 developmental variants. As you read, consider what fits for you (or others), what has remained the same or changed over time, and options for where to go from here.

How INTJs Lead with Heroism

Chart the Process

Reflect on data and perceptions. Often appear focused and preoccupied. Attend to reference points.

Keen Foreseeing
Transform with a meta-perspective.
Introverted Intuiting (Ni)

Withdraw from the world and tap your whole mind to receive an insight. Can enter a brief trance to respond to a challenge, foresee the future, or answer a philosophical issue. Avoid specializing and rely instead on timely "ah-ha" moments or a holistic "zen state" to tackle novel tasks, which may look like creative expertise. Manage your own mental processes and stay aware of where you are in an open-ended task. May use an action or symbol to focus. Sensitive to the unknown. Ruminate on ways to improve. Look for synergy. Might try out a realization to transform yourself or how you think. May over-rely on the unconscious.

What flavor of Keen Foreseeing?

INTJs can express this process in two ways. They likely develop a bias for one way early in life and may develop the other later.

"Visionary" Ni	"Oracle" Ni
Analytic/Yang Style: active, focused, fixed, outward, top down	*Holistic/Yin Style*: receptive, diffuse, flexible, inward, bottom up
Stick to a singular vision of the future to improve self and society. Be certain of a few compelling insights. Don't let go or water down. Turn realizations into principles. Apply many complex concepts. Act as a guiding spirit.	Hold lightly many interrelated insights. Connect to the many facets of the archetypal world. Open to transformation. Respond to others' questions, and innovate for the group. Cultivate an aesthetic or spiritual practice.

How INTJs Give Flexible Support

Expedite Decision Making

Proactively meet goals. Often appear sure and confident.
Organize and fix to get positive results soon.

Timely Building
Measure and construct for progress.
Extraverted Thinking (Te)

Make decisions objectively based on measures and the evidence before you. Focus on word content, figures, clock units, and visual data. Find that "facts speak for themselves". Tend to check whether things are functioning properly. Can usually provide convincing, decisive explanations. Value time, and highly efficient at managing resources. Tend to utilize mental resources only when extra thinking is truly demanded. Otherwise, use what's at hand for a "good enough" result that works. Easily compartmentalize problems. Like to apply procedures to control events and achieve goals. May display high confidence even when wrong.

What flavor of Timely Building?

INTJs can express this process in two ways. They likely develop a bias for one way early in life and may develop the other later.

"Manager" Te	"Builder" Te
Analytic/Yang Style: active, focused, fixed, outward, top down	*Holistic/Yin Style*: receptive, diffuse, flexible, inward, bottom up
Eyes success at a few ambitious goals. Speak logically and confidently. Apply a business mindset to affairs. Manage and drive others as resources to get things done. May put speed and profit above usefulness or accuracy.	Helpful hard worker. Efficient, frugal, economical, and timely. Focus on doing work right. Avoid distractions. Perfect details and optimize functionality. Comfortable with different forms of complexity and multiple projects.

INTJ Self-Portrait

From Conversations*: *What's it like to be you?*

I often feel I am missing something, that I have a perspective or viewpoint that isn't widely shared and that I am decades ahead of my time, maybe more. It's like being caught in a time warp.

I tend to be someone who looks at all the what-ifs, thinking way ahead with a vision of things and anticipating. I'm always interested in extending myself into areas I don't do well in. I'm a good problem solver from that perspective. I like to go through anything I can think of before I act—the implications, what others have tried before and their effect, my options and their consequences, who to mobilize and in what time frame. I like coming up with new ideas about how to approach a situation until I find a solution that feels right. And I like to think that solution will be something that works for everyone. I experience problems as challenges, not as things that can't be dealt with or accomplished. Challenges can always be dealt with.

I am naturally organized, structured, and analytical. If a project enters my mind it immediately assumes the form of its pieces, its basic structure, and what order—first, next, last—it will take to get it done. This isn't something I do, it happens instantaneously without effort. Issues are multifaceted and I try to think from different perspectives, not only my perspectives but others' too. And I've found it's good to gather as many facts as I can. Sometimes there is a piece that needs to be thrown out, or maybe it's the seed of another project.

I won't do something if I feel I can't do it well. I prefer trying something, then critique after the fact. I will integrate the experience and never make the same mistakes again. I am satisfied when things work well, and I like to improve people's lives by reorganizing and introducing things in an understandable way that is explicit and clear and makes sense. Then someone else can come in and take over. I set very high standards for myself, and I believe it is possible to be competent at anything and everything I set my mind to.

* Reprinted from *16 Personality Types: Descriptions for Self-Discovery*

I keep myself very private; that's a part of who I am. I keep people at arm's length. They have to gain my trust and interest. People are curious about me, I think, but only the brave try to figure me out. I feel very serious, but some I meet I just like a lot, and I can be spontaneously playful. I have a sensitivity to people and can feel warm with them, although many perceive me as intimidating, aloof or annoyed, or incredibly calm and competent about everything. People say I ask them good questions, not to make the decision for them, but to help them think through things. I look for systems that will make things better, and I am very much a person who seeks fairness and equality. People are very important, and I want to help them develop the skills they need to get on in life, whatever that means for each one of them.

There's always something to occupy my mind or attention. I must be using my mind in a purposefully creative way, pushing the envelope with the most creatively challenging thing I can do, being the originator of a solution to a problem that doesn't exist yet. It's a complex world, and I believe we each should develop as complex an inner life as possible with the facility to react or initiate in a wide variety of ways. The more successful one is at actively developing all of that and having access to that, the better things can be. If something really interests me I have an incredible ability to stick with it—even though I have a larger perspective, I can be very focused and zero in on a point. I have always seen the world at many levels.

Autonomy is important, to be respected for my own thoughts and feelings, ideas and creativity. I am turned off when people try to discredit my ideas or don't listen before they even understand, or when people don't try to do the best they can or fight against progress. And if the emotional piece is not well managed in my life, or not compartmentalized, work is very difficult. Chitchat is tedious. I don't know what to say, and I figure the other person isn't actually interested in me anyway.

Over time I have built a world-view, like constructing a map of the cosmos, and from this, essentially everything is understandable and anything is possible. All the things I've done, have been self-taught by picking up on or asking myself good, clear, penetrating questions to expose and articulate the hidden structures that underlie the experience of living.

"Visionary Director" (INTJ-D)
more driven and confident than other INTJs
(Dominant subtype)

These INTJ have things worked out. They are relatively fast reacting, can act as skilled managers or executives, and lean on analytical skills, particularly language-based reasoning. They've learned how to be in charge.

Brain-wise, their wiring is biased toward the front, giving them relatively quick responses, and they also often favor the left hemisphere for solid analytical skills. They show a weak or no "starburst" brainstorming pattern. Thus, they lean away from unstructured creativity. Even if they show a weak starburst, it's something they use more in quiet time alone. These INTJs rely on specific brain regions for hypothesizing, imaginative analogies, and so forth to implement their creative side. They also enjoy exceptional speaking skills and self-control. And they tend to have good physical skills for sports and such and can get somewhat competitive.

Compared to other INTJs, Visionary Directors are likely in a large institution or company. That might be the military, hospital, engineering firm, or software house. They typically lead in a conventional office space and/or are focused on technical innovation. Of course, as INTJs, they are still introverts. So, their use of executive and frontal regions—for making decisions, juggling new data, and managing others—has required an effortful learning curve. They have figured out how to balance situational demands versus their values and a desire for things being smooth or absolute. Speaking and listening are comfortable ways for them to act as leaders. And with their more assertive and territorial style, they are comfortable speaking up about someone's misstep, pushing an argument, and confronting leaders.

Outside of work, they enjoy imaginative introverted activities that tap the back of the brain. They are more auditory and less visual than other INTJs and likely enjoy audio books, music, and such. They do have a reflective side distinct from being "on" at work. They remain open to musings or even hobbies that are esoteric or fanciful.

"Creative Enthusiast" (INTJ-C)
more exploratory and social than other INTJs
(Creative subtype)

These INTJs tend to be highly creative in a thoughtful, detailed way, though also somewhat scattered and more generalists than specialists. They've learned how to stir the pot, engage others, entertain, and get things going.

For these INTJs, the brain often shows a strong, solid "starburst" pattern typical of fast intuitive insight. They take in data and quickly play with it in their mind in different ways. To balance this chaos, they have a clear left or front-left brain-wiring bias, with some back-right bias as well. This allows them to organize, present, and act on their thoughts and impressions in a goal-focused way. Thus, they are particularly quick at absorbing and synthesizing a lot of abstract, conceptual material. They easily notice patterns, project into the future how an idea or event will turn out, and then set a goal and focus around it with a confident drive to completion.

Despite their lively, relatively sociable energy and varied hobbies, they still have mediocre emotional and body awareness like other INTJs, as they tend to neglect those areas even as they extrovert ideas. They may develop a circuit or two to handle these in a limited or focused way. Ideally, they incorporate body and emotions into their creative endeavors such as music and seek a healthy, solid basis in life. Similarly, being introverts, executive tasks such as decision making, juggling new, incoming data, and managing others take effort and give mixed results. Oppositely, they tend to seek reward from visual, reflective, and detailed activities that tap their brain's back regions. They also find reward from activities that improve their visual-spatial (biomechanical) understanding in life. They are among the most innovative of all types.

Overall, these INTJs are motivated generalists. They see little difference between their workplace and hobbies. Their intuitive side works across many subjects and contexts, though often in a scattered way that needs constant self-management. They make for interesting conversationalists and stimulating partners.

"Unconventional Guide" (INTJ-N)
more conventional and specialized than other INTJs
(Normalizing subtype)

These INTJs blend in well culturally with brain-wiring that is more the norm of the general population. They are still quirky. They have a clear chart-the-course style that makes them good stewards, monitors, and guides.

Their brain-wiring is relatively even across the brain. That even pattern means every region is connected to its nearest neighbor horizontally or vertically. Often there is also some bias toward the back, middle-back, and/or left hemisphere. Overall, this makes them look like linear, reflective, and analytical thinkers, processing information one step at a time in a rational way. Male INTJs here show a particularly strong linear, deductive style.

These INTJs are more likely to come from a collectivist or a conventional upbringing, perhaps with less education or lower-profile careers, compared to other INTJs. Or conversely, they may work at a high level, busy implementing a big idea in a routine way. The more at odds with their upbringing, the more they have introverted wiring with dense links toward the back of the brain. Conversely, the more they fit with their background, the more the wiring is an even field across the brain.

Compared to other INTJs, they are more in tune with their senses, more patient with analysis of detail, and more likely to be well-socialized. They can hang at the county fair, small-talk about everyday events, and enjoy life's little moments. They are thoughtful, careful speakers. They tend to be particularly visual, and they enjoy reflection and internal sorting. Like other INTJs, executive tasks take effort, though they easily make smart, careful managers.

As for a creative side, they enjoy crafts and likely rely on pencil-paper and familiar frameworks to sketch out ideas. They are less apt than other INTJs to just brainstorm and work out ideas in their head. They remain open to entertaining a wide range of fanciful ideas that they can mull over in their giant database of abstract impressions.

"Eccentric Diamond" (INTJ-H)
more empathic and reflective than other INTJs
(Harmonizing subtype)

These INTJs are the most eccentric and eclectic of their type. They are also the most values- or principles-based of INTJs and the most "out there", living their unique philosophy and desires. They can have a behind-the-scenes quality, observant and driven, yet also tolerant and not pushing themselves onto others.

Their brains rely on one or more diamond-shaped networks that bridge the hemispheres. Thus, their name. The example shows a set of typical networks. Each network includes four to six diverse brain regions that work in concert. These multiple networks tend to not overlap. Each does it own thing and represents a different "mode". And each mode fits a kind of situation or way of thinking and being. Every mode includes a diverse set of skills that link and harmonize a thematic set of values, behavior, speech, perception, feeling, analysis, and so on.

To hold these modes together, there is also often a starburst pattern. It may be strongly active, but usually it is soft, working in the background. Either way, the starburst helps all the regions work in synch. Thus, this INTJ operates from a meta-perspective much of the time, rapidly switching between modes. And if they lack a mode for a situation, their behavior is odd or non-reactive. Moreover, they often lack a "halo" in terms of brain-wiring pattern. That means there is no ring of connections around the perimeter of the brain like many other people have. It's as if typical forms of linear, everyday expected thinking are actively excluded.

Despite their eccentric style, these INTJs have a strong drive to complete goals, and forming and pursuing tasks in service of their goals takes scant effort. Oppositely, staying open takes work because their thinking is already so complex and developed in specialized ways. This variant is most common among INTJs at or after midlife and among those with a mix of analytical and human-centric careers.

Mind Your Neurotic Zone*

Like all types, INTJs have neurotic moments. These erupt when the ego and unconscious clash. While at times uplifting, the result is often anxiety and insecurity. These episodes are also opportunities to learn and grow.

Quiet Crusading
Staying true to who you really are.
Introverted Feeling (Fi)

- **Basic Use**: Adhere to personal beliefs about what's important.
- **Advanced Use**: Evaluate situations and choose what you believe is congruent with your personal identity.
- **Neurotic Use**: Feel extreme loyalty and condemn disloyalty. Tend to be self-righteous or moralistic (especially about hypocrisy) with stubborn black-or-white judgment. Easily repress emotions and pretend they don't care, then have an outburst. Fail to fully hear others' input (notably feelings) and then hurt by the backlash. Endless inner emotional sorting without peace. Easily moody or tense, or suffer chronic low-level depression or anger. Tend to be serious and orderly while pining for joy and freedom. Selfish focus on their own personal wants, goals, values, etc.

Manage Your Energy**

INTJs are private and protective of their energy. This is about more than time, physical space, and resources. Their psyche is like a finely-tuned, highly sensitive antenna that takes in a lot of abstract impressions. Thus, they can be stressed by things that others don't notice. They also trust their capacity for creative flow, but getting into and sustaining flow takes seclusion, which generally requires having room away from others' "auras".

At times, they may feel they lack energy to get off the ground. This can look like procrastination but is due to a lack of information and alignment to deep needs and values. They benefit by setting strong boundaries, being clear to others up front when it's okay to intrude. And, they need positive, healthy people around them who can also facilitate in

* Similar here to cousin type ISTJ.

a gentle, hands-off way when they go overboard.

A big challenge is working at too many goals, and feeling paralyzed to act, or falling into the trap of tunnel vision, pushing themselves beyond healthy limits to complete a huge project. Ideally, they take time to simplify down to what's important right now.

Rather than devoting themselves to a single body-mind practice, they benefit from having a set of several low-impact practices to pick from daily to "cleanse" and reset. Taking off a few weeks at a time, especially alone in nature as "me time" is ideal. Having private time everyday for an hour or two, where they can relax rather than be in work mode or carer mode, is also great. They also benefit when they have a low-maintenance environment and workplace.

Pursue Your Aspirations**

Like all types, INTJs trust and prioritize their heroic strengths. At the same time, they also seek ways to express their opposite. This opposite acts as a bridge to the unconscious, a realm where potential and vulnerability reside. Thus, their opposite is a doorway to growth.

Active Adapting
Immerse in the present context.
Extraverted Sensing (Se)

- **Basic Use**: Notice sensory data in the environment.
- **Advanced Use**: Trust your gut instincts and take action relevant to the moment and current context.
- **Aspirational Use**: Yearn to live freely in the present with tangible and immediate experiences. Enjoy trips into nature. Channel abstract visions into tangible projects or actionable plans. Use insights for personal and interpersonal improvement. Use foresight to predict trends and create products and services for these trends. Stimulate inner growth through rich sensory experiences such as travel. Express deep insights about the human experience through sensory mediums like art, dance, music, writing, or yoga. Can get derailed by concrete details or entertaining pleasures.

** Similar here to cousin type INFJ.

INTJ Reminders*
for Growth and Success

- ☐ Seeing through life's fog, and managing a lot of complexity, are among your top talents.
- ☐ Recruit people who believe in you and your ideas. And show other people your projects—get feedback to keep your vision realistic.
- ☐ Find an environment with the tools and resources to build and test your ideas.
- ☐ A mentor is a good way to get ahead.
- ☐ When possible, consider ways to automate and delegate to free you to focus on what only you can do.
- ☐ Attend to your impact on others, especially in how you communicate.
- ☐ Ask what others may need, and learn "people tools" to change how you feel and understand whom to trust.
- ☐ Try to keep at least three good friends.
- ☐ Remember to give expression to your feelings. And if you allow someone to influence your heart then you will never be alone.
- ☐ You don't need to experiment or push every relationship in order to learn.
- ☐ Treat others as more human than you treat yourself.
- ☐ Account for your health, body, and environment in all plans.
- ☐ Collect the feeling or meaning of each of your life experiences, and have as many kinds of experiences as possible.
- ☐ Consider that there are always more choices.
- ☐ Be ready to rethink what "success" means.

* Adapted from *Quick Guide to the
16 Personality Types in Organizations*

What Now?

Now that you've explored INTJ:

1. How do the strengths and challenges of this type show up in your life?
2. What's an insight or goal you can act on today in some way?
3. See the later chapters to leverage your subtype, neurotic zone, energy, and aspirations.

* Similar here to cousin type ISTJ.

ENTP
Life Paths

ENTP Essentials
Explorer Inventor™
Extraverting • iNtuiting • Thinking • Perceiving

Core Themes

ENTPs are inventive and life-long learners. They explore lots of ideas. They have a talent to build prototypes and launch projects. They enjoy creative problem solving and like to share their insights about life's possibilities. ENTPs are pragmatic as they come up with strategies for success. They enjoy the drama of give and take. They try to be diplomatic, invite others, and host. At some level, they need to feel safe. They are surprised when strategizing a relationship doesn't work.

Unpack the Stack: ENTPs...

Lead with "Excited Brainstorming" (Ne)
Perceive, pursue, and play with life's many potential possibilities, facilitating the promising ones.

Support by "Skillful Sleuthing" (Ti)
Analyze and define situations, solve problems, and apply leverage according to universal logical principles.

Struggle at "Friendly Hosting" (Fe)
Tend relationships, social norms, and people's needs and values as they organize and make thoughtful decisions.

Aspire to "Cautious Protecting" (Si)
Reference a massive storehouse of rich past experiences as they cultivate familiarity, comfort, and stability.

Let's explore...

this type from various angles including 4 developmental variants. As you read, consider what fits for you (or others), what has remained the same or changed over time, and options for where to go from here.

How ENTPs Lead with Heroism

Energize the Process
Seek out stimuli. Often appear random, emergent, and enthusiastic. Attend to the here and now.

Excited Brainstorming
Explore numerous emerging patterns.
Extraverted iNtuiting (Ne)

Perceive and play with ideas and relationships. Wonder about patterns of interaction across various situations. Keep up a high-energy mode that helps you notice and engage potential possibilities. Think analogically: stimuli are springboards to generate inferences, analogies, metaphors, jokes, and more new ideas. Easily guess details. Adept at "what if?" scenarios, mirroring others, and even role-playing. Can shift a situation's dynamics and trust what emerges. Mental activity tends to feel chaotic, with many highs and lows at once, like an ever-changing "Christmas tree" of flashing lights. Often entertain multiple meanings at once. May find it hard to stay on-task.

What flavor of Excited Brainstorming?
ENTPs can express this process in two ways. They likely develop a bias for one way early in life and may develop the other later.

"Marketer" Ne	"Catalyst" Ne
Analytic/Yang Style: active, focused, fixed, outward, top down	*Holistic/Yin Style*: receptive, diffuse, flexible, inward, bottom up
Put on a show. Pitch and juggle many ideas, trusting quantity over quality in search of advantages or gains. Recruit others and rely on strong energy of ideas to shift situations to one's liking. Court uncertainty for progress.	Notice subtle patterns. Negotiate toward a novel win-win outcome with a relaxed, subtle style. Use humor and disguises. Include and promote others. Search for the highest quality potential possibilities for everyone's gain.

How ENTPs Give Flexible Support

Refine Decision Making
Clarify what's universal, true or worthwhile. Often
appear quietly receptive. Trust own judgments.

Skillful Sleuthing
Gain leverage using a framework.
Introverted Thinking (Ti)

Study a situation from different angles and fit it to a theory, framework, or principle. This often involves reasoning multiple ways to objectively and accurately analyze problems. Rely on complex/subtle logical reasoning. Adept at deductive thinking, defining and categorizing, weighing odds and risks, and/or naming and navigating. Notice points to apply leverage and subtle influence. Value consistency of thought. Can shut out the senses and "go deep" to think, and separate body from mind to become objective when arguing or analyzing. Tend to backtrack to clarify thoughts, and withhold deciding in favor of thorough examination. May quickly stop listening.

What flavor of Skillful Sleuthing?
ENTPs can express this process in two ways. They likely develop a bias for one way early in life and may develop the other later.

"Critic" Ti	"Systemist" Ti
Analytic/Yang Style: active, focused, fixed, outward, top down	*Holistic/Yin Style*: receptive, diffuse, flexible, inward, bottom up
Stubborn on principles. Stick to a singular, most worthy framework that can explain everything. Define precisely. Provide expert logic and guidance. Bring order to ideas. Correct errors, poor thinking, and wrong approaches.	Take multiple points of view. Find patterns in the chaos. Notice how systems scale, and apply principles in a fluid way. People, art, nature, and technology all interrelate. Understand and find leverage in the messiness of life.

ENTP Self-Portrait

From Conversations*: *What's it like to be you?*

Life feels like a constant state of moving from one interesting thing to another, and I can get frustrated when there isn't enough time to pursue all those interesting things.

I have a wide range of interests. I love to explore the world, how other people live, what they believe in, and what their lives are like. I have a deep need to understand the human condition and what brings people to life, even above difficult odds. I like it when the conversation goes wherever it wants to go—deep imaginative, intellectual, or philosophical conversation. Going off on one theory or another is fun, but long stories with nothing to learn frustrate me.

Ideas mean change. When I meet people who have interesting ideas, talents, or projects, I want to get to know them and help them make whatever they want to do possibly much bigger, more successful, or more impactful than they had intended. I start aligning with them and building trust because I want to get invited in—to probably change whatever they want to do because I tend to see more possibilities. Then we cook up the project. It's fun to learn. I enjoy that in-the-moment experience of connecting things in my mind. Challenge and intellectual stimulation get me excited.

I just see a different world than the one in which I live, and I admire people who have genuine compassion and a commitment to serve others. I really respect people who have the ability to take the slings and arrows that come with leadership roles and working for change, who can cope with all the misunderstanding and resistance, who can say, "This is an idea whose time has come and we're going to get it done." It's important to me to be in a setting where people are committed, where facts are respected, and where there is a space for people to tell the truth or at least look for the truth—and be open to listening.

Colleagues describe me as someone they can go to when they want an idea or help with an issue or problem they're trying to solve.

* Reprinted from *16 Personality Types: Descriptions for Self-Discovery*

I often can condense or simplify a complex idea. I really often know the right words to use, not necessarily the right empathetic words but the right words. Coaching and giving ideas I do well. Just giving direction is boring. I don't feel things have to be done my way, but they have to be done well.

I am very partner oriented, and being creative together is what makes a relationship alive.

I work a lot, always looking for new projects, something to sink my teeth into, and I am constantly challenging myself to make things better. Things I've already figured out I like to put together in a format or structure, so I don't have to sit down and go through all the nitty-gritty details. I think in terms of the future—why am I here, what is this connected to, where are things going, where did they come from and wouldn't it be better if…? When my intuition is working it produces a lot of excitement and ideas.

I tend to look at things from a very objective basis. Sometimes I don't take the time to stop and thank people and let them know I'm trying to build on what they have already done. When I look at things, I am trying to figure out the system—looking beneath, behind, or above, somehow looking beyond the sensory data to figure out how it all works. I spend a lot of time trying to figure out in my head everything around me. Competence is a must, trying to perfect things, finding a new way. I am hardest on myself, with incredibly high standards, and I hold others to my standards even though sometimes I wish I hadn't. And yet I often seem pretty easygoing.

Fairness and consistency are really important. I feel that people should be treated with respect at all times, and I don't like behavior demeaning to others. When there is conflict I feel a compulsion to figure it out, to resolve it. When I'm personally involved, it can be difficult to initiate a discussion about the conflict. Sometimes I feel inadequate.

I think life is a puzzle and we keep playing with how to fit the pieces together. Something new and challenging is always more interesting to me than something I am already competent at.

"Independent Consultant" (ENTP-D)
more driven and confident than other ENTPs
(Dominant subtype)

These ENTPs are confident, independent experts. They enjoy a lot of variety and life-long learning as they assist people using their keen minds and insightful problem-solving frameworks. They are cheerful, sophisticated, in charge of their lives, and serious when they get down to work.

In terms of brain-wiring, these ENTPs show a clear front bias indicating quick, extroverted responses. They also show an underlying zigzag pattern, which points to an out-of-the-box thinking style, where they connect things in unusual or dramatic ways. Finally, they show a clear right-hemisphere bias, which supports holistic thinking, and a network in the back of the brain for silent observation and quiet "me time". Overall, they are skilled at language-based reasoning, attention to values, listening, and noticing visual and narrative patterns.

These ENTPs tend to work in or pull from the business world, education, and the social sciences. They are confident to meet and advise CEOs and leaders of all kinds. Whatever they do officially, they bring in their extra skills since people (and their issues) are the name of the game. At the same time, they have an independent style, often working as free-lancers while partnering with supportive organizations. Thus, they are great at assisting others' structures and processes, large or small, but they personally like a more unstructured, free-form life. To make this work, they stick to a singular domain of practice, constantly self-enriching their education there to build their appeal and stay fresh.

Behind their professional veneer, they are unconventional. Compared with the Creative variant, these ENTPs do not require as much grounding. However, they still benefit from a home-base, regular travel, educational workshops, and a network of fun colleagues in order to relax, get outside society's boxes, and feed their needs for discourse and discovery.

"Inventive Promoter" (ENTP-C)
more exploratory and social than other ENTPs
(Creative subtype)

These ENTPs are often involved in a myriad of exciting projects and ventures, with minds that easily take in and play with a lot of data and possibilities. They are constantly stirring the pot and getting things going, and they can have trouble focusing and staying grounded.

For brain-wiring, these ENTPs show a strong "starburst" pattern. A starburst correlates with creative brainstorming. It allows all brain areas to fire simultaneously, allowing all of the mind's departments, so-to-speak, to potentially contribute to what's going on. This can lead to surprising leaps of insight and also difficulty staying on one task. They usually have exceptional auditory skills and a weak "halo", or no halo at all, especially when younger. A halo is a classic ring around the brain indicating practical support skills. There is also some right-hemisphere bias that supports holistic thinking and a back (or center-back) bias aids visual-spatial skills.

These ENTPs are hard to miss. They gravitate to entrepreneurship and are busy everyday promoting, talking to people, exploring possibilities, and making deals. They often like technology and innovation. They tend to hype things and jump around multiple businesses. Typically, they have a mix of business, psychology, and/or legal training to support their activities. More than other ENTPs, they can get into difficulties at times with too many deadlines, dicey ventures, and/or legal issues. They aim to meet these challenges—and in general, life's awkward situations—with a characteristic cheer and an endearingly, cheesy sense of humor.

Given their chaotic minds, there's a good chance that they have a strong, grounding hobby such as horticulture, music, martial arts or yoga. A caring circle of friends and family, and a stable institutional or geographic home-base also help them stay grounded. Being in touch with their deepest passions, finding where they feel safe, and being more selective in where they put their energy, all help them focus too.

"Technical Manager" (ENTP-N)
more conventional and specialized than other ENTPs
(Normalizing subtype)

These ENTPs blend well into society. They are relatively structured, comfortable with detail, and organized. They have adopted a chart-the-course style. That said, they are still curious mavericks at heart. They make for even-keeled managers with a talent for rapid troubleshooting.

For brain-wiring, these ENTPs sport an even-field across the brain for a more linear thinking style. They show a halo of support skills for social interaction and structured work. And, there is often a bias toward the back of the brain; they observe and figure out what's going on before opening their mouths. Overall, there is a balance of hemispheres, giving a nice mix of analytic skills and holistic understanding of situations.

Many ENTPs here report a background in science or engineering, though their training might easily be construction, finance, history, linguistics, operations management, or any other area that requires wide knowledge, technical details, and big-picture understanding. They function well in organizations as technical managers or specialists, and they can stay put for years, working through daily to-do lists and juggling surprises, all while staying cool and keeping things moving, fun, and light for themselves and others. They stay organized by having a set up, a system, or set of strategies. They can juggle a lot of complexity. Though aware of rules and the need to avoid trouble, they have little patience for rigidity. They enjoy figuring out and exploiting weak points, and are keen to help friends and clients work around bureaucratic and technical obstacles.

Socially, these ENTPs easily put out feelers with people, playing with whatever others can serve back. They are casual and insightful, maybe with a devilish humor. Often, rather than argue, they ask an incisive question or play devil's advocate. People find them open-minded and full of illustrative anecdotes. They enjoy weekend getaways, or if possible, far-flung travels to experience cultural differences. While relatively sedate, they need entertaining social hobbies or they will fall into unhealthy forms of escape.

"Strategic Humanist" (ENTP-H)
more empathic and reflective than other ENTPs
(Harmonizing subtype)

These ENTPs are supportive facilitators. They are patient, energized by a deep passion and broad principles. They attend to many variables, have a strong theoretical bent, like aiding groups, and are good at asking open-ended questions. They have adopted a more behind-the-scenes style.

Typically, these ENTPs sport a set of distinct, diamond-shaped networks. They switch back and forth between these networks, each corresponding to a mode of observing, analyzing, and interacting. They also often show the type's characteristic zigzag pattern, which supports their creative, quirky, and dramatic style. They may also have a weak starburst pattern which they bring in for brainstorming. With a back bias, they can get particularly reflective. Overall, they blend a mix of left- and right-brain ways of thinking to fully understand situations.

These ENTPs tend to focus on reaching out to, guiding, and inspiring others, particularly in a group setting. They rely on skills they've developed for listening and observing as they work from a sophisticated theoretical basis. They look at situations and systems from multiple angles and at multiple scales, asking questions and suggesting choice ideas. For example, when looking at an economic issue, there is a large scale of national, global and cross-cultural power dynamics; then, there is a mid-scale of finances and functioning of a specific industry or organization; and finally, there are smaller-scale groups within those. They are not dogmatic, loud or pushy. Rather, they are caring catalysts for change.

These ENTPs aim to bring a pragmatic wisdom to others and society, and they are not naive about this big enterprise. They are considerate with serious points behind the inspiring talk, and they delight to help others learn, shift, and grow. They benefit from fun, off-the-wall adventures as breaks as well as from a partner and supportive team to help them stay organized and get what they need.

Mind Your Neurotic Zone*

Like all types, ENTPs have neurotic moments. These erupt when the ego and unconscious clash. While at times uplifting, the result is often anxiety and insecurity. These episodes are also opportunities to learn and grow.

Friendly Hosting
Nurture trust in giving relationships.
Extraverted Feeling (Fe)

- *Basic Use*: Honor others' needs and preferences.
- *Advanced Use*: Connect with people by sharing values and taking on their needs as yours.
- *Neurotic Use*: Prone to blaming others for causing their emotions. Find themselves feeling needy while also meeting others' needs before their own. Tend to self-aggrandize while also being self-critical. Overly nice (or mean) and respectful (or disrespectful), expecting more from others or from themselves. Can find themselves caught up in endless office politics and relationship drama. Can get hyper-focused on societal values and policy issues (for or against those). Tend to over-analyze emotions and interpersonal issues without actually feeling them.

Manage Your Energy**

ENTPs tend to be quite busy with a variety of interests and diverse activities all at once. Imagine multiple songs or devices playing at the same time. This stimulates their creativity and keeps life interesting and meaningful. Everywhere they notice potential possibilities and all of their brain entertains everything that comes in. Needless to say, this can really tax their "batteries"; on average, the brain consumes a quarter of a person's energy!

Often, health and physical activities are not so interesting to them. What is meaningful about kicking around a ball to get it into a net? And doing a forty-minute run on a treadmill sounds boring. They'd much rather be out-and-about and chatting about ideas. Unfortunately, the life

* Similar here to cousin type ESTP.

of the mind easily pulls them away from the physical world, and if they don't care for their health, they will suffer later. This is particularly true as they get older if they rely ever-more on caffeine, sugar, or other stimulants to keep up their high-energy multi-tasking life. For ENTP, they really benefit from something that engages the mind, such as listening to a podcast while exercising, or it might be learning new techniques in martial arts.

The secret for this type is to raise their standards. Over time, they can learn to filter what is worth interacting around and prioritize quality. Ideally, they also benefit from a body-mind practice that encourages them to be present with their body rather than shut it out. What feedback, or wisdom, does their body have? And in terms of work, they benefit by having a solid "container" that holds their diverse interests.

Pursue Your Aspirations**

Like all types, ENTPs trust and prioritize their heroic strengths. At the same time, they also seek ways to express their opposite. This opposite acts as a bridge to the unconscious, a realm where potential and vulnerability reside. Thus, their opposite is a doorway to growth.

Cautious Protecting
Stabilize with a Predictable Standard.
Introverted Sensing (Si)

- *Basic Use*: Recall tangible data and experiences.
- *Advanced Use*: Stabilize a situation by comparing it to what is expected, known, and reliable.
- *Aspirational Use*: Yearn for stability. Find grounding and a sense of safety in past experiences, traditions, and the familiar. Skilled at revitalizing old ideas with new applications, and drawn to reimagine or expand upon established ideas with inventive twists. Ideally, they come to respect proven methods, historical context, and learned lessons. At their best, they acknowledge the wisdom of the past, and existing methods and institutions, as they balance new ideas with universal themes that speak to society at large and the timeless human experience. Can get overly nostalgic or stuck in poor habits.

** Similar here to cousin type ENFP.

ENTP Reminders*
for Growth and Success

☐Yours is a rare mind; use it wisely.

☐Find a place where your brainstorming and insights into possibilities are appreciated and given credit.

☐Be nice and play fairly.

☐In relationships, get feedback on how much the other person wants to do problem solving.

☐Keep your humor.

☐Practice diplomatically articulating your needs, values, and feelings.

☐Focus on what you are the most passionate about.

☐When (or if) you play politics, recognize that being political isn't "the" way but your way.

☐If you cannot pinpoint someone else's strategy or principle, then recognize it as their belief.

☐It's okay to have three jobs at once; just remember to sleep well, taste your food, and breathe deeply.

☐Not everything can be successfully approached using a technique.

☐There are many kinds of intelligence—some aren't cognitive—and it's okay that not all of them can be like yours.

☐Promote the worth of others.

☐Try to name three personal beliefs about major ideas you engage.

☐Affect announces character, so pay attention to nonverbal cues.

☐Recognize that failure can result from over-preparation, as well under-preparation.

☐Practice giving and compassion

* Adapted from *Quick Guide to the 16 Personality Types in Organizations*

What Now?

Now that you've explored ENTP:

1. How do the strengths and challenges of this type show up in your life?
2. What's an insight or goal you can act on today in some way?
3. See the later chapters to leverage your subtype, neurotic zone, energy, and aspirations.

Dario Nardi

INTP
Life Paths

219

INTP Essentials
Designer Theorizer™
Introverting • iNtuiting • Thinking • Perceiving

Core Themes

INTPs like to explore ideas to deepen their expertise. They notice new patterns and elegant connections. They easily cross boundaries of thought. They play with ideas and detach to analyze. They clarify, reference, and define. INTPs have a talent to design and redesign. They are open to try whatever starts up their imagination. They like to reflect on thinking. They hold to core principles and solid models. Making discoveries brings them joy. They struggle to attend to the physical world.

Unpack the Stack: INTPs...

Lead with "Skillful Sleuthing" (Ti)
Analyze and define situations, solve problems, and apply leverage according to universal logical principles.

Support by "Excited Brainstorming" (Ne)
Perceive, pursue, and play with life's many potential possibilities, facilitating the promising ones.

Struggle at "Cautious Protecting" (Si)
Reference a massive storehouse of rich past experiences as they cultivate familiarity, comfort, and stability.

Aspire to "Friendly Hosting" (Fe)
Tend relationships, social norms, and people's needs and values as they organize and make thoughtful decisions.

Let's explore...

this type from various angles including 4 developmental variants. As you read, consider what fits for you (or others), what has remained the same or changed over time, and options for where to go from here.

How INTPs Lead with Heroism

Refine Decision Making

Clarify what's universal, true or worthwhile. Often appear quietly receptive. Trust own judgments.

Skillful Sleuthing
Gain leverage using a framework.
Introverted Thinking (Ti)

Study a situation from different angles and fit it to a theory, framework, or principle. This often involves reasoning multiple ways to objectively and accurately analyze problems. Rely on complex/subtle logical reasoning. Adept at deductive thinking, defining and categorizing, weighing odds and risks, and/or naming and navigating. Notice points to apply leverage and subtle influence. Value consistency of thought. Can shut out the senses and "go deep" to think, and separate body from mind to become objective when arguing or analyzing. Tend to backtrack to clarify thoughts, and withhold deciding in favor of thorough examination. May quickly stop listening.

What flavor of Skillful Sleuthing?

INTPs can express this process in two ways. They likely develop a bias for one way early in life and may develop the other later.

"Critic" Ti	"Systemist" Ti
Analytic/Yang Style: *active, focused, fixed, outward, top down*	**Holistic/Yin Style:** *receptive, diffuse, flexible, inward, bottom up*
Stubborn on principles. Stick to a singular, most worthy framework that can explain everything. Define precisely. Provide expert logic and guidance. Bring order to ideas. Correct errors, poor thinking, and wrong approaches.	Take multiple points of view. Find patterns in the chaos. Notice how systems scale, and apply principles in a fluid way. People, art, nature, and technology all interrelate. Understand and find leverage in the messiness of life.

222

How INTPs Give Flexible Support

Energize the Process
Seek out stimuli. Often appear random, emergent, and enthusiastic. Attend to the here and now.

Excited Brainstorming
Explore numerous emerging patterns.
Extraverted iNtuiting (Ne)

Perceive and play with ideas and relationships. Wonder about patterns of interaction across various situations. Keep up a high-energy mode that helps you notice and engage potential possibilities. Think analogically: stimuli are springboards to generate inferences, analogies, metaphors, jokes, and more new ideas. Easily guess details.Adept at "what if?" scenarios, mirroring others, and even role-playing. Can shift a situation's dynamics and trust what emerges. Mental activity tends to feel chaotic, with many highs and lows at once, like an ever-changing "Christmas tree" of flashing lights. Often entertain multiple meanings at once. May find it hard to stay on-task.

What flavor of Excited Brainstorming?
INTPs can express this process in two ways. They likely develop a bias for one way early in life and may develop the other later.

"Marketer" Ne	"Catalyst" Ne
Analytic/Yang Style: active, focused, fixed, outward, top down	**Holistic/Yin Style**: receptive, diffuse, flexible, inward, bottom up
Put on a show. Pitch and juggle many ideas, trusting quantity over quality in search of advantages or gains. Recruit others and rely on strong energy of ideas to shift situations to one's liking. Court uncertainty for progress.	Notice subtle patterns. Negotiate toward a novel win-win outcome with a relaxed, subtle style. Use humor and disguises. Include and promote others. Search for the highest quality potential possibilities for everyone's gain.

INTP Self-Portrait

From Conversations*: *What's it like to be you?*

I want to know the truth and get down to the bottom of things. It's an internal life, living in the head, theorizing constantly about how things work.

I can link many thoughts and shoot off in multiple directions at once in an attempt to clarify and explain things really well or to try to represent the fullness of who I am and all the different things I can do and can't do. I like to design—not just implementation but the stuff before that. There is a goal, a theme, and I start from that and work through the specifics one by one, keeping the whole thing integrated as I go, until I come up with "the elegant solution." Often when I talk to people they only get from me a few steps—one, thirteen, a hundred. That's all that gets verbalized, and what's very clear to me either I've forgotten or find unnecessary to say out loud, which can come across as confusing at times.

I am very knowledge and big picture oriented. I want to bring everything that can be known into understanding a problem or situation. I enjoy working with those who think like I do but verbalize better. We can end up leaping forward rapidly and building off of ideas, asking questions with an answer in mind but wanting to verify things and learn more. If I am knowledgeable in that area, I always have something to add, to help better understand the idea and add something new. Although sometimes, even when I know we agree, people feel like I am trying to challenge them, which is frustrating because I am just doing it out of excitement. I try to understand all the variables and possible influences and then apply as broad a range of information as I can bring to the problem, to impact why the problem exists. I am interested in developing new skills and trying new ideas with those skills, and I am a good team member, and yet sometimes a little group work can go a long way. Most of all, I love to learn.

Central for me is honesty and integrity, especially intellectual integrity. If it's not an honest approach to the issue at hand or to the rela-

* Reprinted from *16 Personality Types: Descriptions for Self-Discovery*

224

tionship or organization, then it becomes an illusion—it only appears to have substance. I respect people who are genuine, honest, and open and doing what they are good at and what they enjoy and are up front about what is important to them.

I have a penchant for clarity. Some people say I'm hairsplitting, but there is value in precision.

I don't like sloppy thinking, waste, and redundancy, and I am uncomfortable with sending out something that isn't as good as it can be, but it has to go out anyway. I like things thought through. Incompetence just sets me right off. I have very little tolerance or patience, especially if the person is above me or isn't really trying. I don't think I push people any harder than I push myself and most people probably push less, which is where conflict comes in. Some people say my standard may be way out of whack and I assume the other person is competent. I like to avoid conflict at all possible costs, but if it reaches a point where I can't go anywhere unless this gets resolved, then I will jump in and take care of it. That takes me a long time and I will go miles out my way to avoid that. It's an ongoing decision between fairness and not letting people walk all over me.

There is this constant balancing act between self-confidence and questioning myself. Sometimes I feel secure and comfortable about knowing and thinking about and recognizing a lot and knowing how to learn new skills and ideas and concepts. But I have an almost instant ability to detect limitations—not knowing enough, picking out what's missing, adding in an always-present feeling that it's not quite right, and not knowing everything there is to know with insufficient time to learn everything that is important.

I can be seen as too unfeeling, too quick to start into work with not enough basis laid out for the day, and I'm not much for the personal amenities or socializing. Yet it is important that others are aware they are important to me. It's not the first thing, but it's in my awareness. I tend to try solving personal problems all by myself. Then sometimes I wind up without accurate information from others or about how it will affect others. I believe there must be an answer or a solution if I can just figure it out.

."Ambitious Strategist" (INTP-D)
more driven and confident than other INTPs
(Dominant subtype)

These INTPs are comfortable with a managerial or out-front leadership position. They function the same as other INTPs but on a large stage, often acting as a consummate strategist or top consultant. They may start as entrepreneurs but prefer to be with an organization or community that matches their values, and handles execution and details.

In terms of brain wiring, their wiring is biased toward the front and often the left hemisphere. They show a weak or no "starburst" brainstorming pattern, and thus lean away from unstructured creativity. If they show a weak starburst, it's mostly for generating ideas. These INTPs rely on brain regions that support speaking and listening, language-based reasoning, and a balance of flexing to the context while holding to a principle. They also rely on a few back-brain areas to collate data.

They are objective hard-hitters, speaking their mind as needed, particularly when something is counter to their understanding. Thus, when immature, they can be argumentative, critical, and highly skeptical. If something does not follow a core concept for them, then it goes unheard and does not exist. Similarly, they tend to have a stronger physical presence than other INTPs, which can deter others from speaking up. Overall, when they are right, it's truly what others need to hear, even when it's the umpteenth reminder. But when they are wrong, it is a near-hopeless task to shift their perspective, as they expect others to reason things out using their terms.

These INTPs are comfortable with the principles and levers of power. They proceed patiently with an eye for when and where to exert leverage. They strategize how to move people, products, and ideas even as they hold to a core agenda. They don't stray into areas that lack scrutiny and they often prefer a position next to a throne as a respected expert, free of constant Decision Making and safe from scapegoating for mistakes.

"Curious Investigator" (INTP-C)
more exploratory and social than other INTPs
(Creative subtype)

This is the most curious, playful, and funny of the INTPs. They can look like social extroverts in their energy and enthusiasm. They tend to pose lots of questions and offer ideas, and they are often willing to entertain going down a path or three wherever data leads in their aim for understanding. At times, they may not know when to stop since they attend more to the ideas than the individuals or social conventions. Overall, they've learned how to stir the pot, engage others, entertain, and get things going.

For brain-wiring, these INTPs often show a strong, solid "starburst" pattern typical of fast intuitive insights. They take in data and quickly play with it in their mind in different ways. To complement this, they tend to have strong auditory, linguistic, and visual skills. In particular, they often show a strong goal-focused capacity for speaking, attending to word content, and processing more-obvious social feedback.

They enjoy a wide range of interests. Over time they can accumulate an incredible database of eclectic knowledge. For example, they may know hundreds of comic books or anime shows. Or they may be highly familiar with particular painters, musicians, foreign dishes, or so on, knowing many details. At work, they tend to jump around on various projects or various angles on a project, and can find themselves distracted or scattered with difficulty attending to official assignments. Searching the Internet for an answer to a question might lead to hours of exploring that is fascinating and unproductive. Potential patterns fascinate them. They may have a challenging time finding a best-fit home, professionally. Even when they are in a traditional profession with established thinking and norms such as medicine or law, they'll develop a framework and practice in their preferred way.

Despite their more extroverted and open style, make no mistake, these INTPs maintain the type's need to analyze situations and control the integrity and quality of outcomes. It's simply hidden from others' view and drawn out over a longer time frame.

"Exacting Designer" (INTP-N)
more conventional and specialized than other INTPs
(Normalizing subtype)

These INTPs have brain-wiring that is the most typical of the general population. The wiring is relatively even across various regions, and often there is also a bias toward the back and/or left hemisphere, giving them a linear, reflective, and analytical style. They process information one step at a time in a very rational way, often staying with a particular course.

In the workplace, they are quiet, observant specialists. They focus deeply in one area, gaining an incredible degree of expertise. Others may find them boring, and they do enjoy discussing the ins-and-outs of their work because problem solving is both their work and play. They fit well into large, conventional organizations, or at least they favor steady positions, so long as they're given projects that are interesting, or that they can make interesting.

These INTPs tend to favor a single, coherent set of tools and methods that is widely-used and meets professional norms. At the same time, they like to tweak things for incremental gains. For example, they might write software to speed up a common statistics algorithm and share it with a professional forum. They have a heavy investment in their domain and are unlikely to flex to new ways. Their whole brain is wired around what they know. This is also why they can be so fast to spot potential patterns in data and promising leads to solve a problem in their domain.

They are not so social. Their humor tends to be understated. Their words can have multiple, subtle meanings that poke fun even at the very people they are with, without others hearing it, and this is a kind of stress release. They are very patient: their frustrations, particularly with difficult people and institutional rules, can simmer for months or years. They are the most likely to stick to mastering a specific hobby, from playing a musical instrument to doing martial arts, and they can find a lot of enjoyment and stress relief in such hobbies.

"Caring Theorizer" (INTP-H)
more empathic and reflective than other INTPs
(Harmonizing subtype)

This INTP is most often in a people-helping role such as psychologist or diplomat. More than other INTPs, their specialty is human interactions. They may work a bit with other people, maybe everyday, and they keep a behind-the-scenes style, acting as subtle, supportive facilitators.

These INTPs are comfortable with lots of fuzzy input, they tend to focus on methodology over technicalities, and they find clear definitions and models to be essential in this challenging domain. Their memory banks are filled with specific, detailed cases of others' words and behavior patterns. They are patient listeners and observers, can hold multiple models and methods in a light way (not heavy-handed), and they are tolerant, able to shift with others perspectives and needs.

Their brains rely on one or more diamond-shaped networks that bridge the hemispheres. Each network includes four to six diverse brain regions that work in concert. Each does it own thing and represents a different "mode" or "angle", and each fits a kind of situation or way of addressing a problem. Using these, they experiment with questions, correlating and shifting angles until something "lands" to get the needed effect. On the downside, daily details for self-maintenance can be a major challenge. This variant is most common at or after midlife.

These INTPs tend to work at a small, personal scale, one-on-one or in a group setting. They focus on facilitating others' potential rather than calculating odds or gains. They can sit with a person or group in a mindful, patient way, acting as a catalyst for problem-solving to meet the unstated needs in the room. Usually, they don't consciously "experience" the other people emotionally in front of them. The distance they keep can be very helpful when there is a lot of heat and confusion going around. However, the INTP can suffer an odd stress-response afterward. Given their style, Caring Theorists can make for wise, respected community leaders.

Mind Your Neurotic Zone*

Like all types, INTPs have neurotic moments. These erupt when the ego and unconscious clash. While at times uplifting, the result is often anxiety and insecurity. These episodes are also opportunities to learn and grow.

Cautious Protecting
Stabilize with a predictable standard.
Introverted Sensing (Si)

- *Basic Use*: Recall tangible data and experiences.
- *Advanced Use*: Stabilize a situation by comparing it to what is expected, known, and reliable.
- *Neurotic Use*: Lack of action. Just endless researching, listening, etc. Easily caught in bad habits or a routine (for years). Tend to ignore health, presentation, and physical environment; or, settle on one thing and just repeat. Can hyper-focus on odd bodily signals yet don't give consistent care to their actual needs. Strongly accept (or strongly reject) norms such as established tools, historical data, certified experts, social etiquette, etc. Live as an "anchored cloud". Can easily dismiss hard facts, bottom-line consequences, or the material world, where only the meaning/model exists.

Manage Your Energy*

INTPs tend to live in their head, in their imagination. It's so much fun to explore ideas, and dream up and mentally play out possibilities, whether that's reading a book, listening to music, working through a philosophical question, or going down rabbit holes surfing the Internet. But where in any of this is their body, attention to health, or daily material practicalities?

Energy-wise, they can find it pretty difficult to get motivated to actually go out and do something. A great theory or story comes to mind, but writing it down—much less getting it to a marketplace—is a challenge. All of the logistical details and the path to get from A to Z—or even figure out what Z is—feels like a big wall to get over. Their creative

* Similar here to cousin type INFP.

energy then goes nowhere. Ideally, they have a network of peers to keep exchanging ideas and maybe engage in a project together, and their main role is can be input and feedback over doing the nitty-gritty work. Connecting with others can be a particular challenge when their main interest is highly unusual.

The trick is habit-building. If INTPs fall into unhealthy habits, they can remain stuck for a long time in someone else's routine. Oppositely, when they cultivate good habits—write one page, or do one gym or yoga set every day; or post one technical piece, or interview one interesting person every week—then over time they nurture a great habit and accumulate a ton of insights, memories, and maybe materials that benefit them. In terms of work, these habits also reduce worry and self-questioning while building confidence.

Pursue Your Aspirations**

Like all types, INTPs trust and prioritize their heroic strengths. At the same time, they also seek ways to express their opposite. This opposite acts as a bridge to the unconscious, a realm where potential and vulnerability reside. Thus, their opposite is a doorway to growth.

Friendly Hosting
Nurture trust in giving relationships.
Extraverted Feeling (Fe)

- **Basic Use**: Honor others' needs and preferences.
- **Advanced Use**: Connect with people by sharing values and taking on their needs as yours.
- **Aspirational Use**: Yearn to be useful to others and society. Will apply a model, philosophy, set of techniques, or a scientific principle to deal with human behavior. Tend to remain calm and independent when most others fall prey to emotions or group-think. Stay informed about and support social policy causes, often from the sidelines. Uncomfortable in the spotlight. At their best, apply their problem solving skills to aid people, or at least fix things that matter to others. Like to be in a network of fellow experts. Can latch on to someone in a sticky way as an idealized companion.

** Similar here to cousin type ISTP.

INTP Reminders*
for Growth and Success

☐ Observing and asking questions are among your greatest gifts.

☐ Find a comfortable, collegial environment where you can play with and generate ideas.

☐ Locate your own interests.

☐ When explaining something, try to give three complete examples.

☐ Keep an eye on areas where thinking is rigid.

☐ If you express your vision and passion for the potential effect of your ideas and principles, then people will listen.

☐ Maintain openness to what is true socially or psychologically—as well as conceptually.

☐ Try to maintain some links to enjoy life's pleasantries; similarly, design a work area mostly free of mundane demands.

☐ Use multiple models for how to be diplomatic.

☐ Remember that when critiquing others' ideas, your questions about improvement will be received and acted on more often than your criticism.

☐ Acknowledge the physical world, your body, and the worth of anecdotal observation—or you may likely just float away.

☐ Find people who can turn your ideas into useful products that see daylight.

☐ Observe the observational processes of others.

☐ Enjoy the soothing sensation of walking barefoot in the grass.

☐ It's okay to express emotion.

*Adapted from *Quick Guide to the 16 Personality Types in Organizations*

What Now?

Now that you've explored INTP:

1. How do the strengths and challenges of this type show up in your life?
2. What's an insight or goal you can act on today in some way?
3. See the later chapters to leverage your subtype, neurotic zone, energy, and aspirations.

ENFJ
Life Paths

ENFJ Essentials
Envisioner Mentor™
Extraverting • iNtuiting • Feeling • Judging

Core Themes

ENFJs like to communicate and share values. They set goals and seek shared success. They strive to realize dreams—their own and others. They look for ways to grow together. They heed the call to a life's work or mission. They have a talent for noticing potential in others. ENFJs enjoy being creative, using their intuitive intellect. They try to bridge the past and the future. When needed, they can get very precise or technical. They find it hard to live in the present moment, to feel at peace.

Unpack the Stack: ENFJs...

Lead with "Friendly Hosting" (Fe)
Tend relationships, social norms, and people's needs and values as they organize and make thoughtful decisions.

Support by "Keen Foreseeing" (Ni)
Focus on a vision of the future, and on insights and realizations from the inner hidden world of the unconscious.

Struggle at "Active Adapting" (Se)
Enjoy the external world using their five senses and take concrete actions based on options before them.

Aspire to "Skillful Sleuthing" (Ti)
Analyze situations, solve problems, and apply leverage according to universal logical principles.

Let's explore...

this type from various angles including 4 developmental variants. As you read, consider what fits for you (or others), what has remained the same or changed over time, and options for where to go from here.

How ENFJs Lead with Heroism

Expedite Decision Making:
Proactively meet goals. Often appear sure and confident.
Organize and fix to get positive results soon.

Friendly Hosting
Nurture trust in giving relationships.
Extraverted Feeling (Fe)

Evaluate and communicate values to build trust and enhance relationships. Like to promote social/interpersonal cohesion. Attend keenly to how others judge you. Quickly adjust your behavior for social harmony. Often rely on a favorite way to reason, with an emphasis on words. Prefer to stay positive, supportive, and optimistic. Empathically respond to others' needs and feelings, and may take on others' needs as your own. Need respect and trust. Easily embarrassed. Like using adjectives to convey values. Enjoy hosting. May hold back the true degree of your emotional response about morals/ethics, regarding talk as more effective. May try too hard to please.

What flavor of Friendly Hosting?
ENFJs can express this process in two ways. They likely develop a bias for one way early in life and may develop the other later.

"Shepherd" Fe	"Host" Fe
Analytic/Yang Style: active, focused, fixed, outward, top down	**Holistic/Yin Style**: receptive, diffuse, flexible, inward, bottom up
Announce values and prescribe best behaviors. Corral outliers and encourage them to join the group. Actively work to fix relationships. Inspire as an orator. Make sacrifices, and ask others to sacrifice, in a push to meet needs.	Enjoy supporting your community, family, and friends. Value harmony with others over being right. Sensitive to negative feedback. Accommodate people's many differences. Can be self-sacrificing as you even help foes.

How ENFJs Give Flexible Support

Chart the Process:

Reflect on data and perceptions. Often appear focused and preoccupied. Attend to reference points.

Keen Foreseeing

Transform with a meta-perspective.

Introverted Intuiting (Ni)

Withdraw from the world and tap your whole mind to receive an insight. Can enter a brief trance to respond to a challenge, foresee the future, or answer a philosophical issue. Avoid specializing and rely instead on timely "ah-ha" moments or a holistic "zen state" to tackle novel tasks, which may look like creative expertise. Manage your own mental processes and stay aware of where you are in an open-ended task. May use an action or symbol to focus. Sensitive to the unknown. Ruminate on ways to improve. Look for synergy. Might try out a realization to transform yourself or how you think. May over-rely on the unconscious.

What flavor of Keen Foreseeing?

ENFJs can express this process in two ways. They likely develop a bias for one way early in life and may develop the other later.

"Visionary" Ni	"Oracle" Ni
Analytic/Yang Style: active, focused, fixed, outward, top down	**Holistic/Yin Style**: receptive, diffuse, flexible, inward, bottom up
Stick to a singular vision of the future to improve self and society. Be certain of a few compelling insights. Don't let go or water down. Turn realizations into principles. Apply many complex concepts. Act as a guiding spirit.	Hold lightly many interrelated insights. Connect to the many facets of the archetypal world. Open to transformation. Respond to others' questions, and innovate for the group. Cultivate an aesthetic or spiritual practice.

ENFJ Self-Portrait

From Conversations*: *What's it like to be you?*

I really believe everything happens for a reason, to everybody. I'm a human being, there are other human beings around me, and each of us is unique. I trust when something is going to take me to a higher level and I'll bring lots of people along with me—a constant quest of building a strong foundation of self and others from everything I learn. Relationships are about the higher purpose—there is a deep level that needs to be satisfied or there is no point—I need a unique connection or I am unsatisfied. I feel a responsibility to make a difference.

I am empathic. I just get a feeling about people. It's difficult to explain. I have the gift of being able to relate and meaningful communication is a major piece of my life and a major vehicle for growth. I'm good at working with people to improve their behavior and their lives. I'm described as someone who cares, who has an uncanny sense for knowing what others need or what they are about. When I talk to people I'm listening for their stories and their concerns and I experience the joy or stress with them. I remember what's uniquely descriptive of that individual, and I am good at giving praise and pointing out the gifts they bring to their world. If I get vibes that they are not comfortable developing the relationship the way I think it should be, I will back off, but I look for another clue to come back and develop it. What matters is working at making the relationship the best that it can be at whatever level it is, building depth into it.

Honesty is very important. Even if the truth is bad it adds to the depth of the relationship.

I hate unresolved conflict—it makes me sick and can stay with me until it's resolved—and I hate it when people are demeaned or mistreated. My heart goes out to them so I feel it's my responsibility to help, and I will fight on their behalf. It's just something I do, but it hasn't always worked. I end up telling the person what to do and then they do what they want regardless. If I'm really upset, I'll let myself calm down, figure out what I'm going to say, and then confront the situation. I am very careful and aware of my actions or words and what effect they will have on another person, and I am thankful to have learned to take the time to envision various interactions before they happen. I used to push, but now I'm more patient. I'm usually fair, open, and unbiased. I don't understand people who are insensitive to others needs or issues or thoughts or feelings. Either I don't want them in my life or I want to teach them how to care. It bugs me when people don't take the time to understand each other.

I usually put the relationship ahead of tasks I have to do, but I don't have unlimited energy. When I can just be who I am and in a sharing mode and when there is not a task-oriented pressure, that flows better. I try hard to "be there" emotionally for those in my life so I have to constantly set up boundaries so I don't take on their problems. I usually work overtime to make sure I am understood. It is also very important to me for others' to be properly understood, and I expend a lot of time and energy making sure they are understood and comfortable. Being unable to build relationships with those who need it is frustrating.

It's particularly difficult when my needs aren't being met. Sometimes I can't even feel good about myself because I worry that others did not get what they needed. In a group, I need to separate my interests from others or I'll be easily swayed by what they want and how they behave. I can't be successful for myself if I'm trying to fit into someone else's idea of me.

I also tend to take a leadership position—not a strong one always but I'm looked at as a leader. Others having genuine confidence in me is almost as good as having the confidence myself. When someone comes for help, it's a compliment. I listen and feed some things back that maybe they haven't thought about, something that's profound for them. Often people will disregard the information I give them as unimportant only to later request the same information. That energizes me. I try to be a thoughtful good listener, interested, fun, and someone to come up with ideas. Humor is a great teacher and great healer. My favorite thing is to watch someone have an "aha" experience, and I really admire people who have been through something and learned.

"Communications Director" (ENFJ-D)
more driven and confident than other ENFJs
(Dominant subtype)

These ENFJs are charismatic leaders with a clear "in charge" style. They are deeply anchored in their values, what is needed to improve society, and the insights needed to get there. Whatever their profession or age, even if young, they tend to fill roles as liaisons, group leaders, educators, policy gurus, and spiritual guides.

Their brain-wiring has a clear front bias with strong executive and managerial skills. That means balancing the needs of a context with key values. They also sport moderate to strong language-based reasoning. Thus, they are skilled at deduction, step-by-step planning, abstract concepts, and metaphor. They may focus somewhat more speaking and word content or on voice tone and intention depending on their career skills and other factors. Either way, they are naturals at communicating. All of this helps them hold an audience and stay on-message, using words and ideas to inform and sway others. Their weakness is usually poor visual-spatial skills, difficulty being in the moment, and a lack of deep reflection.

Commonly, these ENFJs stick to a few neural "super highways", which gives them a lot of resilience. With their executive and managerial skills, they are dramatic, assertive figures. Being idealistic and anchored in values, they usually use this power in the name of peace, justice, truth and such (as they see it). They do not back off from confrontation, quickly taking in and responding to new information to fit their message and vision. At times, their dominant executive judge may fail like a breaking dam when they can no longer filter out negative feelings or the reality of a bad situation. Overall, finding the humor in situations is a valable way to reduce stress.

Some ENFJs here, who tend to be older, are more relaxed. They are more reflective, better with detail, rely on more-effective mental models, and are more patient when helping others.

"Dramatic Empath" (ENFJ-C)
more exploratory and social than other ENFJs
(Creative subtype)

These ENFJs are passionate creators. They have a dramatic, intuitive, and open-ended style. They excel in areas that require adapting, improvising, and expressing themselves. They can stir the pot in almost any situation.

For brain-wiring, they usually have a soft starburst pattern. That is, all areas of the brain respond, relevant or not, when new input comes. Thus, they tend to be open-minded and exploratory, willing to entertain what-if and try new things. It also indicates an intuitive way of thinking. Moreover, they have excellent auditory skills, attend easily to voice tone and body language, and are goal-focused. All this primes them for diverse social endeavors. Conversely, they tend to lack a halo of links around the brain's perimeter that is common with more linear thinkers. They rely more on holistic understanding over knowledge to get by. Sustaining their attention on mundane tasks can be challenging.

They are collaborative and prefer visceral, in-person activities. They are less adept at directing others or engaging in deep reason. They trust their five senses to feed their intuition, and then rely on direct, face-to-face interaction. They are well-suited to the creative arts such as acting or dance. But really they can thrive anywhere that benefits from their style, whether as a business entrepreneur, journalist, or social influencer. Despite being more exploratory, they may still resist working exemporaneously and benefit from trusting their intuition in the moment.

These ENFJs are sensitive to and respond to emotional extremes. They have less of a need to be in control, and as extroverts, they can throw themselves into a group's life and have a strong catalytic effect. Ideally, they learn to channel their dramatic overtones into creative projects. They are particularly idealistic as they stay open to the whole pallet of human affairs. Work and play, body and spirit all interrelated for them.

"Compassionate Expert" (ENFJ-N)
more conventional and specialized than other ENFJs
(Normalizing subtype)

These ENFJs are inclined to technical work in service to others. They are comfortable taking their time with details and working in a factual, linear way, ideally to help people. Overall, they've adopted a more chart-the-course style.

Brain-wiring is dense toward the back and left, and it is often spread out like an "even field", such that they connect thoughts and skills in pairs like rungs of a ladder as they go through tasks. They have good visual skills with an eye for detail. They quickly notice errors. They listen and speak well. They are fairly contemplative, have a solid command of facts and case studies, and are adept at collating new data with the giant database of what they know as they figure out answers.

Being idealists, these ENFJs need to know they are helping individuals and society. For them, this often shows up as educating people while helping them or directing others to aid those who need it. They have a strong sense of togetherness, of people caring for and relying on each other. They take pride in their gift to help. Compared to other ENFJs, they are more likely in a technical field such as medicine, computing or engineering. In leadership roles, they take a more technical approach, following a model or plan. Even in the arts, they take a conservative, structured approach, such as classical music. They may get rigid here. Often, they come from a traditional or collectivist culture. Whatever their background, they crave societal acceptance of their gifts.

Work and play are kept separate. Among ENFJs, they tend to have strong bodily awareness, which can get quite specific. For example, they might know many dance steps or yoga poses but are uncomfortable with free-form moves. They can consistently attend to particular ailments. Their intuitive side comes to the fore in specific, predictable ways such as through dreams, tarot cards, premonitions of the future, and such.

"Mystical Counselor" (ENFJ-H)
more empathic and reflective than other ENFJs
(Harmonizing subtype)

These ENFJs are quietly sophisticated. They are naturals as counselors and therapists, trusting intuitive modes of thinking to listen, offer insight, and foretell the future. They often work behind the scenes in a private, careful, and patient way.

For these ENFJs, brain-wiring tends to show up as diamond-shaped patterns, which are unique networks that stretch across the brain's hemispheres. Alternatively, they show one diamond network and also many zigzag connections. Either way, there is a lot of cross-hemisphere activity as they bring together diverse brain skills into a cohesive way of understanding situations. For example, while listening to someone, they may receive a striking visual image of what that person suffered as a child and bring that up for discussion. Because these diamonds and zigzags are unusual, the ENFJ's way of thinking—experiencing the world—can feel equally unusual. They may sink into a particular oracle-like mode for their best work. And they can really bring up a dramatic twist, connecting data points that others don't recognize. At their best, they can shift perspectives to truly relate to other points of view.

Despite their whole-brain pattern, they still tend to have decent executive function. They can take in and respond to events in a goal-focused, cohesive way. However, they are not so adept at managing others. And, they lack the "halo" of social skills that society expects of people. Overall, they are more listeners than talkers, and more reactive than proactive, often waiting for the right insight to come or the right mode to get into. Career-wise, they might be an artist, counselor, or even a monk or psychic. Their kind of wisdom does not often fit easily in society.

More than other ENFJs, they are comfortable with time alone reflecting, imagining, meditating, divining hidden meanings, and working with symbols, archetypes, and ideas. They tend to seek flow rather than control. They accept and accommodate. And they trust the abstract meaning world more than the everyday, "common sense" one. In this sense, they may seriously struggle with life's ordinary demands.

Mind Your Neurotic Zone*

Like all types, ENFJs have neurotic moments. These erupt when the ego and unconscious clash. While at times uplifting, the result is often anxiety and insecurity. These episodes are also opportunities to learn and grow.

Active Adapting
Immerse in the present context.
Extraverted Sensing (Se)

- *Basic Use*: Notice sensory data in the environment.
- *Advanced Use*: Trust your instincts and take action relevant to the moment and current context.
- *Neurotic Use*: Put health/body in danger. (e.g. skip sleep or meals). Judge something or try to control it rather than experience it. Easily give in to impulses to quickly take actions (even if it's the wrong action). Tend to view all outcomes of their actions as reversible or fixable. Set unrealistic/grandiose plans, yet easily distracted and drawn into adolescent fun. Feel exempt from life's rules due to secret shortcuts. (e.g. "The Secret" style thinking). Get a genius insight while resisting feedback, viewing it as the final answer with no more questions or ideas needed.

Manage Your Energy*

ENFJs tend to set lofty goals and map out big plans for themselves and other people. As part of this, they tend to live in their head, in a realm of high ideals. At the same time, they can get easily side-tracked by fun physical and social activities. While juggling all of this, they can abuse their health. They may repeatedly injure themselves during risky adventures. They may skimp on diet and, especially, sleep. Quality sleep is absolutely essential for sustainable energy and a clear head!

Another challenge: They tend to try to control or judge experiences rather than be open to the beauty or possibilities of a moment. They have clear goals with ideas for how to fill them, and they can feel impatient with a lot of energy to simply actualize those. This leads to tension when

* Similar here to cousin type ENTJ.

others resist their expectation or plan, and also they may miss opportunities to genuinely relax. For ENFJs, they can get caught up in the drama and emotion of a situation, which can be really stressful. As part of this, they can quickly get hands-on to take a helpful action that they think is what's needed, without really checking to confirm first.

They benefit by getting out in nature, ideally with friends, in a way that they must leave work and technology behind. Ideally, a physical activity so absorbs their attention that they entirely forget about their problems and goals. They also benefit from keeping up several body- and health-practices rather than relying on one, since they can easily get stuck in a favorite way of thinking. Finally, they benefit when their work is grounding, when they can experience life "on the front lines" and get a lot of practical feedback to balance the big dreams.

Pursue Your Aspirations**

Like all types, ENFJs trust and prioritize their heroic strengths. At the same time, they also seek ways to express their opposite. This opposite acts as a bridge to the unconscious, a realm where potential and vulnerability reside. Thus, their opposite is a doorway to growth.

Skillful Sleuthing
Gain leverage using a framework.
Introverted Thinking (Ti)

- *Basic Use*: Adhere to definitions and philosophical principles.
- *Advanced Use*: Analyze a problem using a framework, and find an angle or leverage by which to solve it.
- *Aspirational Use*: Yearn for a consistent, universal philosophy underlying life's squabbles and troubles. Try to see an issue from multiple angles and from voices of all involved in order to find equitable solutions. Drawn to use analytical rigor and a logical framework that can help people live better. Willing to specialize deeply to do that. Generally, aspire to analyze situations logically, draw boundaries, and balance their empathy and caregiving with objective outcomes. Tend to admire intellect, scholarship, and deep thinking. May over-apply leverage to move themselves and others in social systems.

245   ** Similar here to cousin type ESFJ.

ENFJ Reminders*
for Growth and Success

☐Leading people to a new horizon is among your finest gifts.

☐Maintain multiple sources of intuitive insight.

☐It's okay to sense what others don't, but stay practical.

☐Arrange your life and career so that you are rewarded for your creative endeavors.

☐You shouldn't have to discard parts of yourself just to please someone else; nor should others have to discard parts of themselves to please you.

☐If it feels like people are hurting you, then voice which of your values they are violating.

☐Exercise and other physical activities are a great way to relax.

☐Be more open to people's values—people sense if you like them or not.

☐If your dreams guide your daily choices, then don't expect the fruits of a conventional life at the end of the rainbow.

☐Remind yourself that your unconscious is in charge of your personal growth.

☐Life has a way of unfolding according to its own design.

☐Stay curious. Try to ask open-ended questions.

☐If you want someone to change, really notice what they do to show they care.

☐Consider that some people aren't rude, they're just different.

☐Disillusionment leads to negativity and the misinterpretation of others' intent.

☐Remember your power.

* Adapted from *Quick Guide to the 16 Personality Types in Organizations*

What Now?

Now that you've explored ENFJ:

1. How do the strengths and challenges of this type show up in your life?
2. What's an insight or goal you can act on today in some way?
3. See the later chapters to leverage your subtype, neurotic zone, energy, and aspirations.

INFJ
Life Paths

INFJ Essentials
Foreseer Developer™
Introverting • iNtuiting • Feeling • Judging

Core Themes

INFJs focus on personal growth. They have a talent for foreseeing. A flash of insight comes and they know what will happen. They can sustain a vision while honoring the gifts of others. They need a sense of purpose and take a creative approach to life. INFJs can get into exploring issues to bridge differences and connect people and ideas. They can get analytical when problem solving. Living an idealistic life often presents them with a great deal of stress and a need to withdraw.

Unpack the Stack: INFJs...

Lead with "Keen Foreseeing" (Ni)
Focus on a vision of the future, and on insights and realizations from the inner hidden world of the unconscious.

Support by "Friendly Hosting" (Fe)
Tend relationships, social norms, and people's needs and values as they organize and make thoughtful decisions.

Struggle at "Skillful Sleuthing" (Ti)
Analyze situations, solve problems, and apply leverage according to universal logical principles.

Aspire to "Active Adapting" (Se)
Enjoy the external world using their five senses and take concrete actions based on options before them.

Let's explore...

this type from various angles including 4 developmental variants. As you read, consider what fits for you (or others), what has remained the same or changed over time, and options for where to go from here.

How INFJs Lead with Heroism

Chart the Process

Reflect on data and perceptions. Often appear focused and preoccupied. Attend to reference points.

Keen Foreseeing
Transform with a meta-perspective.
Introverted Intuiting (Ni)

Withdraw from the world and tap your whole mind to receive an insight. Can enter a brief trance to respond to a challenge, foresee the future, or answer a philosophical issue. Avoid specializing and rely instead on timely "ah-ha" moments or a holistic "zen state" to tackle novel tasks, which may look like creative expertise. Manage your own mental processes and stay aware of where you are in an open-ended task. May use an action or symbol to focus. Sensitive to the unknown. Ruminate on ways to improve. Look for synergy. Might try out a realization to transform yourself or how you think. May over-rely on the unconscious.

What flavor of Keen Foreseeing?

INFJs can express this process in two ways. They likely develop a bias for one way early in life and may develop the other later.

"Visionary" Ni	"Oracle" Ni
Analytic/Yang Style: *active, focused, fixed, outward, top down*	***Holistic/Yin Style***: *receptive, diffuse, flexible, inward, bottom up*
Stick to a singular vision of the future to improve self and society. Be certain of a few compelling insights. Don't let go or water down. Turn realizations into principles. Apply many complex concepts. Act as a guiding spirit.	Hold lightly many interrelated insights. Connect to the many facets of the archetypal world. Open to transformation. Respond to others' questions, and innovate for the group. Cultivate an aesthetic or spiritual practice.

How INFJs Give Flexible Support

Expedite Decision Making
Proactively meet goals. Often appear sure and confident.
Organize and fix to get positive results soon.

Friendly Hosting
Nurture trust in giving relationships.
Extraverted Feeling (Fe)

Evaluate and communicate values to build trust and enhance relationships. Like to promote social/interpersonal cohesion. Attend keenly to how others judge you. Quickly adjust your behavior for social harmony. Often rely on a favorite way to reason, with an emphasis on words. Prefer to stay positive, supportive, and optimistic. Empathically respond to others' needs and feelings, and may take on others' needs as your own. Need respect and trust. Easily embarrassed. Like using adjectives to convey values. Enjoy hosting. May hold back the true degree of your emotional response about morals/ethics, regarding talk as more effective. May try too hard to please.

What flavor of Friendly Hosting?
INFJs can express this process in two ways. They likely develop a bias for one way early in life and may develop the other later.

"Shepherd" Fe	"Host" Fe
Analytic/Yang Style: active, focused, fixed, outward, top down	*Holistic/Yin Style*: receptive, diffuse, flexible, inward, bottom up
Announce values and prescribe best behaviors. Corral outliers and encourage them to join the group. Actively work to fix relationships. Inspire as an orator. Make sacrifices, and ask others to sacrifice, in a push to meet needs.	Enjoy supporting your community, family, and friends. Value harmony with others over being right. Sensitive to negative feedback. Accommodate people's many differences. Can be self-sacrificing as you even help foes.

INFJ Self-Portrait

From Conversations*: *What's it like to be you?*

The quest for more knowledge, the meaning of life, the philosophical questions—my mind is always occupied, and what's exciting is when I get to follow through with an insight and do something. I am an abstract future thinker, looking at things from different perspectives. I'm about the relationships and possibilities and enjoy anything with deeper meaning that leaves me wondering, with more questions to ask and things to untangle. Connecting for me means being able to intuitively ask questions of people to get them to go deeper into the things they are talking about.

Inspiring others, helping them find their purpose or meaning, being a different kind of leader from what's traditional—that's really gratifying. I just do that naturally. The challenge is opening up people's minds to have their own original thoughts. I'm a listener and guide.

I think I am a mystery to people. They never really understand me and part of me enjoys that. More often though, I long to be understood.

I tend to approach my day with a structured way of getting things accomplished. People see me as organized, thorough, and easy to get along with, pulling my own weight and eager to help out when called upon. But I'm not as outgoing or as critical as I may sometimes appear. I need a balance between people contact and working on creative projects and will break away from interactions when I get tired out. If I don't have some long-term goals, then what's the point?

I tend to intuitively read people very quickly, but I have to be cautious not to make assumptions. I'm an observer. I get a feeling when people are interesting, and I watch from a distance, make some assessments about the situation, and then approach them and engage in conversation. I put a little bit out and a little more and see how that goes. Do I trust and like them, are they who they say? I have a few deep friendships. A friendship comes best when it is worked to develop that investment. I quickly pick up on sincerity and withdraw if the person is superficial or obviously doesn't care. When I see people who abuse their power or won't stand behind what they say, that ticks me off. It's about integrity. I feel other people's feelings, and taking on that burden can make me too intense and serious, where I can't be spontaneous and fun loving.

I like whatever gets us to think beyond the box, where people can function better because they are not afraid to say things they really feel. I have a lot of imagination and by and large can amuse myself. I love independent projects and reading and writing. I do my best thinking alone, and I like getting out in nature, being alone to go inside and center myself. I have always been drawn to the spiritual. Everywhere, I see life in symbols. Symbols give me focus. Sometimes the connections and perceptions in my mind are so abstract there are no words to explain. A lot of times I just know something and can't explain it—a premonition that's hard to articulate. If it's strong I usually say something or explore where it's coming from, but I will keep it to myself if people don't seem to understand. Informed decisions require lots of information and looking at a situation from as many different points of view as possible. I find it amusing, the absurdity in everyday situations.

It is painful when there is conflict or when I offer advice and someone chooses not to take it. For me, I have to prepare myself for what is going to happen so I can either support people in a positive way or get away and wait out the inevitable heavy duty stuff before returning to fix things. How will it impact me and the people in my life? Will it put me in another place or another level where I can grow more? Not knowing the right thing to say and do is stressful.

Everything revolves around growth. Caring is about the ability to help others grow. What I bring is caring about people, not things. If we spent more time trying to understand each other's point of view, to communicate more effectively, we would grow. In an honest, open, sincere relationship, I can accomplish anything. My challenge is to create those kinds of relationships. I respect most the person who is willing to come forth and be an individual—to make the world a better place, or make a difference in a person's life, where we reach each other's hearts.

."Bold Educator" (INFJ-D)
more driven and confident than other INFJs
(Dominant subtype)

These INFJs are outspoken, even daring, and willing to ruffle a few feathers, albeit in an eloquent way. They are strong, thoughtful, and deeply attendant to values.

Brain-wise, their wiring is biased toward the front and they may show a weak "starburst" brainstorming pattern too. Thus, they are relatively quick in addressing what they see in situations and—given a little extra time—bringing in fresh ideas. They can be smooth managers. They can grow to be paragons of emotional intelligence, aware of where they and others are coming from and how they can manage relationships diplomatically. In support of this, they often have strong auditory skills. They strive to use the spoken (and written) word to its best effect.

As INFJs, they are still reflective thinkers. They keep refining the expression of their values and principles. Their relatively quick responses come from the time they spend processing the new with the old, or the recent with the timeless, to express what's of eternal value. This verbal and visual process results in maps or montages of meanings. And, rather than hide or downplay their insights, they tend to pronounce them.

They stay engaged with the world, take chances, and like an audience. They can put themselves out there in a new place or in the public eye, in an audacious way, even when they feel nervous inside. At their best, they are articulate proponents with compelling stories and diverse interests. At times, they can look vulnerable or brittle, but they possess—mentally and emotionally—a hidden strength of character. They can call out and really critique people, ideas, and institutions. The price: when least expected, stress or depression comes home to slam them hard.

These INFJs can make fine advisers, educators, leaders, managers and teachers. Whatever their medium or venue, they aim to inspire people to live together better. They also enjoy taking more of a lead in their romantic, family, and community lives as a central respected figure.

"Passionate Creator" (INFJ-C)
more exploratory and social than other INFJs
(Creative subtype)

These INFJs trust in the power of flow to channel a hidden muse. They are curious and imaginative, love learning, and are often well-traveled with a bohemian flair.

In terms of brain-wiring, they usually show a strong starburst pattern. This indicates a creative, intuitive mind. Like a set of antennas, they take in everything around them and synthesize it to learn or create something new. At times they feel like a sponge, soaking up everything to get a holistic picture of what's going on. Or, the starburst promotes a Zen-like state of creative flow like weaving a great tapestry from many threads. They manage a mass of details, definitions, images, and diverse ideas to craft something compelling. Or they feel blocked or lazy and nothing comes.

Besides the starburst and flow, they apply executive skills to direct and shape the output of their intuition. They also often have dense auditory links, especially if playing music is a passion. They are usually skilled with abstract concepts, metaphor, and humor. And they enjoy a hidden talent for analysis to manage complexity, like a conductor managing an orchestra. They may rely on a set of rote steps or templates to shape their creative work, whether guitar chord patterns or film editing techniques. On the downside, these INFJs have more difficulty getting by with mundane daily tasks, as they lack the full halo of connections that most people rely on. They can look scattered.

These INFJs are usually in the creative arts, especially music, and they are often into travel, foreign languages, cross-cultural exploration, and life-long learning. In the arts, they are more likely into jazz or improv than memorizing classics. They seek their own style. The same if they venture into the sciences. They can make caring and enthusiastic teachers, and their passion for learning never ends.

"Enduring Associate" (INFJ-N)
more conventional and specialized than other INFJs
(Normalizing subtype)

These INFJs show brain-wiring that is more typical of the general population. That said, they are still their own unique creature inside, just with a mainstream "costume" to help them work hard to realize their dreams.

For brain-wiring, these INFJs show a mix of linear connections. Most often, they possess a halo of conventional skills to excel in the classroom and the workplace. Yet the rest of the brain within, is a mass of zigzag connections. Because these zigzags are unusual and specific to them, the INFJ's way of processing life is equally unusual. When they experience a situation, their understanding and reaction can feel like a leap or turn of thinking. To work with this inner life, they tend to have good, even remarkable, self-management skills. This self-conscious emotional intelligence is often right-brained. That is, it feels both symbolic, valuable, and meaningful. In terms of other skills, they are adept with language, and they tend to tap this in a practical way such as writing reports with an audience in mind. Being introverts, of course, they have a deep reflective side. They value having time to get sorted and draw inspiration from their well of feelings, facts, ideas, stories, and values.

More than other INFJs, they have high endurance in pursuit of goals, which should be clear and compelling. They rely on multiple touch points to push forward to success. Even when one source of motivation fails them, they turn to others. They find their inner strength as best they can to keep moving and working. It can feel like a noble pursuit.

With their endurance, intuitive intellect, and desire to succeed, they often reach a high position. They can get through medical school, layers of corporate management, the complexities of engineering, a terrible disease, or a similar demanding goal. Invariably, the path runs through an institution or traditional practice. Prestige often acts as a compass. Along the way, they bring a warm passion for helping others.

"Prophetic Councilor" (INFJ-H)
more empathic and reflective than other INFJs
(Harmonizing subtype)

These INFJs are ethereal, far-seeing, philosophical, poetic, and soulful. They have sophisticated, even quite unique, brain-wiring that sets them apart.

In terms of brain-wiring, they show a mix of complex patterns. They sport a diamond-like network, or two, that spans the hemispheres. This supports a specialized skillset that mixes analytical and holistic approaches. They may also tap a soft starburst pattern where all brain regions engage at once in a flow state. Often, they sport a zig-zag of connections too that reflect unusual ways of thinking. They can go from A to B, then M, and back to C. They may easily also have their own pattern of wiring that, really, doesn't much look like anyone else's. They have strong visual skills invariability tied to a brain region that aids narrative, symbols, and visual patterns. They are also usually attentive to voice tone and social feedback. They are sensitive to what's going on with others. All of this is often disconnected from executive regions. Generally, they are not as adept at language as other INFJs. And they lack the typical suite of skills that others have to get by easily in daily life. Thus, their intuitive side lies behind a curtain.

They may be in any profession but advising others is a de facto forte. A discipline like counseling or healthcare fits them, as do mystical or shamanic arts. They are sensitive to artistic quality. They have a knack for cross-cultural understanding and can hold multiple points of view with detachment. Whatever their role, everything feels interrelated and is a challenge to communicate directly. Thus, they can look passive. They often prefer to work solo, one-on-one, or as a revered guest.

To understand these INFJs, look at the small things. They are quiet, considerate, and concerned for others' well-being. They are fine hosts and romantic partners with thoughtful gifts and personalized touches. They take an interest in the esoteric and are connected to a spirit world of sorts.

Mind Your Neurotic Zone*

Like all types, INFJs have neurotic moments. These erupt when the ego and unconscious clash. While at times uplifting, the result is often anxiety and insecurity. These episodes are also opportunities to learn and grow.

Skillful Sleuthing
Gain leverage using a framework.
Introverted Thinking (Ti)

- *Basic Use*: Adhere to definitions and philosophical principles.
- *Advanced Use*: Analyze a problem using a framework, and find an angle or leverage by which to solve it.
- *Neurotic Use*: Can get hypercritical yet are also personally quite sensitive (even to small slights). Tend to get stuck in analysis paralysis. Constantly grapple with vague big ideas without getting clarity. Prefer simple mental models except a specialty to endlessly tweak and elaborate on (word-smithing, etc). Strongly favor (or reject) intellectual or cultural elitism (e.g. fetishize scholarship/education). Easily define personal or local experiences as part of some global/grand drama. Feel a strong inner/outer split (e.g. warm on the outside while cold inside, or vice versa).

Manage Your Energy**

INFJs are private and protective of their energy. This is about more than time, physical space, and resources. Their psyche is like a finely-tuned, highly sensitive antenna that takes in a lot of abstract impressions. Thus, they can be stressed by things that others don't notice. They also trust their capacity for creative flow, but getting into and sustaining flow takes seclusion, which generally requires having room away from others' "auras".

At times, they may feel they lack energy to get off the ground. Often, this looks like procrastination but is due to a lack of information and alignment to deep needs and values. They benefit by setting strong boundaries, making it clear to others up front when it's okay to intrude.

* Similar here to cousin type ISFJ.

And, they need positive, healthy people around them who can also facilitate in a gentle, hands-off way when they go over-board. Constantly attending to others' needs and emotions can be a challenge, and they can find themselves staying up nights, finding it hard to sleep, as they mull over a problem. Ideally, they take time to clarify the best principles to approach life's varied situations.

Rather than devoting themselves to a single body-mind practice, they benefit from having a set of several low-impact practices to pick from daily to "cleanse" and reset. Taking off a few weeks at a time, especially alone in nature as "me time" is ideal. Having private time everyday for an hour or two, where they can relax rather than be in work mode or carer mode, is also great. They also benefit when they have a low-maintenance environment and workplace.

Pursue Your Aspirations**

Like all types, INFJs trust and prioritize their heroic strengths. At the same time, they also seek ways to express their opposite. This opposite acts as a bridge to the unconscious, a realm where potential and vulnerability reside. Thus, their opposite is a doorway to growth.

Active Adapting
Immerse in the present context.
Extraverted Sensing (Se)

- **Basic Use**: Notice sensory data in the environment.
- **Advanced Use**: Trust your gut instincts and take action relevant to the moment and current context.
- **Aspirational Use**: Yearn to live freely in the present with tangible and immediate experiences. Enjoy trips into nature. Channel abstract visions into tangible projects or actionable plans. Use insights for personal and interpersonal improvement. Use foresight to predict trends and create products and services for these trends. Stimulate inner growth through rich sensory experiences such as travel. Express deep insights about the human experience through sensory mediums like art, dance, music, writing, or yoga. Can get derailed by concrete details or entertaining pleasures.

** Similar here to cousin type INTJ.

INFJ Reminders*
for Growth and Success

☐ Own your ability to reframe a situation or interaction as one of your greatest gifts.

☐ Find an arena where your foresight is valued.

☐ Allow time to enjoy talking for fun with people whose interests and visions lie in the future.

☐ To live in the moment, remember to share what you and others are hearing, seeing, and feeling right now.

☐ Have a safety net (time and space) to retreat to when overwhelmed by stress and the physical world.

☐ Remember that theories are nice tools to further exploration.

☐ If your understanding of something doesn't suggest how change or growth is possible, then add more depth and experience to that understanding.

☐ Balance what is supportive, friendly, and safe with what challenges the thinking behind your opinions.

☐ Have outlets, ideally creative ones, to express life's many layers and levels.

☐ Try to imagine sometimes that you are like everyone else.

☐ After a period of personal growth, check for external evidence of change.

☐ Keep in mind that learning "how" to think is more useful than "what" to think.

☐ Consider, you can manifest what most others can only imagine.

* Adapted from *Quick Guide to the 16 Personality Types in Organizations*

What Now?

Now that you've explored INFJ:

1. How do the strengths and challenges of this type show up in your life?

2. What's an insight or goal you can act on today in some way?

3. See the later chapters to leverage your subtype, neurotic zone, energy, and aspirations.

ENFP
Life Paths

ENFP Essentials
Discoverer Advocate™
Extraverting • iNtuiting • Feeling • Perceiving

Core Themes

ENFPs explore perceptions and try out stories. They often see what's hidden and voice what's really meant. They notice others' potential and like to inspire. They ask what-if and fly with creative new ideas. They want goodness and happiness. ENFPs strive to honestly believe in and live with themselves. They have a talent to bring about ideal or magical moments with someone. When needed, they can organize and manage a lot. They often feel restless with a hunger to discover their true direction.

Unpack the Stack: ENFPs...

Lead with "Excited Brainstorming" (Ne)
Perceive, pursue, and play with life's many potential possibilities, facilitating the promising ones.

Support by "Quiet Crusading" (Fi)
Listen to their feelings, convictions, and conscience to make choices that align with their identity and beliefs.

Struggle at "Timely Building" (Te)
Utilize measurable data, tools, resources, and efficient procedures as they organize and make effective decisions.

Aspire to "Cautious Protecting" (Si)
Reference a massive storehouse of rich past experiences as they cultivate familiarity, comfort, and stability.

Let's explore...

this type from various angles including 4 developmental variants. As you read, consider what fits for you (or others), what has remained the same or changed over time, and options for where to go from here.

How ENFPs Lead with Heroism

Energize the Process

Seek out stimuli. Often appear random, emergent,
and enthusiastic. Attend to the here and now.

Excited Brainstorming

Explore numerous emerging patterns.

Extraverted iNtuiting (Ne)

Perceive and play with ideas and relationships. Wonder about patterns of interaction across various situations. Keep up a high-energy mode that helps you notice and engage potential possibilities. Think analogically: stimuli are springboards to generate inferences, analogies, metaphors, jokes, and more new ideas. Easily guess details.Adept at "what if?" scenarios, mirroring others, and even role-playing. Can shift a situation's dynamics and trust what emerges. Mental activity tends to feel chaotic, with many highs and lows at once, like an ever-changing "Christmas tree" of flashing lights. Often entertain multiple meanings at once. May find it hard to stay on-task.

What flavor of Excited Brainstorming?

ENFPs can express this process in two ways. They likely develop a bias for one way early in life and may develop the other later.

"Marketer" Ne	"Catalyst" Ne
Analytic/Yang Style: active, focused, fixed, outward, top down	*Holistic/Yin Style: receptive, diffuse, flexible, inward, bottom up*
Put on a show. Pitch and juggle many ideas, trusting quantity over quality in search of advantages or gains. Recruit others and rely on strong energy of ideas to shift situations to one's liking. Court uncertainty for progress.	Notice subtle patterns. Negotiate toward a novel win-win outcome with a relaxed, subtle style. Use humor and disguises. Include and promote others. Search for the highest quality potential possibilities for everyone's gain.

How ENFPs Give Flexible Support

Refine Decision Making
Clarify what's universal, true or worthwhile. Often appear quietly receptive. Trust own judgments.

Quiet Crusading
Stay true to who you really are.
Introverted Feeling (Fi)

Listen with your whole self to locate and support what's important. Often evaluate importance along a spectrum from love/like to dislike/hate. Patient and good at listening for identity, values, and what resonates, though may tune out when "done" listening. Value loyalty and belief in oneself and others. Attentive and curious for what is not said. Focus on word choice, voice tone, and facial expressions to detect intent. Check with your conscience before acting. Choose behavior congruent with what's important, your personal identity, and beliefs. Hard to embarrass. Can respond strongly to specific, high-value words or false data. May not utilize feedback.

What flavor of Quiet Crusading?
ENFPs can express this process in two ways. They likely develop a bias for one way early in life and may develop the other later.

"Quester" Fi	"Romantic" Fi
Analytic/Yang Style: active, focused, fixed, outward, top down	**_Holistic/Yin Style_**: receptive, diffuse, flexible, inward, bottom up
Pursue a singular life quest or truth. Aim for moral clarity. Dedicated to a congruent set of beliefs. Align quest and core personal identity. Listen to a select voice like one's own conscience. Contain your feelings.	Live a life of deep quiet feeling. Listen to and harmonize with many voices. Pursue multiple soft quests. Allow room for inner and outer conflicts. Identity is subtle, diffuse, and varies in the context of each relationship.

ENFP Self-Portrait

From Conversations*: *What's it like to be you?*

I have to be directly in contact with people and know that somehow I am influencing what happens for them in a positive way. That is a kind of driving force in my life, actualizing potential, giving encouragement, letting people know what I think they can do. I have been told I have this uncanny ability to absolutely zero in on and intuit what people need. I sometimes recognize something about them that they have not said to anybody else. And they say, "How did you know?"

I see myself as a facilitator. It's not about imposing what I want to see happen, although I have some grand ideal of everyone having a better life or feeling better or dealing with a particular issue. Being able to understand people in depth gives me a feeling I have been friends with them forever, and when I act too much that way, they may not be able to handle it. But I feel sad when I see potential in someone and they are either denying it or not able to access it in some way. I'm very sensitive too, but sometimes easily discouraged, and I still go on thrilled to meet new people, with an interest in assisting them in whatever they are seeking. I give them both knowledge and meaning. I bring a fresh perspective and my appreciation for people's goodness.

If I'm stuck for hours working at a monotonous task, I get peculiar, zonky, and weird. I get very tired if I can't get out and exchange information. I'll lack bounce, the bubbling of ideas that makes me run through life. I absolutely have to have a fulfilling job or I get depressed. I want to use my talents, make a difference, and have autonomy. If not, I struggle to retain a sense of self and it's like my spirit is dying.

People talk about being drawn to me. Friends are so important to me and I have good intentions. I like to think I'll do whatever I can do to hold on to them, but often I don't get around to writing or calling. They know that if they create a friendship with me, then the friendship is going to be intense and loyal and I will be there for them when they really need

* Reprinted from *16 Personality Types: Descriptions for Self-Discovery*

me. And I can engage with people that I care about who are a distance away and feel like they are a part of my life on an ongoing basis, picking up a lot of feeling from what they write or when they call. It would be easier to spin straw into gold than be totally alone.

As a kid I did a lot of imaginary things. It's like acting. I am very enthusiastic about many different things and very romantic. I have a child-like quality and like to get others roped into that too. Fun is a feeling of satisfaction as opposed to just an activity, the feeling of being able to smile all the time and get others to smile. What's fun is watching other people find out they can really do something they otherwise never thought of themselves as capable of doing.

I have a strong sense of ethics and fairness and I can be a little too aware of an imbalance. I am a perfect mimic. I can be someone else and get enormous insight about that person, and I want to tell them about it. I admire authenticity, the person who can just be, and speaking the truth with clarity and tact, to get this magic bond where we are transfixed in that moment. That's something I seek.

The way to tick me off is to either do something really unethical or question my integrity. I get very annoyed when people jump me for not doing things their way, but I often don't defend myself because I fear losing control. I'd rather be in control when I talk to them about the situation. They don't know what effect they're having and it tears me up inside. It makes me crazy if I am in conflict with someone who wants to walk away and I need to engage with them until we work it out. I need to be supported, not just always the giver and catalyst. And I need contact—emotional, intellectual, just words—for fun and connection.

I remember this wonderful little boy, but he was conning everyone. I kept looking straight at him, "in the soul," and finally he put his hands up over his eyes and said, "You've got to quit looking at me like that. I can look at people like that, but you can't look at me like that." And I completely understood him and I said, "I know who you are, and it's not bad. It's good, you're good, and you have promise." That's what people don't want to hear—I see you, I value you, I care what you'll become, and I wish to be a part of that if you need me.

"Crafty Producer" (ENFP-D)
more driven and confident than other ENFPs
(Dominant subtype)

These ENFPs are confident, entertaining, and relatively quick decision-makers. They make good managers and leaders. They tend to seek out, rope in, and direct others with high potential to bring about a memorable, compelling result. They have found their "in charge" voice.

In terms of brain-wiring, these ENFPs sport strong links in the front of the brain. That includes good executive skills. They can focus and decide based on new information as it comes in. They tend to be talkative, can follow a metaphor or line of reasoning, and are moderately perceptive, though not as much as other ENFPs. Importantly, in a leadership role, they easily juggle the needs of the context with their values, likes, and dislikes to keep things moving. In their endeavors, they tend to be well-rounded jack-of-all-trades but not exceptional. They "remake" frames rather than break them.

Many of these ENFPs have a soft starburst pattern. Thus, creative thinking fills a support role; for example, they brainstorm ways to solve a problem, but what's central is getting a solution. They can easily follow a style or template, improvising to get the most out of its potential. They are quick to try out things, notably in a managerial, producer or executive role. They trust their intuitive response, yes or no, right away to go with a result, or they will turn to someone they believe can help or at least back up their intuition.

With their confident style, they can dominate the scene, talking a bit, and miss nuances or key points. In this sense, they can come off as egotistical or not as smart or ethical as they think. On the other hand, their confident excitement brings in a lot of acquaintances. They are persistent, and their mainstream way of doing things can reach a wide following. Finding conventional rewards and success comes more easily to them than other ENFPs. Whether they acknowledge others' contributions and share their success signals their character.

"Eclectic Wanderer" (ENFP-C)
more exploratory and social than other ENFPs
(Creative subtype)

These ENFPs are notably outgoing, positive, adaptable, and energetic with a welcoming, cheerful style. They are truly capable of perceiving and entertaining a lot at once. They tend to be wanderers, exploring all that life has to offer. They love to stir the pot and challenge norms.

For brain-wiring, they always have a strong starburst pattern. Every region lights up, relevant or not, to fully consider whatever stimuli come in. Every input is like a potential secret letter that everyone must see. Thus, their brains are very active and they tend to notice a lot of interesting connections. They will go out of their way to evoke new input, and will try stuff just to see what results. They trust their talent to adapt, noticing ideal moments to move, and finding ways to use their skills on the go to swing things their way. They can handle a lot of complexity, playing with possibilities until something helps bring things down to a concrete form.

Besides brainstorming, most have remarkable rapport-building skills with quick, uncanny insights into voice tone and body language. They easily notice visual and narrative patterns. They usually have fair executive skills: they can stay with a task when it is clear with a simple, obvious end goal. Otherwise, focusing and making decisions are challenges, and they can get off track or fall into a funk.

Among these ENFPs, social and artistic interests come first, even with technical tasks, and they often pursue multiple careers, perhaps moving back and forth. They look gifted in each, and they may or may not succeed in a practical way. They self-motivate only in spurts, and at most they can pursue a big, vague dream. Settling down can be a big challenge. When they do, they are energetic and quirky partners, parents, and colleagues. They have a rebellious streak. They really benefit when they have people they care about in their life who help ground them.

"Secret Agent" (ENFP-N)
more conventional and specialized than other ENFPs
(Normalizing subtype)

These ENFPs have brain-wiring that is more the norm of the general population. They come off as patient, reflective, technically adept, traditional, and well-mannered, with a quiet charm. They bring organizational skills, a team-player mindset, and a more chart-the-course style.

Brain-wiring consists of many linear connections toward the left, back, and maybe middle of the brain. Thus, they are more technical, grounded, and linear thinkers than other ENFPs. They tend to be strongly visual and fairly factual. They may have trained as an engineer, lawyer, photographer, programmer, scientist, soldier, or such. A traditional cultural background also encourages this brain-wiring. If they are in the arts, which they may well be, their approach is more physical or technical such as computer graphics. They rely on specific brain regions to engage in hypothesizing, imagining, and so on.

Their skills and style mirror their brain-wiring. They tend to be quieter, more structured, and have more of a critical eye than other ENFPs. They can come up with designs and plans, they use charts or diagrams, and they want those to be logical and straight-forward. Not having these can feel stressful though using them is a learned skill. They are patient to work through problems and tend to keep a lid on their enthusiasm. They chuckle rather than burst with excitement. They are less random but still subtly playful. They also understand the value of working on a team, supporting others, and communicating in a clear, effective way. They enjoy family life and traditional cultural activities, though often with a twist.

Being ENFPs, their skills serve an idealistic interest. Hidden behind their commercial or conventional presentation are deep passion and a desire to impact others and the culture. They work well with and easily touch the general populace. Their biggest contribution can be making something a new standard or tradition that the average person can relate to.

"Dedicated Advocate" (ENFP-H)
more empathic and reflective than other ENFPs
(Harmonizing subtype)

These ENFPs have many subtle tones. They offer a dedicated heart, are sophisticated thinkers, and are often older and wiser, if not literally, then in the way they come off. They can really apply themselves to a deep cause with warmth and caring. They've taken on a flowing, relaxed, behind-the-scenes style.

In terms of brain-wiring, these ENFPs can show one of two patterns, or a blend of both. They may have a strong right-hemisphere bias that supports a really holistic or artistic style. Or, the brain-wiring consists of a mass of diamond-shape networks. Each network operates on its own, bringing together a diverse range of skills for them to work from. This allows them to sink fully into a particular way of thinking and acting as they fill their key roles. For example, as a therapist, they integrate their natural ENFP talents with all of their career knowledge to work in a deep way. These diamond networks are also very fast. Some ENFPs show both neural patterns, or also a "starburst" to weave it all together. Regardless of the pattern, they tend to have strong anchoring in their identity and beliefs.

These ENFPs tend to be older, having had access to and experience in the best aspects of their profession and what life has to offer. They hail from a wide range of professions from acting and business to engineering and psychotherapy; what stands out is the high quality of their work and their sophisticated understanding. Whatever their job, they are great with complex information and can be incredible transformers.

Personally, these ENFPs tend to be peaceful with integrity. They ponder a lot, ask deep philosophical questions, enjoy discovery through discussion, and act as advocates for enduring changes. With their quieter style and high standards, they tend to keep a small social circle and are deeply loyal to their intimates, able to endure much.

Mind Your Neurotic Zone*

Like all types, ENFPs have neurotic moments. These erupt when the ego and unconscious clash. While at times uplifting, the result is often anxiety and insecurity. These episodes are also opportunities to learn and grow.

Timely Building
Measure and construct for progress.
Extraverted Thinking (Te)

- *Basic Use*: Follow steps, points, and time tables.
- *Advanced Use*: Create structure, reason by measures and evidence, and implement complex plans.
- *Neurotic Use*: Tend to under- or over-manage. Easily frustrated or feel lost in logistical and technical details such as paperwork. Can panic at deadlines. Under or over explain, either losing others when they think they're clear, or fear they're confusing when it's clear. Reject hierarchy/authority figures and rules, yet also easily buy into or ignore institutional failures. Confuse being blunt—or making up reasons—for actual reasoning with evidence. Troubleshooting (under-do or over-do). Easily take a "consequences be damned" attitude. Struggle to stay detached or objective.

Manage Your Energy**

ENFPs tend to be quite busy with a variety of interests and diverse activities all at once. Imagine multiple songs or devices playing at the same time. This stimulates their creativity and keeps life interesting and meaningful. Everywhere they notice potential possibilities and all of their brain entertains everything that comes in. Needless to say, this can really tax their "batteries"; on average, the brain consumes a quarter of a person's energy!

Often times, health and physical activities are not so interesting to them. What is meaningful about kicking around a ball to get it into a net? And doing a forty-minute run on a treadmill sounds boring. They'd much rather be out-and-about and chatting about ideas. Unfortunately,

* Similar here to cousin type ESFP.

the life of the mind easily pulls them away from the physical world, and if they don't care for their health, they will suffer later. This is particularly true as they get older if they rely ever-more on caffeine, sugar, and other stimulants to keep up their high-energy multi-tasking life. For ENFPs, they really benefit by having an interesting, low-stress person to exercise with, such as a personal trainer or gym buddy. Putting together a favorite music list, and being in an appealing environment, also help.

The secret for this type is to raise their standards. Over time, they can learn to filter what is worth interacting around and prioritize quality. Ideally, they also benefit from a body-mind practice that encourages them to be present with their body rather than shut it out. What feedback, or wisdom, does their body have? And in terms of work, they benefit by having a solid "container" that holds their diverse interests.

Pursue Your Aspirations**

Like all types, ENFPs trust and prioritize their heroic strengths. At the same time, they also seek ways to express their opposite. This opposite acts as a bridge to the unconscious, a realm where potential and vulnerability reside. Thus, their opposite is a doorway to growth.

Cautious Protecting
Stabilize with a Predictable Standard.
Introverted Sensing (Si)

- **Basic Use**: Recall tangible data and experiences.
- **Advanced Use**: Stabilize a situation by comparing it to what is expected, known, and reliable.
- **Aspirational Use**: Yearn for stability. Find grounding and a sense of safety in past experiences, traditions, and the familiar. Skilled at revitalizing old ideas with new applications, and drawn to reimagine or expand upon established ideas with inventive twists. Ideally, they come to respect proven methods, historical context, and learned lessons. At their best, they acknowledge the wisdom of the past, and existing methods and institutions, as they balance new ideas with universal themes that speak to society at large and the timeless human experience. Can get overly nostalgic or stuck in poor habits.

** Similar here to cousin type ENTP.

ENFP Reminders*
for Growth and Success

- ☐ Your greatest gifts are silent.
- ☐ Find and stay with what creates inspiring moments for you.
- ☐ Give people you encounter a second evaluation—to perceive what you missed the first time.
- ☐ Keep up with friends.
- ☐ It's okay to need inspiration for yourself.
- ☐ In a conflict, say something about yourself, too.
- ☐ Have a work environment where you can be involved in numerous projects and flow creatively.
- ☐ Find times to let up on the need for constant change.
- ☐ Words are only words, so be honest about whether actions match intentions.
- ☐ Don't let who you think you are get in the way of what you can be.
- ☐ A good direction in life is to make something totally novel into a new tradition.
- ☐ Trust that at some points, you can safely be yourself when people get close.
- ☐ Be sure you like who you're with.
- ☐ Practice patience with those who complain while doing nothing about it.
- ☐ In any situation, try to always recognize at least three interpretations grounded in common sense.
- ☐ Beware of unhealthy habits.
- ☐ Good empathic connections require compassion.
- ☐ Consider that thinking everything is in the mind might be wishful thinking.

* Adapted from *Quick Guide to the 16 Personality Types in Organizations*

What Now?

Now that you've explored ENFP:

1. How do the strengths and challenges of this type show up in your life?
2. What's an insight or goal you can act on today in some way?
3. See the later chapters to leverage your subtype, neurotic zone, energy, and aspirations.

INFP
Life Paths

INFP Essentials
Harmonizer Clarifier™
Introverting • iNtuiting • Feeling • Perceiving

Core Themes

INFPs need a quest or core meaning. Yet they tend to go with the flow. They have a talent to listen in order to help, noticing what sits behind what's said. They explore moral questions, enjoy uncovering mysteries, and relate through stories and metaphors. INFPs have a way of knowing what is believable. They seek to balance opposites. To get to really know oneself again is a beautiful moment. They can manage others pretty well. They struggle with structure and getting their lives in order.

Unpack the Stack: INFPs...

Lead with "Quiet Crusading" (Fi)
Listen to their feelings, convictions, and conscience to make choices that align with their identity and beliefs.

Support by "Excited Brainstorming" (Ne)
Perceive, pursue, and play with life's many potential possibilities, facilitating the promising ones.

Struggle at "Cautious Protecting" (Si)
Reference a massive storehouse of rich past experiences as they cultivate familiarity, comfort, and stability.

Aspire to "Timely Building" (Te)
Utilize measurable data, tools, resources, and efficient procedures as they organize and make effective decisions.

Let's explore...

this type from various angles including 4 developmental variants. As you read, consider what fits for you (or others), what has remained the same or changed over time, and options for where to go from here.

How INFPs Lead with Heroism

Refine Decision Making
Clarify what's universal, true or worthwhile. Often appear quietly receptive. Trust own judgments.

Quiet Crusading
Stay true to who you really are.
Introverted Feeling (Fi)

Listen with your whole self to locate and support what's important. Often evaluate importance along a spectrum from love/like to dislike/hate. Patient and good at listening for identity, values, and what resonates, though may tune out when "done" listening. Value loyalty and belief in oneself and others. Attentive and curious for what is not said. Focus on word choice, voice tone, and facial expressions to detect intent. Check with your conscience before acting. Choose behavior congruent with what's important, your personal identity, and beliefs. Hard to embarrass. Can respond strongly to specific, high-value words or false data. May not utilize feedback.

What flavor of Quiet Crusading?
INFPs can express this process in two ways. They likely develop a bias for one way early in life and may develop the other later.

"Quester" Fi	"Romantic" Fi
Analytic/Yang Style: active, focused, fixed, outward, top down	**Holistic/Yin Style**: receptive, diffuse, flexible, inward, bottom up
Pursue a singular life quest or truth. Aim for moral clarity. Dedicated to a congruent set of beliefs. Align quest and core personal identity. Listen to a select voice like one's own conscience. Contain your feelings.	Live a life of deep quiet feeling. Listen to and harmonize with many voices. Pursue multiple soft quests. Allow room for inner and outer conflicts. Identity is subtle, diffuse, and varies in the context of each relationship.

How INFPs Give Flexible Support

Energize the Process

Seek out stimuli. Often appear random, emergent,
and enthusiastic. Attend to the here and now.

Excited Brainstorming
Explore numerous emerging patterns.
Extraverted iNtuiting (Ne)

Perceive and play with ideas and relationships. Wonder about patterns of interaction across various situations. Keep up a high-energy mode that helps you notice and engage potential possibilities. Think analogically: stimuli are springboards to generate inferences, analogies, metaphors, jokes, and more new ideas. Easily guess details. Adept at "what if?" scenarios, mirroring others, and even role-playing. Can shift a situation's dynamics and trust what emerges. Mental activity tends to feel chaotic, with many highs and lows at once, like an ever-changing "Christmas tree" of flashing lights. Often entertain multiple meanings at once. May find it hard to stay on-task.

What flavor of Excited Brainstorming?

INFPs can express this process in two ways. They likely develop a bias for one way early in life and may develop the other later.

"Marketer" Ne	"Catalyst" Ne
Analytic/Yang Style: active, focused, fixed, outward, top down	**_Holistic/Yin Style_**: receptive, diffuse, flexible, inward, bottom up
Put on a show. Pitch and juggle many ideas, trusting quantity over quality in search of advantages or gains. Recruit others and rely on strong energy of ideas to shift situations to one's liking. Court uncertainty for progress.	Notice subtle patterns. Negotiate toward a novel win-win outcome with a relaxed, subtle style. Use humor and disguises. Include and promote others. Search for the highest quality potential possibilities for everyone's gain.

INFPs In Their Own Words

From Conversations*: *What's it like to be you?*

I have a very internal focus. I think I look at my-self through other people's eyes, but sometimes I can lose touch with how things work for me. Then I can get introspective, going very deep and staying there, not coming out too quickly or easily. Somehow I find it very difficult to put into words and communicate the things that really matter to me. Most people don't have the foggiest notion about what goes on with me.

I like harmony and seek consensus and do well with the deep issues. My values and the things that are important to me often feel outside the mainstream in the sense that I feel impinged upon and uncomfortable with so much of what goes on. I'm too private to push my values on to other people, but I am convinced that one ought to be congruent in their own life if they are going to expect congruence from others. In a sense I hold other people to that standard, and I worry about my own incongruities, inconsistencies, and contradictions. Groups can be hard. I can put myself in the group process so rapidly and so completely, and it's important not to get sucked in. I need to be predictable about what I believe.

I am a global thinker and I like to learn interactively. My thoughts need to be connected with some person or value. On reflection, don't all thoughts have to be connected to something? I feed new information into other things I've read and my thoughts, and I can have a marvelous time just sitting with ideas. And I like to discuss or write things because I seem to have a lot in my head and I've got to get it out. I love bringing together different eclectic ideas and seeing what's similar. I like to have my own ideas, hear others ideas, and have ideas challenged, bantering back and forth. Chitchat has no interest for me. I tend to do a lot of mental rehearsal and play in problem solving, and the fun part is figuring out how to do something. Motivation comes when something has real meaning or value for me, and while I enjoy ideas, I don't like having my values challenged.

For me, asking questions is just a different form of being quiet, a

* Reprinted from *16 Personality Types: Descriptions for Self-Discovery*

way to explore an inner thought stream or check out of reality and back into my thoughts. Sometimes I chuckle at myself that there is really no sequential way that I work though tasks.

I have always trusted my intuition, even before I was aware of it. I enjoy talking to people. It's interesting to learn about them, where they're coming from and how they invent their reality. And I have an innate talent for reading between the lines—to hear what hasn't been said—and a sense of what needs to be said and done. I tend to form impressions right away about people, and most of the time I feel pretty good about my impressions but sometimes I am way off. At least if the people have good intentions, I can relax.

I enjoy seeing people enjoy who they are, and I get a lot of joy helping others discover that they have value. Being able to help someone in their darkest hour, to communicate across differences and find common ways of working together, that is very satisfying because then there is a real sense of closeness and acceptance and a genuine pursuit of helping people heal and achieve their goals. I hold on to relationships even though we may go long periods without seeing each other, and I cherish those long associations.

I'm concerned about how others feel when they are around me. Lack of honesty or ethics or integrity in interactions—when someone is saying one thing but doing another—really puts me off. So does when someone doesn't honor, or accept as valid, my communication or feeling as I try to talk to them about something that matters to me. And I don't need to talk about myself. I don't enjoy it. Sometimes I'm frustrated trying to communicate, and sometimes a metaphor or a joke or a story is a way to effectively express myself so what I'm saying can be heard by someone who hears or experiences things differently.

I don't know what I am going to do next, but I trust in myself that something will come in as a new idea, with challenge and inner meaning. Whatever it is, it will be right. Although I would never actually say it, it feels as though I am grounded in the very being of who I am when I talk like this.

"Noble Champion" (INFP-D)
more driven and confident than other INFPs
(Dominant subtype)

These INFPs really show strong character. They hold themselves together with endurance toward their goals and ideals, which can feel like a quest or even a crusade at times. They can become remarkable managers and leaders with an in-charge feel.

Brain-wise, the wiring is densest toward the front. Thus, they are relatively quick to process new information, sharing their reaction or stating a value at stake. They are strong speakers and writers, and attentive listeners and readers with exceptional language-based reasoning skills, all woven into a tapestry. They are particularly good at communicating with a purpose in mind such as explaining a key idea or tuning in to someone's real agenda.

Ideally, they find ways to balance the various demands of a situation with their identity, checking that decisions match their goals and values. Often, they rely upon templates: ways of thinking and working that they can draw on to quickly do something. To really use their imagination, they must turn it on or wait for it to wake up. This process is often vaguely visual.

Being INFPs, they still need quiet time. In those moments, they ponder ideas and feelings, comparing what's new with to what is already in their memory storehouse. They check for what aligns and may simply screen out what does not. They are persistent and consistent as they work toward what are inevitably noble, humanistic ends. Focus and certainty often frames them as ethical and moral examples. Other times, they can come off as overly idealistic, preachy, rigid or extreme.

These INFPs tend to excel in public-facing and administrative jobs. Their specific interests vary, but they keep at whatever it is. Business, education, law, music, psychology, and social work are popular choices. They usually have musical talent, which they may or may not choose to develop.

"Curious Dreamer" (INFP-C)
more exploratory and social than other INFPs
(Creative subtype)

These INFPs are delightfully playful. They bring curiosity, fun, and a bubbly imagination. They trust the gift of magic while exploring life's many questions. They can seem more extroverted or get-things-going than they truly are.

For brain-wiring, they show a strong "starburst" pattern. That is, they accept and ponder over everything that comes in. This really helps them think outside the box and allows anything to reveal its potential meaning. This also makes it harder to focus, attend to particulars, or even stick to one course or career. That said, they are well-suited to the arts, travel, and working with small groups, as their diffuse psyche allows them to attend to many people and ideas at once. Given time, they may excel in a more technical field such as film-making, philosophy, or journalism, as these are forever ripe with new questions and possible projects, to feel inspired, bold and fresh.

Besides the starburst, these INFPs often have some dense right-brain connections. They are good with concepts, humor, and abstract language, easily attend to voice tone and intention, and have a way of working with stories, symbols and patterns, especially in a visual way. They tend to be decent speakers, though they prefer to communicate to share and learn rather than be academic or preachy. Often, despite their eclectic interests, their brain-wiring tends to lack a "halo"; thus, they tend to have holes in their education and skills, and can find it hard at times to do something that most others can do. When push comes to shove, they can still usually buckle down so long as goals, values, and the environment all gel.

Rather than try to force themselves to fit an ideal, they allow themselves to flow through life, exploring to touch the essence of the human condition. They love stories. They value freedom. Others with true eyes and ears grow with them. They benefit from a stabilizing person in their lives. Though they may lack solid anchoring, they are a rich soul in any endeavor.

"Faithful Supporter" (INFP-N)
more conventional and specialized than other INFPs
(Normalizing subtype)

These INFPs function well in mainstream society. They have brain-wiring that is more the norm of the general population. They tend to work hard, are extremely loyal to loved ones and friends, and do their best to be beacons of calm. They have adopted a chart-the-course style.

Their brain-wiring is relatively even across various regions, giving them a more linear style and an even distribution of skills. Imagine checkered farm fields. Every skill is connected to every other skill in some way, though the INFP may need to walk a lot down particular mental paths to get from here to there in a satisfying way. They tend to rely on patience and hard work. They excel at speaking and listening, especially listening, as well as reading. They also usually excel at language-based reasoning such as linear deduction and abstract concepts. On the minus side, body-kinesthetic skills are mediocre. Although they possess endurance, they must take extra care to stay safe when doing physical activities.

What stands out, brain-wise, is their capacity for contemplation. Facts, figures, symbols, metaphors, memories, stories—they ruminate long and deep with these. They may also show a back-brain bias, in which case they can come off as notably introverted until they open up around what's interesting and important to them. This also means they may react slowly as they aim to thoroughly understand something and find ways to give genuine, practical help.

When given a chance to shine, these INFPs can get into top colleges and jobs. Or if not, they usually find a place to prove their value in a traditional career, even a highly technical one, or in a large institution. Ideally, their job taps their imagination and people skills. Whatever their role, they may easily downplay—even sacrifice—themselves for the greater good. With their patience, they can be among the most thoughtful, caring, and stubborn of types.

"Empathic Counselor" (INFP-H)
more empathic and reflective than other INFPs
(Harmonizing subtype)

These are the most multi-faceted, sophisticated, and tolerant of all INFPs. More than others of their type, they work "behind the scenes" even when right in front of someone.

Often, their brains show a small set of diamond-shaped networks. Each diamond reflects a different mode, a specific way of acting, feeling, perceiving, and deciding. These networks bridge the hemispheres for a mix of analytical and holistic skills. This is the fruit of years of life. Moreover, underneath these specialized networks, a bed of zigzag connections brings in other skills for listening, speaking, language-based reasoning, internal awareness, and observational skills. These zigzags link brain regions that don't normally dance together; thus, these INFPs can make dramatic, intuitive leaps going from A to X to M. Taken together, their way of thinking is complex and unusual.

These INFPs are natural humanists or therapists. Overall, they tend to be more right brained, giving them a clear holistic style. With another person, they easily notice clues to work off of, to help in terms of energy and emotions in an open-ended way. They are exceptional at processing a complex interplay of many clues, and they easily recall a person's behavioral patterns from one meeting or situation to the next, which provides a profound historical insight into that person's journey and psychology. They also have a nose for understanding symbolic imagery and the unconscious. It's all a bit like reading a fine character novel. In the same way, they can appreciate whole complex human systems from couples and families to institutions and cultures. This ability to deeply understand—and at times, help gently shift—people and systems easily leaves them humbled and hesitant to judge others or rely on any form of dogma.

These INFPs are usually older or more mature for their age or have a multi-cultural perspective. They excel in areas like international relations and family counseling. As for themselves, their rich inner world, including their spiritual life, is almost beyond words to share. That's what serious (and humorous) novels, plays, and films are for.

Mind Your Neurotic Zone*

Like all types, INFPs have neurotic moments. These erupt when the ego and unconscious clash. While at times uplifting, the result is often anxiety and insecurity. These episodes are also opportunities to learn and grow.

Cautious Protecting
Stabilize with a predictable standard.
Introverted Sensing (Si)

- *Basic Use*: Recall tangible data and experiences.
- *Advanced Use*: Stabilize a situation by comparing it to what is expected, known, and reliable.
- *Neurotic Use*: Lack of action. Just endless researching, listening, etc. Easily caught in bad habits or a routine (for years). Tend to ignore health, presentation, and physical environment; or, settle on one thing and just repeat. Can hyper-focus on odd bodily signals yet don't give consistent care to their actual needs. Strongly accept (or strongly reject) norms such as established tools, historical data, certified experts, social etiquette, etc. Live as an "anchored cloud". Can easily dismiss hard facts, bottom-line consequences, or the material world, where only the meaning/model exists.

Manage Your Energy*

INFPs tend to live in their head, in their imagination. It's so much fun to explore ideas, and dream up and mentally play out possibilities, whether that's reading a book, listening to music, working through a philosophical question, or going down rabbit holes surfing the Internet. But where in any of this is their body, attention to health, or daily material practicalities?

Energy-wise, they can find it pretty difficult to get motivated to actually go out and do something. A great theory or story comes to mind, but writing it down—much less getting it to a marketplace—can be a challenge. All of the logistical details and the path to get from A to Z—or even figure out what Z is—feels like a big wall to get over. Their creative

* Similar here to cousin type INTP.

energy then goes nowhere. What works well is having a quest, a meaningful, heart-first prompt to spread some "good news" (or urgent bad news) to encourage action, change, and growth. Some kind of routine, even setting aside ten minutes a day, helps too.

The trick is habit-building. If INFPs fall into unhealthy habits, they can remain stuck for a long time, especially in someone else's routine. Oppositely, when they cultivate good habits—write one page, or do one gym session or yoga set every day; or post one technical piece, or interview one interesting person every week—then over time they nurture a great habit and accumulate a ton of insights, memories, and maybe materials that benefit them. In terms of work, these habits also reduce worry and self-questioning while building confidence. Having a few milestones along the way can also help.

Pursue Your Aspirations**

Like all types, INFPs trust and prioritize their heroic strengths. At the same time, they also seek ways to express their opposite. This opposite acts as a bridge to the unconscious, a realm where potential and vulnerability reside. Thus, their opposite is a doorway to growth.

Timely Building
Measure and construct for progress.
Extraverted Thinking (Te)

- **Basic Use**: Follow steps, points, and time tables.
- **Advanced Use**: Create structure, reason by measures and evidence, and implement complex plans.
- **Aspirational Use**: Yearn to channel their deeply felt emotions and convictions into a productive life. Establish a nonprofit, design a set of tools or methods or a platform, follow a strict training regime, or manage an effective business venture—aims that align with their values. Enjoy producing creative compositions (art, music, etc.) to put out in the world. Love to see objective validation, such as scientific measures. Harbor a hidden drive for effective organization, objective structure, and impactful execution. Can occasionally become overly critical, fixated on success metrics, or subtly controlling.

** Similar here to cousin type ISFP.

INFP Reminders*
for Growth and Success

☐ Your gift is to really go the heart of any issue, if you dare.

☐ Connect with people who create the kind of organization where you can be empathic.

☐ With a project, try to do a little work every day.

☐ If you're going to use an idea ethically, then seriously learn the specifics.

☐ Try to gather three facts about important situations, even if you must ask.

☐ It's okay to imagine "as if" you had a certain plan.

☐ Try to stay "tuned in" to alternate beliefs.

☐ When something seems unbelievable, consider what is really an aspect of your identity and what is simply a hasty evaluation about its worth.

☐ Good reasoning involves considering multiple counter-arguments.

☐ Ground your beliefs in the lives of many real people.

☐ Don't get seduced by the "dark side" of a reactionary identity.

☐ If you wait to hear what sounds good, consider how you can work out the negative feelings.

☐ Attend to your health and physical environment—it's not as scary as you imagine.

☐ If you can't "be there" emotionally for a person, then introduce them to someone who can.

☐ Realize that your words may cause people to reconsider who they are and what they believe in.

* Adapted from *Quick Guide to the
16 Personality Types in Organizations*

What Now?

Now that you've explored INFP:

1. How do the strengths and challenges of this type show up in your life?

2. What's an insight or goal you can act on today in some way?

3. See the later chapters to leverage your subtype, neurotic zone, energy, and aspirations.

6

Coaching the Subtypes

Coaching Applications

As promised, there are practical applications. Specifically, let's focus on three: We can bust stereotypes, help people more easily locate their best-fit 4-letter type code, and better coach people for their "best life fit", especially regarding career options.

Busting Stereotypes

First, we can bust some biases and stereotypes. Specifically, we can soften the type community's long-standing Intuiting bias. The community is populated heavily by—and seemingly for—those with an Intuiting preference. A way around this is to showcase more diversity among people with a Sensing preference. By looking at subtypes, some people may even discover that they have a Sensing preference after all! Just imagine, there are Creative ISTJs, Normalizing ENFPs, Dominant ISFJs, and Harmonizing ENTJs, to name just a few examples. Just browsing through the subtypes can help us see the multiple facets of every type.

Locating Best-Fit Type

Second, when we know about the subtypes, we can help people better get to their best-fit type.

For example, let's say you meet a client who is a dancer. She's perfectionistic and works within a large school as a teacher, and at first blush, she sounds like she has ISFJ preferences. But she actually self-sorts to ISFP. Where can we go from here? Consider that anyone can be perfectionistic within their domain, teaching is not related to type, and being in a large organization is not type-specific either. What we're seeing here is development within a context. Odds are, she will fit well with the Normalizing ISFP profile.

In short, thinking in terms of development, and subtypes, helps explain sometimes why there are some ISFPs and ISFJs—or any other two types—who look like each other and find it difficult to land on a best-fit type. Or, maybe they find it easy but defy our first impression, because there are Creative ISFJs and there are Normalizing ISFPs, and so on.

By the way, there is a rule of thumb: When a person is debating between two or more types, and their subtype is fairly clear, they will likely relate to that subtype across all of the appealing types.

For example, someone might relate clearly to Harmonizing, and let's say specifically to Harmonizing for INFP, INFJ, ENFP, and INTP. But when we ask them to look at the other subtypes, they will likely say, "Yes, I can see that about myself too", but only for their actual type, not the other options. This person might relate fairly well to all facets of INFP, including even Dominant INFP, but certainly not to Dominant INFJ, Dominant INTP, and so on.

Hopefully, this makes sense. It's a little trick to help people more easily locate their best-fit type.

Coaching Career Options

Because subtype relates so strongly to career, this is a great way to help people find better fits there. Not every ISTJ is suited, or wishes, to work as an accountant in a large organization. That's Normalizing. There are three other options. You can present all 4 subtypes as options to help a person understand what taking different paths will look like. Everyone can be creative, a leader, or so on.

Just reading about the 4 subtypes for one's type can put options in context. This works because career is actually about more than job activities and skills. It involves the kind organization we work in, including its size (large, small, or independent), how we relate to others and society, our values, and even our physiology at times.

A person's subtype is not a guide to the future. It simply represents where the person has been, likely in the past few years, and where he or she is as of today. If someone isn't happy with a situation, such as being bored in a current, longtime corporate job, then the person's calling may lie in a different subtype. In this case, while this dissatisfied person may identify with Normalizing for now, wanting more personal interaction points to Harmonizing, more creativity or variety points to Creative, and more of a leadership role, or climbing up independently, points to Dominant. This reminds us that subtype is developmental, with choices going forward.

Three Example Applications with Type

To get specific, let's look at three example applications of using the subtypes rather than simply working the 16 types alone.

Case #1: Better Explain Differences

Joan scored as "ISTJ preferences" in her workplace. She was entirely new to the idea of a personality type code, and was skeptical, but the plain meaning behind each letter made sense for her. Yes, she was more of an introvert (the "I" in the code), she considered herself naturally practical and organized (the "S" and "J" in the code), and she has striven to stay objective ("T"), though at times she could "falter", as she thought of it, and get quite soft and sentimental ("F", not "T").

What irked her: Three teammates also scored as ISTJ. While one of them was indeed a comrade in spirit, a "sister from another mother" as they joked, the other two were a mystery. Of those two, one eventually identified with a different type. Okay. But the last one, Maria, was steadfast on ISTJ. And indeed, when Joan thought about it, yes, she and Maria focused on data and made decisions in quite similar ways, but Maria somehow had developed a more creative side. She felt freer to be funny, asked more questions, gave bright artistic ideas, and was generally more social. Over her life, she'd also traveled a bit more. What explained this?

Happily, the team learned about subtypes. Joan identified as Normalizing ISTJ while Maria said she resonated with the Creative ISTJ. The curtain of confusion lifted, and Joan felt a lot more comfortable with her type as a home base. Joan also saw for the first time, through Maria as an example, how she could potentially stretch in life to be more creative.

Case #2: Sort Between Many Options

Marko struggled to decide between two personality types—well, three or four to be frank. Mostly, he joked that he was somewhere "on a spectrum", moving between ENTP, INTP, INFP, and even INTJ. The only thing he was sure was the "N" for Intuiting. And as befitting that preference, he treated the whole thing as a bit of fun, and a natural limitation of any model with *just* 16 types. Even when he learned about the "cognitive functions" that underly the type code, and saw that "Extraverted Intuiting" was a fine fit for him, none of the types perfectly did it. And he wasn't about to fool himself or settle for someone else's convenience.

Then Marko learned about subtypes. He was a bank manager, and when tasked to rank the subtypes, he put Dominant first, Normalizing second, and Creative third. As he read more, among the Dominant profiles, ENTP did not fit at all. Marko was confident, but not such an extrovert. And although he could see INTP and INTJ, what really stood out was the Dominant INFP. He marveled: *Wow, INFPs can be leaders too!* In fact, INFPs are usually portrayed as artists, counselors, and such. No wonder Marko was thrown off.

Looking back, as a kid, Marko was not so confident and driven. He was more shy and very imaginative. But being the oldest child in a large family that lost a parent early had pushed him to take more responsibility, to find his inner strength and march himself forward to a point that was now quite comfortable.

Case #3: Pick a Smarter Path

Pat was unhappy at work. This she knew. As a teen, a school counselor had taken her through a careers session and helped her see that she had "ESTJ" preferences. Yes, she was a super-organized go-getter, no doubt about it. And the career options that went with it were practical. A bank operations manager sounded right, so off she went.

However, on the job in banking, she was bored too quickly. She enjoyed learning and tackling new problems, and needed more variety. When the bank rolled out a personality profiling session, she found ESTP and ENTJ better fits. Not perfect, but better. However, when the facilitator explained the theory in more detail, and they did group activities, Pat circled back to ESTJ, deciding that she was just "different".

Later, looking at the subtypes, Pat put a finger on the Creative ESTJ. It was a light-bulb moment. Importantly, knowing her subtype gave her a much better idea of where she needed to go career-wise. Apparently, the singing career she left behind in high school and almost forgotten about was right for her after all.

Frequently Asked Questions

As you or a client or friend explores the subtype descriptions, you will likely encounter a number of questions. Below are answers to the most commonly asked. Of course, they are short. If a person wants to know, for example, the brain-imaging database behind these, then you will find more detailed information after this Q&A.

1. What if I identify with more than one subtype? Ideally, rank them from 1st to 4th. If you're unsure what's 1st, look at which subtype is LEAST like you (4th). Whatever is diagonally opposite that is likely 1st.

2. Are there more than 4 subtypes? Brain wiring varies tremendously. Every person is different in some way even within the "normal" range. You can view these 4 as cardinal points on a compass. Hypothetically, we could get more detailed with blends of subtypes.

3. Is it more accurate to use "variant", "subtype", "facet" or some other term? The word "subtype" is easy to understand. But it is also misleading. It sounds like a box. The word "variant" suggests a variation on the type's core themes, which is more accurate. "Facet" also works, though it is used in other type literature.

4. Can subtype change? To-date, researchers observe that brain-wiring is reliable (consistent) for about 2 years. Also, the distribution of subtypes changes by age cohort. For example, middle-age people are more likely than others to show a Harmonizing pattern.

5. What are these descriptions based on? They are based on multiple sources, namely brain imaging by the author using EEG technology. For the main analysis, there were 444 subjects total over 16 types, with 15 to 65 people of each type. Since then, the database has grown to over 600 people. The extra data has been a great way to assess the descriptions in action and tweak if needed.

6. Can you tell me more about the neuroscience? An EEG reports activity from the brain's neocortex, or outer layer, which is the most thick in humans and reflects higher thinking skills. For this research, subjects go through a diverse protocol of tasks for 30 minutes or 1 hour to stimulate their brain in multiple ways. Later analysis using two common methods (called FFT and "Hebbian Learning") shows which brain regions are most active, densely connected, and so on.

7. Should I try to be all four subtypes or is it best to focus on one? If you are satisfied with your life situation, then it's likely best to build off of your strengths and cover blind-spots.

8. How does this relate to other personality models? These parallel the work of Dr. Victor Gulenko, Dr. Helen Fisher, and Dr. Richard Nisbett. See page 40 for more information.

9. What if I don't relate to the career or role options in my subtype? The jobs mentioned are based on people who voluntarily participated in the brain-imaging study, they likely paid for it, and opportunities were often at conferences. Thus, there is a bias toward certain careers such as psychologist. That said, we did get people who were in almost every area.

10. How do the demographics shape up in terms of age, gender, type and so forth? Notably, there were more people with Intuiting preference over Sensing preference, contrary to the general population. Still, there were enough people to do analysis. Though there were somewhat more women than men, the trend by sex mirrored known demographics except for the SFP types (who were more male, rather than female).

11. How did you validate people's 4-letter Myers-Briggs type codes? The majority of participants were professionals and long-time type users. However, when there was uncertainty or the person did not know, I used the CPA (www.keys2cognition.com) or the NPI (www.careerplanner.com). In some cases, people could not settle or they changed their type after the fact, and those were noted in the data.

12. Is there a best way to determine someone's subtype? The best way is a brain-imaging session. Otherwise, you can go through the 4 subtypes, self-reflect, and get input from others who know you. If you know a person's 4-letter type code, they can read the four descriptions for their type as well as adjacent types (e.g. for INTJ, also read INTP, ENTJ, ISTJ, etc.) They should be able to relate to their subtype even for the adjacent types, as well as their own.

13. How do the subtypes match up in relationships? The research did not look closely at relationships. However, for couples and long-time friends and associates who participated, similar brain-wiring was typical and a sign for satisfaction in the relationship.

14. Can I take deliberate steps to shift my subtype? Yes, though you likely need to be patient. You can identify a hobby or other activity that interests you and likely uses a brain network like another subtype. For example, one-on-one time with other people is more Harmonizing. You can then practice that activity and allow it to take up more of your time. You can also simply switch careers or such but that is a big change!

15. Should I maximize my subtype or learn to flex to different subtypes? Most societies reward people for specialization. But personal growth often relies on learning to flex, and that requires taking risks. Experiment, think carefully, and have a strong foundation. Hopefully, over a lifespan, you have a chance to explore all four.

16. What role does opportunity or socio-economic status play? Brain wiring reflects habits, and if a person lacks the opportunity to play particular roles, such as being in a leadership position, or feeling safe in close relatiobships, then the person won't yet have a chance to develop that side.

17. What do the subtypes have in common? Dominant and Creative are more outgoing (assertive or expressive, respectively). In contrast, Normalizing and Harmonizing are more reserved. Then, Dominant and Normalizing are both more analytic, and Creative and Harmonizing more holistic. Finally, Dominant and Harmonizing have an "attract" dynamic (far range and close range, and to each other). In contrast, Creative and Normalizing have an "oppose" dynamic (in-group versus out-group, and they oppose each other.)

18. Which is more important, my personality type (4-letter code) or my subtype? The 16 types are psychological in nature. Each is an enduring and systemic pattern of functioning. In contrast, subtypes represent more observable and changeable qualities such as the size of the organization we work in. Both are important!

Coaching the Dominant Subtype

Overall, Dominants will challenge more than others of their type, confront with counter-points, seek to interact as an equal or a superior, try to direct their own unconscious, and maybe "win" at the interaction. The cost of their strong ego is lower awareness than the other subtypes.

Build Respect: Recognize their desire to be seen as equals or act as leaders. Respect their input while being firm in your expertise.

Challenge Them: These individuals may respond well to being challenged in constructive ways. Setting clear goals and boundaries can motivate them.

Stay Neutral: Avoid getting caught up in power struggles. Maintain a neutral and calm demeanor even when they test boundaries.

Promote Self-awareness: As they have lower awareness, gently point out inconsistencies or contradictions in their actions or thoughts to promote self-reflection.

Helpful Questions

Where are they working? Are they in a managerial or other leadership position, or in an environment that allows them to "step up" a ladder or "step in" to critical roles? If they work independently, how often are they engaging with leaders?

How challenging and influential is their job role? Ideally, their decisions—or at least their feedback– have an obvious impact on others. And ideally, their role falls within a sweet spot that engages them while also staying within their competence.

How are their relationships? They can come across as charismatic, with a vision and a lot of caring. But they can also come across as impatient, critical, or bullying. They may also focus so much on the big picture that they treat close relationships as resources or convenient refuges.

What if they overplay their hand? They tend to be in more visible roles, and their failures can look bigger. Yet, oftentimes, they may simply move "horizontally" to another job without taking full responsibility or learning a lesson to carry forward.

Where to improve? Teamwork and leadership training, ethical conduct, finding ways to get honest feedback, managing the pitfalls of power, being more transparent and accountable, and inviting others to help lead.

Coaching the Creative Subtype

Overall, Creatives will be more interested but also easily distracted, jumping to a variety of topics, and act engaging and yet somehow still evade you as they try to make interaction more "interesting" or "fun". The cost of their curiosity is difficulty sticking to developing new habits.

Engage Creatively: Integrate creative tools or techniques into your sessions. This can range from art to brainstorming exercises.

Structure with Flexibility: While it's crucial to provide structure, allow room for them to explore and deviate occasionally.

Short, Focused Tasks: Break down tasks or goals into smaller, more manageable parts. This allows them to see progress without feeling overwhelmed or losing interest.

Highlight Importance of Consistency: Emphasize the value of consistent effort and how small habits can lead to significant changes over time.

Helpful Questions

Where are they working? If they are working in a large organization, do they at least have the freedom within it to do their own thing? Otherwise, they will likely feel smothered after a while or neglect their duties.

How varied and rewarding is their job role? They may change jobs or careers rather than finding a "container" or "vehicle" for all of their interests, and thus miss the benefit of longterm investment. If the workplace is stifling, their talents will be rejected. Higher ups may not see their value.

How are their relationships? Relative to others of their type, they enjoy having new experiences, traveling around, meeting new people, and so on. Ideally, they find time to nurture long-term relationships, be more intimate, and also take a step back from their creative "fugues".

What if they get into trouble? Being a rebel, or taking a carefree attitude, can lead to financial, health, or legal troubles. They should mind their limits here.

Where to improve? Finding a "vehicle" for all of their interests, developing a strategy or plan to sustain independence, dealing with addictive things, showing they are reliable (not erratic), really committing to quality deliverables, and building in fitness and health routines so they don't burn out.

Coaching the Normalizing Subtype

Overall, Normalizers will be more linear than others of their type, prefer specific explanations and steps, and will be willing to put in effort if someone higher up supports it, or the group as the whole is engaged, though they may not view personal growth as especially relevant.

Provide Clear Steps: Offer step-by-step guidance and procedures. They thrive with clarity and specifics.

Leverage Group Dynamics: Whenever possible, arrange for group settings and group exercises. They find motivation and reassurance from the collective, even if they operate more on their own within the group.

Use External Validation: Cite experts, studies, or authoritative figures that support your advice or guidance. As part of this, be sure the purpose and benefits are clear.

Acknowledge Their Effort: Recognize and commend the work they put in, even if they downplay its importance.

Helpful Questions

Where are they working? If they are working independently or in a very small organization, they likely are not getting the support or long-term benefits that they could. At the least, can they join a network or umbrella service? Ideally, they find a very supportive space.

How routine, stable, and supported is their job role? In an erratic environment, or in one that demands they flex a lot, or think "out of the box" or keep up with innovations, they likely want to look for more predictability or regularly update their skill set.

How are their relationships? They like to have around them people with similar interests, needs, and values. That includes a spouse who can at least flex to the Normalizing style. Also, they may want to mind their kids' subtypes and not push Normalizing onto others.

What if they don't fit? "Normalizing" may mean implementing something new into an organization, community or society. In that case, they best be realistic about their goals and where they are likely to end up.

Where to improve? Speaking up for oneself, building a supportive personal network independent of work and family, remembering that not everyone likes "togetherness", engaging in "perspective shifting" to others' POVs, and getting more comfortable with trying new ideas or activities.

Coaching the Harmonizing Subtype

Overall, Harmonizers will be the most engaged and reflective, talking about their and others' psychology, and able to view themselves more objectively than others of their type. However, they are peculiar, less likely to follow typical body language cues, and may go off on tangents.

Active Listening: This group is reflective, so listen actively and validate their feelings and needs.

Adapt Non-Verbals: Since they may not always follow typical body language cues, pay close attention to their unique non-verbal signals.

Allow for Tangents: While it's essential to guide them back on track, occasionally exploring tangents can offer valuable insights into their thought processes.

Promote Grounding Techniques: Given their propensity for abstract and relational thinking, introduce them to grounding techniques to help them stay present and focused.

Helpful Questions

Where are they working? Regardless of the workplace, do they at least have a few close, comfortable relationships there? Working independently or with little recognition or intimacy can demoralize them.

How personal and complex is their job role? They are sophisticated thinkers and often have a honed skillset. But are they putting that to use? They are often good in diplomatic and cross-cultural roles.

How are their relationships? They usually get on well among colleagues. However, in situations outside of their comfort zone, they can behave oddly, which contrasts their usual sensitivity to people. This may show as less eye contact, a quiet voice, or other ways to be less noticed or to encourage getting close.

What if they feel wounded or unsafe? This is an opportunity for them to ask for help from others, though doing that is a paradox of sorts. Help them to get more direct when needed and take more of the advice they would normally give others.

Where to improve? Decision-making, confidence building, leveraging core competencies, dealing with aggressive people, getting out there and getting noticed when appropriate, managing boundaries, sorting what is really worth caring for, and mentorship opportunities.

Four Body-Mind Exercises

There is a lot more to the mind or personality than the brain. There is the whole nervous system which runs through the body and its many organs and other systems. The emerging wisdom is that thought, behavior, memory, emotion, and breathing all interrelate. For example, traumatic events are "stored" in the body as much (or more) than in the conscious mind. This reminds us that the subtypes are more than brain wiring, hormone levels, and demographics. The subtypes show up in how we breathe, move, pose ourselves, and many other facets of expression.

Here are 4 activities that you can try, alone or with others, as a way to viscerally experience the subtypes. Give at least 5 minutes to each. There is more explanation on the coming pages.

	Goal-focused, repeated sequence, strict	Open-ended, variable flow, loose
Fast breath, eyes open, and outward focus	**Dominant** Do rapid "breath of Fire" while standing with eyes open, focused on a target, repeatedly throwing punches, shooting arrows, or anchoring hands solidly at hips, repeating a mantra around a clear goal.	**Creative** Dance, moving to the rhythms of mostly upbeat, ever-changing music, and ideally part of a group moving around. Keep changing it up, allowing the music to move you. It's fine to sing a song.
Slow breath, eyes closed, and inward focus	**Normalizing** Sit with eyes closed and do "box breath" (a 4-step process), cycling through a mantra, and focus each step with a *mudra* (hand positions) and visualization (such as 4 seasons, 4 elements, etc.)	**Harmonizing** Sit quietly and keep slowing your breath as you listen to richly-texture nature sounds (or similar), letting whatever visuals to come up without dwelling on any, as if observing yourself dream.

Below are more detailed instructions for the four exercises. All four mostly align with *kundalini* style yoga, and if you are new to breathwork and yoga, you can find video examples on the web. Specifically, text in bolded blue points to specific terms that you can look up. Of course, the best way to experience these would be in a guided live workshop.

Dominant: To start, stand with feet, hips, and shoulders squared, with your hands on your hips as if standing your ground. Ideally, play some energetic, warrior music in the background.

Then begin breath of fire. This is breathing from the diaphragm, repeatedly moving your belly button back toward your spine, then releasing, as if your lungs are an accordion. You may begin slowly, but accelerate if you can, knowing you can slow down when you need a rest.

As you go, you can adopt two other stances. Either throwing punches, alternating left and right arms—remember to keep the rest of your body aligned and balanced. Or reposition your legs to take archer pose, fix your gaze on a steady point a moderate distance away, and repeatedly set and release your arms as if drawing a bow and releasing arrows. When you get tired of one sequence, you can switch to the others.

Notice that the dominant style changes up its action. Otherwise, it can be exhausting.

Creative: Put on a mix of fun dance tunes, ideally with strong base, rhythm, and lyrics in a language you don't know, and allow some space to dance freely. If you can dance with friends, all the better.

Now stand and allow the rhythm to move you. If you execute dance steps, then you are missing the point of this subtype exercise; that said, if you are particularly proficient in multiple dance styles, and comfortable improvising, then feel free to do so. Otherwise, this is like ecstatic dance.

You might also try improvisational contact dance. That is, you and another person continuously keep in some kind of physical contact no matter how minimal, as you dance. Which points you keep contact with, such as hands, hips, feet, etc can and likely will shift; remember, you want to allow yourself to flow, not impress others with a performance.

As you dance, you may close your eyes generally, but do open them at times to avoid injuring yourself or others.

Finally, feel free to sing, even if done quietly or with made-up lyrics. Allow words to come to mind and flow through you rather than focusing on correctly recalling lyrics to a specific song.

Normalizing: Sit comfortably with spine straight, chin slightly tucked in, and shoulders squared. Use a cushion or supportive block if needed. Play soft, repetitive music without lyrics in the background.

Begin a box breath. This is a 4-step breathing exercise that you repeat multiple times, as if cycling through seasons. Before you start, select a number from 5 to 10. A higher number if more challenging.

Now, move in 4 parts. First, empty your lungs and breathe in sips that number of times, sipping evenly to fill your lungs by the end of the count. Second, hold your breath for the same duration. Third, release out puffs for the same count. And fourth, hold your breath again, this time with empty lungs. Repeat the process for the exercise's duration.

You are welcome to increase or decrease the number, from say 5 to 8, or 10 to 15, or 12 to 6. If you find that you've started a cycle that is too ambitious, do your best to finish it and then ramp down.

As you do the box breath, add a *mantra* (special phrase), *mudra* (special hand position), and visualization. For example, you might cycle through the words "spring, summer, fall, winter", each time visualizing that season, or the words "birth, life, death, rebirth". As for the hand positioning, either keep the arms and hands in the same place or move them in a cycle, such as resting in your lap for part 1, bringing them to your heart for part 2, raising them like antennae for part 3, and bringing them down to prayer position for part 4.

The more complex and repetitive, as if building a habit and following a routine, the closer to Normalizing you will be.

Harmonizing: Last but not least, sit comfortably, or even lie down. Close your eyes and keep slowing your breath as you listen to richly-texture nature sounds (or similar music, possibly with lyrics).

As with Normalizing, you may try a variety of hand positions, but do not follow a plan and move them only when you tire or feel inspired. Meanwhile, focus your attention on the music, allowing yourself to notice the notes, instruments, texture, and so on. Also allow whatever visuals to come up without dwelling on any, as if observing yourself dream.

This is similar to mindfulness meditation but less strict.

If trying these makes anything clear, it's that "facet" or "variant" is a better term to use than "subtype." Truly, we can access different sides of ourselves simply by tuning in to our bodily energy.

7

Navigating Your Neurotic Boundary

Neurotic Episodes

Everyone has neurotic moments. These are times when we behave strangely, out of character and yet we can think of similar instances in the past. Such strange, or neurotic, moments are not just random. They erupt for a reason and can serve an important function.

Let's consider some examples. Take Jane, an office worker. She suddenly felt envious of a colleague for no substantive reason she could think of, and even accidentally embarrassed herself by saying something rude—the words just popped out! Meanwhile, her boyfriend Romero became so involved in an exciting project that he forgot to exercise, sleep, or even eat for three days, and then he panicked that he had a disease even as he was bragging to his friends that he didn't need sleep. Then there was Talia, Jane's friend, who was certain that her parents were trying to "gaslight" her, only to get feedback from trusted friends like Jane that suggested she herself was the one engaged in gaslighting.

Many more examples are possible, and we will explore a wide range in this chapter, using personality type as a guide to likely neuroses. But before we jump in, let's define what we're talking about and how we can effectively respond to neuroses.

What's Neurotic?

Neuroses erupt when the ego and unconscious clash, particularly when we're under stress. While at times uplifting, the result is often anxiety, confusion, and insecurity, to name a few symptoms. These episodes are also opportunities to learn and grow.

Neurotic here is used in the broad way used by Dr. Jung and others in the early 20th century. When caught in a neurotic episode, we find ourselves inhibited in some areas of life, such as too nervous to speak in front of a group, although overall we are still functional. Typical neurotic experiences include anxiety, an attention deficit, chronic anger, depression, group think, hyperactivity, hallucinations, hypochondria, magical thinking, mania, obsessions or compulsions, paranoia, rage, repetitive thoughts or feelings, tunnel vision, and so on.

Neurotic Episodes: Arrive, Subside, and Return*

Neuroses can be brief or ongoing, obvious or in the background, but mostly they erupt as episodes, and an episode can last a few minutes or hours, or weeks or months or maybe more. If an episode is rare, we may simply say, "That was not me", or "I was beside myself". Whereas, if it's chronic, we may weave a story around it, making it an understandable part of who we are, complete with labels and coping tools, and so on.

For example, we might refer to "my anxiety" like we might say, "my dog" or "my garden" and have a whole routine or set of strategies including medication, attention to triggers, and so on.

The term "episode" reminds us that it comes and goes. We have opportunities to reflect after an episode and make observations and adjustments in preparation for future episodes. However, we need to be clearly aware of what has happened. That's why having a model is so useful. Based on your personality type, you can read what likely happens, which makes it easier to notice, talk about, and perhaps shift out of it.

In terms of personality type, the most likely indicator is our "third function" or "tertiary function". In the stack of processes, it ranks third. For example, ESTP's favorite processes are a heroic Extraverted Sensing (1st) and a supportive Introverted Thinking (2nd). This leaves Extraverted Feeling (3rd) as the most likely source of a neurotic episode. This said, other functions including the aspirational 4th function can get involved. Given this rubric, a knowledgeable person with ESTP preferences can thus guess at his or her likely neurotic issues.

But let's not get too complacent! The nature of these episodes, rooted as they are in the clash of ego and unconscious, always have the potential to surprise us. Once we've figured out how something works and how to "manage it", then it is part of the ego, and we can be misled. This is why, no matter how experienced or practiced we are in dealing with neuroses, our own and others, there are moments when we will suddenly, surprisingly realize that one is playing out, perhaps in a novel way, but still the same thing. Only when we deal with the challenges underlying the neurosis can we find ourselves... free of it, most likely, and also rewarded with a new neurosis to deal with soon down the line.

* Special thanks to Alex Booth and Elise V Allan for ideas here.

Addressing Neuroses

The next two pages summarize typical neurotic manifestations of the 8 cognitive processes, and afterward, you will find in-depth discussion for all 16 types. Remember that you're not looking at your favorite functions, but at your "tertiary" (3rd) function.

As you read, you can ask yourself, "What am I noticing about my life that relates to my neurotic zone?" You may even be able to take a mindful approach, observing yourself experiencing these neurotic behaviors, as if watching a fictional character. And as you observe, appreciate that like the tide (in and out) or phases of day and night (light and dark), these episodes come and go. And when we act simply as a witness, magic can happen: we begin to loosen up and see changes in our lives.

Neurotic episodes are opportunities for growth and change. In fact, they are necessary! Every episode is an attempt by the psyche to improve our situation, fumbling and ineffective as it might seem to be, in order to express and deal with something that needs conscious attention.

What can you do? First, a neurotic episode is a chance to tip your hat to life's humor or absurdity, rather than castigate yourself for an all-too-human experience. Second, you can "factualize" what's going on ("this is the fact of what happened,"). That helps you move past a general feeling of confusion or frustration and take advantage of an opportunity presented by the episode. Third, you can ask, is this is a time to let go of something, to simplify, or to add or build something? Another option: You can ask, "What did I learn from this?" Of course, psychotherapy, and practices like mindfulness and active imagination, can also help you safely work with neuroses, turning underlying issues into ingredients for change—for example, to recount and take action after a nightmare rather than ignore it or get caught up in a neurosis of endlessly analyzing it. Overall, by taking these kinds of steps, you can direct your energy away from the neurosis and toward options for a better path.

Overall, the confusion inherent in any neurotic situation can give way to a reorganization of "you", and the net result is generative, even if small. Conversely, if we remain blind to these episodes, ignore or resist them, then the result is developmental arrest.

Neurotic Se (mainly ENTJ and ENFJ)

Put health/body in danger. (e.g. skip sleep or meals). Judge something or try to control it rather than experience it. Easily give in to impulses to quickly take actions (even if it's the wrong action). Tend to view all outcomes of their actions as reversible or fixable. Set unrealistic/grandiose plans, yet easily distracted and drawn into adolescent fun. Feel exempt from life's rules due to secret shortcuts (e.g. "The Secret" style thinking). Get a genius insight while resisting feedback, viewing it as the final answer with no more questions or ideas needed.

Neurotic Si (mainly INTP and INFP)

Lack of action. Just endless researching, listening, etc. Easily caught in bad habits or a routine (for years). Tend to ignore health, presentation, and physical environment; or, settle on one thing and just repeat. Can hyper-focus on odd bodily signals yet don't give consistent care to their actual needs. Strongly accept (or strongly reject) norms such as established tools, historical data, certified experts, social etiquette, etc. Live as an "anchored cloud". Can easily dismiss hard facts, bottom-line consequences, or the material world, where only the meaning/model exists.

Neurotic Ne (mainly ESTJ and ESFJ)

Deliver nasty humor (e.g. hurtful zingers). Quickly reject or even belittle creative, unfamiliar, and outside-the-box thinking. Drawn to meddle in other people's affairs, often leading to unpleasant surprises. Can get inventive with details to help (but also limit) others. Or similarly, strive to keep things light and safe (but rigid) no matter what. Struggle to bring diverse data points into a cohesive focus. Engage in conversational "trolling" (to reveal others' character, make a point, feel superior, etc). Can easily role-play spirituality as mere rituals.

Neurotic Ni (mainly ISTP and ISFP)

Overly negative theorizing (particularly about everyday situations). Find it hard to perceive their own psychological projections, accusing others of their own faults. View themselves as stupid (or conversely, as super genius). Manic excitement around a vision of an amazing outcome or future but quickly give up on it. Make wild inferences based on one or two data points. Can be incredibly confidently wrong (brash and dismissive based on some deep assumption). Anti-social spirituality. Easily drawn into what most others see as marginal, weird or extreme.

Neurotic Te (mainly ESFP and ENFP)

Tend to under- or over-manage. Easily frustrated or feel lost in logistical and technical details such as paperwork. Can panic at deadlines. Under or over explain, either losing others when they think they're clear, or fear they're confusing when it's clear. Reject hierarchy/authority figures and rules, yet also easily buy into or ignore institutional failures. Confuse being blunt—or making up reasons—for actual reasoning with evidence. Troubleshooting (under-do or over-do). Easily take a "consequences be damned" attitude. Struggle to stay detached or objective.

Neurotic Ti (mainly ISFJ and INFJ)

Can get hypercritical yet are also personally quite sensitive (even to small slights). Tend to get stuck in analysis paralysis. Constantly grapple with vague big ideas without getting clarity. Prefer simple mental models except a specialty to endlessly tweak and elaborate on (word-smithing, etc). Strongly favor (or reject) intellectual or cultural elitism (e.g. fetishize scholarship/education). Easily define personal or local experiences as part of some global/grand drama. Feel a strong inner/outer split (e.g. warm on the outside while cold inside, or vice versa).

Neurotic Fe (mainly ESTP and ENTP)

Prone to blaming others for causing their emotions. Find themselves feeling needy while also meeting others' needs before their own. Tend to self-aggrandize while also being self-critical. Overly nice (or mean) and respectful (or disrespectful), expecting more from others or from themselves. Can find themselves caught up in endless office politics and relationship drama. Can get hyper-focused on societal values and policy issues (for or against those). Tend to over-analyze emotions and interpersonal issues without actually feeling them.

Neurotic Fi (mainly ISTJ and INTJ)

Feel extreme loyalty and condemn disloyalty. Tend to be self-righteous or moralistic (especially about hypocrisy) with stubborn black-or-white judgment. Easily repress emotions and pretend they don't care, then have an outburst. Fail to fully hear others' input (notably feelings) and then hurt by the backlash. Endless inner emotional sorting without peace. Easily moody or tense, or suffer chronic low-level depression or anger. Tend to be serious and orderly while pining for joy and freedom. Selfish focus on their own personal wants, goals, values, etc.

Neurotic Extraverted Sensing (Se)
(mostly ENTJ and ENFJ)

When Extraverted Sensing dominates the neurotic boundary, it often shows as being impulsive, having a great appetite for success, and inviting excessive risks. This applies most to those who are developing this process, ENTJ and ENFJ, and also at times to INTJ and INFJ—or really any type, even those who prefer the process.

With Se, our aim is to immerse in the present context, allowing individuals to notice sensory data in the environment. In its basic use, Se helps us to be fully present, taking in our surroundings and experiencing the world through our senses. In its advanced use, Se empowers us to trust our instincts and take action relevant to the moment and current context.

However, when Se erupts as a neurotic episode, individuals may exhibit a range of problematic behaviors. For example, those with a neurotic Se easily put their health and body in danger. They engage in risky behaviors, such as skipping sleep or meals, in pursuit of immediate gratification or excitement or just to feel like they are doing something. This disregard for their physical well-being can lead to long-term consequences and compromise their overall health.

Individuals with a neurotic Se want to enjoy fun experiences but also tend to judge or try to control those rather than fully immersing themselves. They can struggle to embrace the present moment as it is, constantly evaluating and critiquing their surroundings. This hinders their ability to fully engage with their environment and enjoy the experiences it offers. At the same time, those with a neurotic Se also tend to set unrealistic or grandiose plans but easily become distracted and drawn into more immediate and superficial pleasures. They struggle to stay focused and committed to long-term goals, succumbing to impulses and distractions. This inconsistency can hinder their personal growth and limit their ability to achieve their aspirations.

Similarly, those with a neurotic Se can easily give in to impulsive actions, even if they are inappropriate or counterproductive. They may struggle to exercise self-control, driven mainly by immediate desires or sensations. This can lead to hasty decision-making and a lack of consideration for the potential consequences of actions. They may also tend to view the outcomes of their actions as reversible or fixable. They may underestimate the long-term impact of their choices, assuming that any negative consequences can be easily improved. This can lead to a lack of foresight, lasting mistakes, and responsibility for the repercussions of their actions.

Individuals with a neurotic Se may also develop a belief that they are exempt from life's rules due to "secret shortcuts" or magical thinking. That is, they rely on unrealistic or superstitious beliefs to guide their actions, thinking that they can bypass the usual constraints or principles that govern life. This can lead to irrational decision-making. At the same time, they easily resist feedback, despite having moments of genius insight. They become overly confident in their own ideas and resist input from others. This closed-mindedness can hinder their growth and prevent them from considering alternative perspectives or improving their understanding.

In conclusion, while Se is a valuable process for experiencing the present moment and taking action, it can manifest as neurotic episodes, particularly for ENTJ and ENFJ. By acknowledging the pitfalls of a neurotic Se and striving for self-awareness, impulse control, and a balanced approach to risk-taking, individuals can harness the positive aspects of Se while maintaining their well-being and fostering personal growth.

Neurotic Introverted Sensing (Si)
(mostly INTP and INFP)

When Introverted Sensing dominates the neurotic boundary, it often shows as laziness, stubbornness, awkward social behavior, absent-mindedness, and self-neglect This applies most to those who are developing this process, INTP and INFP, but also at times to ENTP and ENFP—or really any type, even those who prefer the process.

With Si, our aim is to stabilize with a predictable standard, allowing us to draw upon past experiences and memories that helpfully inform our present actions and decisions. In its basic use, Si helps us recall tangible data and experiences. In its advanced use, Si empowers us to bring stability to situations by comparing them to what is expected, known, and reliable. In practice, Si is mostly about assurance, comfort, convenience, predictability, safety, and security.

However, when Si erupts as a neurotic episode, individuals may exhibit a range of problematic behaviors. For example, those with a neurotic Si may engage in a lack of practical action, spending excessive time researching, listening, or seeking information—perhaps all quite fascinating—without taking meaningful steps forward. This can lead to a sense of paralysis and hinder progress or personal growth.

Individuals with a neurotic Si may easily become caught in bad habits or routines that persist for extended periods, often years. They may resist change or new experiences, preferring the comfort and familiarity of established patterns. This resistance to novelty can limit their personal and professional development.

Furthermore, those with a neurotic Si may ignore their health, physical presentation, or the state of their physical environment. They may overlook or neglect their well-being, appearance, or the tidiness of their surroundings, leading to a lack of self-care and a less-than-optimal living or working environment. Alternatively, they may settle on one way of doing things and repetitively adhere to that approach, resisting opportunities for growth or adaptation.

Individuals with a neurotic Si easily hyper-focus on odd bodily signals or sensations, yet they may not consistently address their actual needs. For example, they can get overly concerned with perceived bodily abnormalities or symptoms, leading to excessive worry or hypochondria. However, despite these signals, they may not consistently prioritize or take appropriate care of their physical health or well-being. In fact, they invest in odd solutions that don't actually help.

Moreover, those with a neurotic Si may strongly accept—or conversely, strongly reject—particular societal norms, such as established tools, historical data, certified experts, or social etiquette. Similarly, they can rigidly adhere to traditional practices—or oppositely, resist any deviation from what is considered conventional or accepted. This either/or approach can hinder their ability to adapt to new circumstances or embrace alternative approaches.

Furthermore, individuals with a neurotic Si may live as an "anchored cloud," remaining tethered to their inner world of memories, experiences, ideas, and subjective interpretations. They may rely heavily on personal meaning and internal models, sometimes dismissing or disconnecting from the hard facts, bottom-line consequences, or the material world. This disconnects them from objective reality and hinders effective decision-making or problem-solving.

In conclusion, while Si can be a great process for drawing upon past experiences and stabilizing situations, it can manifest as neurotic episodes, particularly for INTP and INFP. Acknowledging issues and taking small steps toward new habits can help. And with greater self-awareness, and a balanced approach to routine and novelty, individuals can harness the positive aspects of Si while fostering personal growth and adapting to new circumstances.

Neurotic Extraverted Intuiting (Ne)
(mostly ESTJ and ESFJ)

When Extraverted Intuiting dominates the neurotic boundary, it often shows as strange, unpleasant, and deceptive behavior that is otherwise atypical for them. This applies most to those who are developing this process, ESTJ and ESFJ, and also at times to ISTJ and ISFJ—or really any type, even those who prefer the process.

With Ne, our aim is to explore emerging patterns and possibilities, helping us notice abstract patterns as they emerge. In its basic use, Ne helps us to generate ideas, connect concepts, and explore various potential outcomes. In its advanced use, Ne empowers us to shift the dynamics of a situation and explore imaginative possibilities beyond the current reality.

However, when Ne erupts as a neurotic episode, individuals may exhibit a range of problematic behaviors. For example, those with a neurotic Ne may engage in serving up nasty humor, resorting to hurtful zingers or offensive jokes. This behavior suggests an excessive need for attention or a desire to assert superiority through humor, and it can harm relationships and create a negative atmosphere. As part of this, they may engage in conversational "trolling," using provocative or manipulative tactics to elicit reactions from others. This behavior stems from a desire to reveal others' character, make a point, or feel superior. However, it can strain relationships, create tension, and hinder effective communication. Similarly, those with a neurotic Ne may be drawn to meddling in other people's affairs, often leading to unpleasant surprises. They may have a tendency to involve themselves in the personal lives or decisions of others, believing they have major insights or perspectives to offer. However, this can infringe upon others' autonomy and create conflicts or unintended consequences.

Individuals with a neurotic Ne can quickly reject or belittle creative, unfamiliar, and outside-the-box thinking. In particular, they resist ideas that challenge their existing beliefs and practices, dismissing them without due consideration. When in authority, this translates into blocking and limiting others. This rigidity can hinder growth and limit the potential for novel and innovative solutions.

Individuals with a neurotic Ne may get inventive with details to help others, but ironically, this can also limit their growth and potential. They provide solutions or suggestions that are overly specific or restrictive, inadvertently stifling others' creativity or problem-solving abilities. Similarly, they may strive to keep things light and safe, maintaining a rigid and predictable environment, even in situations that could benefit from more flexibility or exploration.

Those with a neurotic Ne may struggle to bring diverse data points into a cohesive focus. They can have difficulty synthesizing information from multiple sources or perspectives, leading to scattered thinking or an inability to form clear conclusions. This can hinder effective decision-making and create confusion in discussions or analysis.

Finally, individuals with a neurotic Ne may easily fall into role-playing spirituality as mere rituals. They may engage in spiritual practices or traditions without truly embracing their deeper meanings or principles. This superficial approach to spirituality can limit personal growth and prevent genuine exploration and understanding.

In conclusion, while Ne is a great process for exploring possibilities and generating ideas, it can manifest as neurotic episodes, particularly for ESTJ and ESFJ. By recognizing the potential pitfalls of a neurotic Ne and striving for self-awareness and respect for diversity in people and ideas, individuals can harness the creative potential of Ne while maintaining positive relationships and fostering personal growth.

Neurotic Introverted Intuiting (Ni)
(mostly ISTP and ISFP)

When Introverted Intuiting dominates the neurotic boundary, it often shows as delusions of worthlessness or grandeur. This applies most to those who are developing this process, ISTP and ISFP, and also at times for ESTP and ESFP—or really any type, even those who prefer the process.

With Ni, our aim is to "transform with a meta-perspective", which in practice means having profound insights and realizations. In its basic use, Ni helps us to receive "aha!" moments and flashes of intuitive understanding. In its advanced use, Ni empowers us to pursue a greater level of awareness, leading to personal transformation and shifts in the very way we think, feel, and behave.

However, when Ni erupts in a neurotic episode, individuals may exhibit a range of problematic behaviors. For instance, those with a neurotic Ni may engage in overly negative theorizing, particularly about everyday situations. This shows up as a tendency to foresee the worst possible outcomes and dwell on pessimistic scenarios, which can contribute to a generally negative outlook on life.

Furthermore, those with a neurotic Ni may view themselves as either stupid or as super geniuses. They may oscillate between feelings of inadequacy and low self-esteem, questioning their own intelligence and abilities, while also experiencing episodes of grandiosity and an inflated sense of superiority. As part of this, they exhibit manic excitement around visions of amazing outcomes or future possibilities—deeply enthralled by their ideas and what will surely happen, but quickly lose interest or give up when faced with the realities of implementation. This pattern of enthusiasm followed by disillusionment can hinder progress and create a cycle of unfulfilled potential.

Those with neurotic Ni also tend to struggle with psychological projection. That's when they easily project their own faults, insecurities, or shortcomings onto others, leading to a pattern of accusing others of behaviors that actually reflect their own inner conflicts. This lack of self-awareness can strain relationships and hinder personal growth.

Moreover, a neurotic Ni can lead individuals to make wild inferences based on limited data points. They may jump to conclusions or form strong beliefs based on insufficient evidence, neglecting to consider alternative perspectives or additional information. This can contribute to misunderstandings and misguided decision-making. As part of this, they exhibit a strong sense of confidence in their assumptions, even when they are objectively wrong. They may appear brash and dismissive, disregarding alternative viewpoints or feedback based on deep-rooted assumptions that are not grounded in reality. This can hinder collaboration and lead to misunderstandings and conflicts.

Finally, individuals with neurotic Ni may have a tendency toward antisocial spirituality. They are drawn to engage in behaviors or embrace beliefs that are considered unusual, extreme, or unconventional by societal standards. This may result in a sense of isolation or alienation from mainstream social circles.

In conclusion, while Ni is a powerful process for gaining insights and pursuing personal transformation, it can manifest as neurotic episodes, particularly for ISTP and ISFP. By striving for self-awareness, balanced thinking, and openness to alternative perspectives, individuals can harness the transformative potential of Ni while maintaining a sane, satisfying life and realistic expectations.

Neurotic Extraverted Thinking (Te)
(mostly ESFP and ENFP)

When Extraverted Thinking dominates the neurotic boundary, it often shows as anxiety in "time and task" situations, or when providing evidence, reasons, and effectiveness. This applies most to those who are developing this process, ESFP and ENFP, and also at times to ISFP and INFP—or really any type, even those who prefer the process.

With Te, our aim is to measure and construct for progress, focusing on following steps, points, and timetables. In its basic use, Te helps us to work efficiently and effectively by adhering to efficient processes and guidelines. In its advanced use, Te empowers us to create structure, reason using measures and evidence, and implement complex plans, ultimately facilitating achievement and growth.

However, when Te erupts in a neurotic episode, individuals may exhibit a range of problematic behaviors. For instance, those with a neurotic Te may tend to under-manage or over-manage situations. They may struggle to strike the right balance between providing guidance and micromanaging, which can lead to frustration and confusion among coworkers. Similarly, individuals with a neurotic Te may also find themselves easily overwhelmed or lost in logistical and technical details, such as paperwork. They may easily feel flustered—or feel a sense of dread or panic—when faced with deadlines or when confronted with intricate procedures, hindering their ability to work efficiently and causing additional stress.

Furthermore, those with a neurotic Te may struggle in their communication style. They may under-explain or over-explain, which can result in miscommunication. This can occur when they assume others are following their logical thought process without providing sufficient context or "how to", or when they overcompensate by providing too much information, confusing or frustrating others.

Individuals with a neurotic Te may exhibit a complex relationship with hierarchy, authority figures, and rules. They may easily reject hierarchical structures and resist authority figures; yet paradoxically, they may also easily buy into or ignore institutional failures. This contradiction may stem from their tendency to question and challenge the status quo while simultaneously wanting structure and guidance.

Moreover, neurotic Te may cause individuals to confuse being blunt or making up reasons over actual reasoning based on evidence. They may prioritize efficiency and straightforwardness at the expense of diplomacy or thorough analysis. This can lead to misunderstandings and strained relationships, as well as a lack of well-founded decision-making. Similarly, neurotic Te can impact troubleshooting. Individuals may under-do or over-do their efforts when problem-solving, either failing to invest sufficient resources to address an issue or becoming excessively fixated on details that are not critical. This can impede progress and hinder effective solutions.

Lastly, those with a neurotic Te may struggle to maintain detachment and objectivity in their decision-making. They may become overly invested in the outcomes or attached to specific methods, compromising their ability to adapt or consider alternative perspectives.

In summary, while Te is a great process for measuring progress and implementing plans, it can manifest as neurotic episodes, particularly for ESFP and ENFP. Staying alert to the warning signs of neurotic Te, and trying techniques for mental relaxation and mental focus, can help. And by striving for self-awareness, individuals can navigate their endeavors more effectively and cultivate a healthier approach to problem-solving and decision-making.

Neurotic Introverted Thinking (Ti)
(mostly ISFJ and ISFJ)

When Introverted Thinking dominates the neurotic boundary, it often shows as poor reasoning that is distorted, simplistic, or overwrought. This applies most to those who are developing this process, ISFJ and INFJ, and also at times to ESFJ and ENFJ—or really any type, even those who prefer the process.

With Ti, our aim is focused on finding leverage using a framework, mainly by adhering to definitions and philosophical principles. In its basic use, Ti helps us to analyze problems and situations using logical frameworks, seeking consistency and coherence. In its advanced use, Ti empowers us to identify angles or leverage points to solve complex problems by applying an analytical framework.

However, when Ti erupts in a neurotic episode, individuals may exhibit a range of problematic behaviors. For example, those with a neurotic Ti may become hypercritical, often scrutinizing ideas, concepts, and arguments with excessive intensity. They jump swiftly to critiquing and may fail to ask even basic questions that, if answered, would alter their response. At the same time they may also be personally quite sensitive, even to small slights or criticisms—a thin skin—which can lead to a heightened emotional response.

Individuals with a neurotic Ti may also struggle with analysis paralysis, constantly grappling with vague big ideas without gaining clarity or reaching a decisive conclusion. They may become trapped in an endless cycle of questioning and overthinking, which can keep them up at night and leave them unsettled for far longer than needed. This can hinder progress and practical decision-making.

Furthermore, those with a neurotic Ti may exhibit a preference for simple mental models, except in areas of their specialty where they continuously tweak and elaborate. They may engage in excessive word smithing or refining of their ideas, seeking perfection or exhaustive precision in their chosen field. While such specialized knowledge is often commended, it may be based on a poor paradigm, or worn or wielded as a badge of superior social status, rather than used for problem solving. Similarly, neurotic Ti can also manifest in a strong inclination towards favoring or rejecting intellectual or cultural elitism. Individuals may fetishize scholarship and education, valuing intellectual prowess and knowledge as a means of establishing personal worth. They may also define personal or local experiences as part of a global or grand drama, attributing significance to everyday occurrences that may not warrant such overarching narratives.

Furthermore, individuals with a neurotic Ti may experience a strong inner/outer split. That is, they may easily appear warm and friendly on the outside while feeling emotionally detached or cold internally, or vice versa. This inner conflict between their external and internal experiences can contribute to a sense of disconnection or difficulty in reconciling their emotional states.

In conclusion, while Ti is a great process for analysis and problem-solving, it can manifest as neurotic episodes, particularly for ISFJ and INFJ. By recognizing the potential pitfalls of a neurotic Ti and cultivating self-awareness, emotional resilience, and a balanced approach to analysis and decision-making, individuals can navigate their intellectual pursuits more effectively and find greater peace and clarity of mind.

Neurotic Extraverted Feeling (Fe)
(mostly ESTP and ENTP)

When Extraverted Feeling dominates the neurotic boundary, it often shows up as social and relationship chaos. This applies most to those who are developing this process, ESTP and ENTP, and also at times to ISTP and INTP—or really any type, even those who prefer the process.

With Fe, our aim is focused on nurturing trust in giving relationships. Individuals who rely on Fe as a primary function aim to honor the needs and preferences of others. In its basic use, using Fe helps us to build connections with others through warmth, empathy, and understanding. In its advanced use, Fe empowers us to share values and take on the ideas, needs, allegiances, concerns, and values of others as our own—or asking that of others—to create a sense of shared experience, camaraderie, and supportive connections.

However, when Fe erupts in a neurotic episode, individuals may exhibit a range of problematic behaviors. For example, those with a neurotic Fe may be prone to blaming others for causing their emotions, rather than taking responsibility for their own feelings. They may feel needy while also prioritizing the needs of others over their own, leading to feelings of resentment or burnout. They may also vacillate between self-aggrandizement and self-criticism, leading to a lack of clarity or confidence in their own abilities.

On top of these internal struggles, those with neurotic Fe may also struggle between extremes in their relationships. They may be overly nice or mean—or overly indifferent or caring, utilitarian or romantic, terse or effusively communicative—depending on the situation or their mood, and may have quite high expectations of themselves and others. This can lead to disappointment or frustration when those expectations are not met, and may contribute to a sense of disconnection from their own emotional experience.

Individuals with a neurotic Fe may also find themselves caught up in office politics and relationship drama. They may become hyper-focused on societal values and policy issues, either for or against them, and may feel a strong sense of urgency or responsibility to promote their beliefs. However, this can also lead to a sense of detachment from their own inner emotional landscape, as their focus is directed outwards rather than inwards.

Finally, those with a neurotic Fe may struggle to fully experience and process their emotions. They may over-analyze their emotions and interpersonal issues without actually feeling them, leading to a sense of disconnection from their own emotional experience and a lack of intimacy or closeness in their relationships with others.

In sum, while Fe is a great process for building connections and nurturing trust in giving relationships, it can also manifest as neurotic episodes, particularly for ESTP and ENTP. By becoming more aware of how and when neurotic Fe plays out, and working to develop a greater sense of self-awareness and emotional regulation, individuals can begin to find greater balance and fulfillment, particularly in their personal and professional relationships.

Neurotic Introverted Feeling (Fi)
(mostly ISTJ and INTJ)

When Introverted Feeling dominates the neurotic boundary, it often shows up as rigid moralism or intense waves of private suffering. This applies most to those who are developing this process, ISTJ and INTJ, and also at times to ESTJ and ENTJ—or actually any type, even those who prefer the process.

With Fi, our aim is staying true to our personal beliefs and values, adhering to an internal compass of what is important. In its basic use, Fi helps us to evaluate situations and make choices based on what we believe is congruent with our personal identity. In its advanced use, it empowers us with a sense of authenticity and individuality, enabling us to live our core principles throughout our lives.

However, when Fi erupts in a neurotic episode, individuals may exhibit a range of problematic behaviors. For example, those with a neurotic Fi may experience extreme loyalty and condemn disloyalty, often having a strong sense of right and wrong. They may become self-righteous or moralistic, especially when confronted with hypocrisy, and make stubborn black-and-white judgments that leave little room for nuance or understanding.

One notable challenge for individuals with neurotic Fi is the tendency to repress emotions and pretend to not care, only to have occasional—and often surprising—outbursts or emotional breakdowns. They may struggle to fully acknowledge and express their own emotions, which can lead to a buildup of unresolved feelings that eventually manifest in unexpected and intense emotional releases.

Furthermore, those with a neurotic Fi may fail to fully hear or consider others' input, particularly when it comes to emotions. They may be so focused on their own internal values and beliefs that they overlook or dismiss the feelings and perspectives of others. As a result, they may inadvertently hurt others and face a backlash due to their lack of empathy or understanding.

When caught in neurotic Fi, people may also engage in endless inner emotional sorting without finding peace. They can experience moodiness or chronic low-level depression and anger due to the ongoing struggle to align their external reality with their internal values. They yearn for joy and freedom but find themselves bound by their serious and orderly nature, leading to feelings of frustration and longing.

Another challenge is a potential selfish focus on one's own personal wants, goals, and values. While it is important for individuals to prioritize their own needs and maintain personal integrity, a neurotic Fi may result in excessive self-centeredness, disregarding the needs and values of others in favor of their own. This can strain relationships and hinder effective collaboration with others.

Taken overall, while Fi is a great process for maintaining personal authenticity and upholding one's values, it can manifest as neurotic episodes, particularly for ISTJ and INTJ. By recognizing and listening to the deeper emotions and needs within oneself, and working towards developing greater self-awareness, emotional regulation, and empathy for others, individuals can navigate life more harmoniously, with inner peace, balancing self-expression and consideration for others.

8

The
Yin and Yang
of Type

Two Sides of the Same Coin

We can express each of the eight cognitive processes in two broad ways. The neuroscience data points to two sides, and Jung's scholarship around yoga exposes two energies: *yang* and *yin*. Thus, each of the eight processes comes in two styles: Analytic (or yang), and Holistic (or yin).

We can cluster people based on their brain wiring. Brain wiring is how different regions of the brain connect and work together as in a so-cial network. To keep it simple, we can sort brain wiring into two groups, *Analytic* and *Holistic*. To understand these terms, imagine driving a car. You keep up two kinds of attention. One kind is focused, such as looking for specific signage as part of following directions to reach a goal. It is more "left brain". The other kind of attention is global as you attend in a diffuse way to the whole traffic environment, so you can respond to any-thing that comes up. It is more "right-brain". Brain wiring reflects habits over a long period of time, and generally, brain data is reliable for two years, which suggests that people can and do change their style, though that may require effort.

There are statistical trends. Among youth (age 15-25), a person's style *tends* to link to biological sex. This is no surprise since the adolescent brain is inundated with sex hormones and shaped by social expectations. Soon, however, among adults (age 25+), these two styles correlate strong-ly to career choice instead. The Analytic style *tends* to be in business, law, science, or technology, whereas the holistic style *tends* to be in the arts, humanities, and social services. Though we should be careful to say, it's less about what you do, and more about how you do it. And of course, every person has a unique brain. The links are statistical. Happily, the data also suggests that people can flex moderately well with context. You might show one style at work and another style at home. This may explain why among older people (age 55+), differences in style tend to disappear altogether. Likely, we integrate the styles as we find balance in life.

The next 2 pages list the key qualities of each style. After that, a chart offers snapshots of all eight processes with both styles. Finally, you can dig really deep over the course of two dozen pages. As you read, consider that for each process, you likely develop a bias for one style early in life, and later you may be able to develop the other style.

Analytic Style

1. More goal-focused, seeking a desired outcome, filtering out distractions, and presenting poise, drive, clarity, and confidence.

2. Take a top-down approach to situations. Apply a pre-existing idea or process to drive or manage the situation.

3. Consider situations in a complex way, bringing in a handful of most relevant variables or viewpoints while excluding less relevant ones.

4. Better at quickly solving known problems, and using known tools.

5. Often more visual, such as noticing body language, charts, etc. and more likely to represent problems and find solutions in a visual-spatial way, such as using diagrams.

6. Attend more to word content, facts, rules, methods, numbers, deduction, labels, and similar specifics.

7. A more literal thinker, and also more likely to limit thinking and ideas to the current specific context. Opens up with analogies.

8. With practice, can switch between multiple ways of reasoning, willfully applying a different method at a needed time.

9. More comfortable working in a hierarchy, with set leadership, and with known tasks.

10. Blind to its own biases, even their own analytic bias. Can be quite confident and may think of themselves as very smart while unaware of what they're doing wrong or don't know.

11. Likely careers include business, engineering, finance, law, military, the "hard" sciences, and technology.

Whether Sensing or Intuiting, the Analytic style focuses more on the central figure or subject in a scene rather than in the background or context. For example, while driving a car, you might focus most on signs or obstacles directly related to their journey.

Whether Thinking or Feeling, the Analytic style takes a more calculated or mental approach. With Thinking, it's the usual set of analytical skills involving criteria, definitions, and measurement. With Feeling, this means sticking to an explicit set of values or a dogma, or issuing goals or a call to action for a group.

Holistic Style

1. More open-ended, seeking input and reflecting on data without filters, while attending, patiently and curiosly, to the flow of the events.

2. Take a bottom-up approach to situations. Stay open to discovering ideas and methods to synthesize a solution.

3. Consider all aspects of a situation at once; thus, may be connecting or relating seemingly unrelated variables or viewpoints.

4. Better at finding novel solutions, and coming up with new tools.

5. Often more auditory, such as noticing voice tone, musical harmony, etc. and more likely to represent problems and find solutions in a narrative way, with stories.

6. Attend more to tone, intention, ethics, artistry, emotional impact, expressiveness, humor and metaphor.

7. A more figurative thinker (e.g. metaphors), and also more likely to limit thoughts to one's identity, values and likes.

8. With practice, can vary how much or how little they engage a situation using their favorite broad reasoning style.

9. More comfortable working in an egalitarian way, with various people helping to lead, and unclear tasks.

10. More aware, often keenly, of their own biases including the analytic versus holistic bias. But may not be sufficiently empowered or confident to make a choice or change.

11. Likely careers include the arts, social services, humanistic pursuits, multiculturalism, and the "soft" sciences.

Whether Sensing or Intuiting, the Holistic style focuses more on the background or context of a scene rather than the obvious central figure. For example, when watching a stage play, you might attend to all aspects of the experience, front and back, on and off stage.

Whether Thinking or Feeling, the Holistic style takes a more loose, organic approach. With Feeling, it's the usual skills involving attention to the entire set of relations, emotions, values, and cues. With Thinking, this means holding lightly a variety of methods and models that complement each other.

Analytic/Yang Style	**Holistic/Yin Style**
active, focused, fixed, foreground subject, top-down	*receptive, diffuse, flexible, background context, bottom-up*

Sensing (S): Tangible, concrete, and experiential awareness

"Mover" Se	"Sensate" Se
Physically active. Move, and move others. Aggressive style. Tackle problems directly. Alert for relevant data. Court danger. Focus on actionable options for tangible, bottom-line results. Impulsive, strong, and can be crude.	Absorb sensory experiences. Enjoy life's pleasures. Trust rich sensory data. Prefer fun, relaxing activities. Attend to others' motion and get in synch with them. Sensual style. Appreciate beauty. Artistic, graceful, and inviting.

"Defender" Si	"Hearth" Si
Act as an anchor. On guard, and guard others. A firm sense of culture and history. Stick with the strongest impressions from your upbringing. Prefer convenience and familiarity. Block big changes. Traditional. Aim to civilize.	Maintain home and traditions. Draw on a big memory bank of sense impressions. Feel grounded. Adapt to the group's changes and flex to others' will. Prefer comfort and safety. Sensitive to subtle sensory variations.

Thinking (T): Assess & organize according to criteria, logic or principles

"Manager" Te	"Builder" Te
Committed to succeed at a few ambitious goals. Speak logically and confidently. Apply a business mindset to affairs. Manage and drive others as resources to get things done. May put speed and profit above usefulness or accuracy.	Helpful hard worker. Efficient, frugal, economical, and timely. Focus on doing work right. Avoid distractions. Perfect details and optimize functionality. Comfortable with different forms of complexity and multiple projects.

"Critic" Ti	"Systemist" Ti
Stubborn on principles. Stick to a singular, most worthy theory that can explain everything. Define precisely. Provide expert logic and guidance. Bring order to ideas. Correct errors, poor thinking, and wrong approaches.	Take multiple points of view. Find patterns in the chaos. Notice how systems scale, and apply principles in a fluid way. People, art, nature, and technology all interrelate. Understand and find leverage in the messiness of life.

Analytic/Yang Style	Holistic/Yin Style
active, focused, fixed, foreground subject, top-down	*receptive, diffuse, flexible, background context, bottom-up*

Intuiting (N): Symbolic, abstract, and conceptual awareness

"Marketer" Ne	"Catalyst" Ne
Put on a show. Pitch and juggle many ideas, trusting quantity over quality in search of advantages or gains. Recruit others and rely on strong energy of ideas to shift situations to one's liking. Court uncertainty for progress.	Notice subtle patterns. Negotiate toward a novel win-win outcome with a relaxed, subtle style. Use humor and disguises. Include and promote others. Search for the highest quality potential possibilities for everyone's gain.

"Visionary" Ni	"Oracle" Ni
Stick to a singular vision of the future to improve self and society. Be certain of a few compelling insights. Don't let go or water down. Turn realizations into principles. Apply many complex concepts. Act as a guiding spirit.	Hold lightly many interrelated insights. Connect to the many facets of the archetypal world. Open to transformation. Respond to others' questions, and innovate for the group. Cultivate an aesthetic or spiritual practice.

Feeling (F): Assess & organize according to appropriateness, values or worth

"Shepherd" Fe	"Host" Fe
Announce values and prescribe best behaviors. Corral outliers and encourage them to join the group. Actively work to fix relationships. Inspire as an orator. Make sacrifices, and ask others to sacrifice, in a push to meet needs.	Enjoy supporting your community, family, and friends. Value harmony with others over being right. Sensitive to negative feedback. Accommodate people's many differences. Can be self-sacrificing as you even help foes.

"Quester" Fi	"Romantic" Fi
Pursue a singular life quest or truth. Aim for moral clarity. Dedicated to a congruent set of beliefs. Align your quest and core personal identity. Listen to a select voice like one's own conscience. Contain your feelings.	Live a life of deep quiet feeling. Listen to and harmonize with many voices. Pursue multiple soft quests. Allow room for inner and outer conflicts. Your identity is subtle, diffuse, and varies in the context of each relationship.

Yang and Yin in Depth

Let's take a look at the two sides of each of the 8 Jungian functions: the Analytic or *yang* style, and the Holistic or *yin* style.

These are based on grouping the types by their favorite functions and teasing out the meanings based on their favorite brain networks, neocortex regions, and responses while trying various tasks such as meditating, solving math problems, drawing, and so forth.

These descriptions are also based on a web interview and presented in a first-person style, which allows personal stories, impressions, and more nuanced explanations. As you read, consider yourself, people you know, and the society you live in.

Extraverted Sensing (Se)

Extroverted sensing (Se) has two sides. It can show up as a mover with a more aggressive and analytical style, or as a sensate with a more receptive and sensual style. People who prefer Se usually show both sides, as suiting their mood and the situation. Though they still have a preference. When there is a strong bias—one-sidedness—then the result is trouble. As for everyone else, we all use Se in some way, even unconsciously, and likely have unconscious conditioning or habits around it.

Analytic/Yang Se – The Mover

Yang Se is about force, strength, and moving things. It's physically active with an aggressive style. This Se user sees a problem and just goes to tackle it. They tune their senses to whatever relevant data comes in about what they can do now, and they take action.

These Se users are okay with danger. "Yes! Let's go bungee jumping!" Or "Let's scuba dive and pet sharks!" (that's a real thing). One time, I was on a busy street with an ISFP friend. An officer in the street was helping to direct traffic from a narrow median. The ISFP just jaywalked to that median, to right where the officer stood. He said hello to the officer and continued jaywalking. I walked with him and didn't say anything.

I thought, only an Se user could do that! But that's not entirely true. Everyone does Se in some way, and if they favor the yang side, they will have confidence to "just do it" – to read the situation's limits and be an "alpha". They focus on what is actionable, the bottom line results, and what they can get away with. They like to be impressive and can come off as aggressive, and are maybe rude or crude.

A great example is Donald Trump. Not that every yang-Se user is just like Trump. A person could have different political beliefs and so forth. In any case, yang Se can be particularly offensive to people who have yin Se, particularly if that yin-Se is in shadow (deep in the unconscious). The offended part of the personality will react, "Oh, this is a horrible, violent person!" And that, my friends, is a type bias.

Here is another story. I was in Costa Rica casually filming two martial arts friends as they sparred. They sparred vigorously as usual. A gal came over, sat to watch, and afterward remarked, "Wow, why are you guys so angry and violent?" They casually replied, "We're not." They didn't experience it that way. They were simply expressing themselves physically. Consider, an Intuiting (N) type can deliver over-the-top abstraction, and a Feeling type can deliver over-the-top drama. Similarly, Se users can deliver over-the-top action. In the case of martial arts, discipline intersects with action, and that discipline matures the analytic, yang Se.

By the way, what I describe here is close to Socionics' definition of Se. Socionics is the Eastern European lineage of type after Dr. Jung. Many of its definitions are similar to the Western lineage popularized by Myers-Briggs, but in some cases—as with Se—they differ.

Holistic/Yin Se – The Sensate

In the Myers-Briggs tradition, Sensing in general is defined as "taking in information through the five senses." This sounds passive or weak compared to yang Se. Yet actual ESFPs and ESTPs are often active and strong! They are not just sitting in a chair, observing. Maybe to no surprise, Isabel Briggs Myers favored yin Se; and moreover, Se was a shadow function for her, as she had INFP preferences. She wrote what she knew. Thus, in her type lineage, Se has a strong yin flavor that needs balancing out.

So what is this yin side of Se? It's about being more diffuse and receptive. It's about absorbing sensory experiences. It is the artist who absorbs the rhythms and hues of a landscape and expresses that through art. It is about enjoying life's pleasures. Notice I said "pleasures", not "comforts". Pleasure is more stimulating and doing what we like in the moment, familiar or not. Imagine a friend saying, "Let's take a road trip!" He ends up slowly traveling through Thailand for a while, experiencing the jungle and the beaches and clubs there. It's mostly about absorbing the sensory experiences: surfing, watching the sunset, dropping in on a party, dancing, drumming, and (maybe) smoking ganja. There's a fun, relaxed feeling, and there's a lot of attending to other people's motion, getting in sync, and being in flow.

One year, at the Burning Man desert art festival, I visited a camp to try "improvisational contact dance". Rule one: You stay physically in touch with your partner at all times, with any part of your bodies, even if that's elbow and knee or whatever. And rule two: you both keep moving to the music, which was mostly slow. It was not electronic dance, though it could be. The idea was to stay in sync with somebody else physically. It was very sensual. So, if analytic yang Se can be "sexual", then holistic yin Se is "sensual". That is, yin Se appreciates beauty and grace, and is fashionable, artistic, and inviting to the senses. Remarkably, this Se user often doesn't even need to do much. There's something about their style, the way they carry themselves, and the way they attend to others at a sensory level, that's inviting. They're also the kind of person who's just happy to lie in the sun at the beach with a drink and suntan. That's their idea of fun.

Sorting Flavors of Se

To sum up, there's yang and yin Se. Both sides orient to the outer world, to concrete practical data, whatever is there as a relevant option in the environment. The question is simply if they take a more imposing or receptive approach. And this bias does not link to having Thinking or Feeling or any specific type. A specific ESTP guy might be holistic, while a specific ISFP gal might be analytic.

The analytic, yang side runs to the top of the hill, drawing his sword to engage in battle, or to engage in business, sports, music, or whatever.

Maybe others follow based on his sheer guts, animal magnetism, and display of force. Even on holiday, yang Se may say, "Let's go jet-skiing!" And if they don't go, or do something that provides an equal adrenaline rush or thrill, they'll be disappointed. Yang Se can show in non-physical ways, too, as a vigorous marketing campaign or an aggressive sales pitch.

In contrast, the holistic, yin side is like the stereotypical painter or dancer—appreciate the beauty of the moment and of movement, the pulse of life, and flow with that. It basks in subtleties of experience. At times it can look like introverted Sensing (Si) because it is more passive, which is somewhat like being introverted. But actually, yin Se is directly and acutely connecting to the outer world—that is, chartreuse is a color to be felt and tried out, not simply a specific stimulus that evokes a memory and set of feelings and preferences that come with that memory (which is Si).

By the way, analytic Se is a little bit more interested in "the facts at hand" compared to holistic Se, simply because facts are more eagerly processed by the analytical mind. That said, facts are more than words and figures. Facts can include the tastes of different beers, or whatnot.

Finally, remember that the yin and yang sides of Se explain well the differing definitions of Se between Socionics and Myers-Briggs. Attending to the two sides also helps people sort their best-fit type so they don't miss out on recognizing who they are simply because of a stereotype.

Introverted Sensing (Si)

Let's get into one of society's most common functions: Introverted Sensing (Si). It's particularly important to talk about the two sides of Si because these folks, the SJ types, are so numerous. They are many tens of millions in America, not to mention probably 1 billion people around the world. Type materials often describe them in a stereotypical way. For the more extroverted—ESTJ or ESFJ—type tends to exaggerate the dominant function in a negative way; for example, describing ESTJ as just a finger-wagging flavor of Extraverted Thinking. Of course, there are less stellar individuals we can all point to who are like this simply because this function is so common. But it's far from the whole picture.

Analytic/Yang Si – The Defender

One side is the yang version of Si. I describe it like a defender, anchor, guard, or protector. These Si users have a solid, firm sense of culture and history, can talk about it and take pride in it, and see it as something very important. It's not just that they're an anchor.

As my grandmother with ESTJ preferences would say, it's as if at any moment, society can regress into barbarism because of human nature, though probably not overnight. We enjoy all of these institutions, which took centuries to build to tame the worst side of our nature and channel our potential. She was clear about what the institutional strengths and weaknesses are, and what's important from culture and history, and what to stick to. So these Si users hold strong impressions about these, usually from their upbringing, though they can come later in life too if really impactful. They hold strong impressions about the things that they're (we're!) going to guard, protect, and rely upon. They're like the pillars in the Acropolis: some of them may crumble, and the roof may come down, but we can still hold firm to the image of the Acropolis and what it stood for in its golden age—democracy, education, science, philosophy, and all of those things.

If you look at what's going on with yang Si, the not-so-hidden agenda aims to civilize, and to be civil. That doesn't necessarily mean nice, traditional, or orderly. It just means civil. And they're not necessarily hysterical about safety. They know there are times when you need to court danger or go to war. So let's do that smartly and purposefully! At the same time, they do prefer familiarity, safety, and convenience, and they are going to block big or dangerous changes. And they do tend to be traditional. Again, it's around this organizing sense that's deep within them, a very firm sense of history and culture—grounded in all of the personal impressions associated with those.

There are competing definitions of Si. Often, what we see is "sequencing", "recalling", "comparing", "stabilizing", or "comforting". All of these are behaviors that support Si as a form of consciousness. Specifically, sequencing and recalling factual details show up with the yang version of Si. It's an analytical, left-brain approach to dealing with the psychological impact of sensory impressions.

Holistic/Yin Si – The Hearth

Now, there's another version of Si, a holistic or yin version, which is not anchored in one specific or particular thing. Instead, it comes off as very grounded—in everything. There's home, the workplace and the community and traditions, and then there's an enormous database of personal memories. And it's not just a select few of those that act as pillars. It's the entire vista, the entire museum of everything that's from their life. And that provides a very grounded, comforting feeling.

There's no one thing you can ever point to with yin Si. We can pull this or that leg from their chair of life, and the chair still stands. Of course, they're likely not going to enjoy the loss, but at least that chair has a thousand legs. Thusly, they're more adaptable to changes because they have a receptive style, and because they have a wide grounding in all of their memories. They can say, for example, "Okay, today's fashion is different, and now people wear black lipstick or funny shoes, or we're all supposed to wear a mask now." Whatever it is, it's just one more thing that goes into their database, the sense-experience database. Of course they prefer things to be safe and comfortable and familiar, and they may not be quick at all to adopt a new practice or style, but they can roll with it, or at least endure it.

These Si users are highly sensitive to subtle sensory variations because their database is so big and things are not just pushed into a box. Asking, "Is it black or white?" is the yang version of Si. This yin version sees a pallet of 64 million colors, tastes, textures, and sounds. Eevery color or such differs a tiny bit; and every color, or pattern of colors, evokes something different within them and others. At the same time, they're pretty comfortable flowing with the culture and where the culture changes, provided it's not too fast, as pallet is rich in options.

They will surely complain along the way if things are too abrupt and too different. They will grumble like Marge Simpson. But nonetheless there is a grounded-ness that you can't take away. Rather than a knight in armor, they are the hearth. That's the word that I use. The hearth warms the home, and they can be a hearth almost everywhere they go as long as it's within their range of experience. Another word I might use is table. They are the table where everyone meets and finds nourishment.

Sorting Flavors of Si

Firstly, when I talk about memories or "impressions", I'm talking about how Jung described Si. People argue about how to define introverted Sensing. Well, just go read the book, please. Go back to Psychological Types, Chapter X. Jung talks clearly. Si is a lot about building up a giant database of sensory impressions. And those impressions easily override actual, later tangible experiences. Think of a person who got sick after eating sushi, and will forever experience sushi in that way, regardless of how it actually tastes now, what restaurant they go to, or whatever—there's just an overriding sense experience that happens. In short, as Jung said, Si is a subjective, personal relationship to the sensory world.

Second, based on brain imaging, the resulting neural maps show just as much variety among Si folks as everyone else. There are ISTJs with a creative starburst neural pattern, and ISFJs with a dominant frontal-cortex bias, and so on. And when we look at their professions, from painter to accountant and dozens of others, we see that the Si folks come in all flavors as richly as everyone else.

Third, when we consider both sides of Si, we see it is both an anchor and a home for people. That sounds so wholesome! But of course, children are impressionable, and a person's childhood is not necessary wholesome. Nor are the impacts necessarily conscious. People hold all sorts of attitudes, attractions, and preferences based on impressions provided by family and society, pleasant or not, healthy or not, rational or not. So for all of the folks, especially with an Intuiting preference, who tend to downplay or deride Si, remember: You've got Si too! The question is what kind, and about what! And it may be that someone actually has a Si preference—say, ISFJ instead of INFJ. And that's okay. When we acknowledge the subjective aspect of Si, we give it all the dimensions that it's due.

Extraverted Intuiting (Ne)

Extraverted Intuiting (Ne) is a favorite dinnertime topic. I was just staying for a couple of weeks with Antonia Dodge and Joel Mark Witt of

Personality Hacker at their farm in Gettysburg, Pennsylvania, and they have ENTP and ENFP preferences. She's the ENTP and he's the ENFP. And they have different versions of Ne, in a non-stereotypical way. Even though he's ENFP, with a Feeling preference, he identifies with the analytic version of Ne. And even though she's ENTP, with a Thinking preference, she identifies with the holistic version of Ne. (Note: They've talked about this on podcasts, and I'm not giving away something personal here.) What do these two sides of Ne look like?

Analytic/Yang Ne – The Marketer

Analytic or yang Ne is like the person who's pitching the wonders of Barnum and Bailey Circus. They're juggling all of these different (and often unusual) ideas, and they're putting on a show with those while looking for a return. There's a large number of potential possibilities, and a lot of excitement around those, and they're throwing whatever comes against the wall to see what sticks.

Yang Ne users do a lot to make interesting things happen in an open-ended way. Sometimes, these sound too interesting. As in, when you listen to them, you easily wonder about the story they're telling: "Is that real, or did he sort of do that, or is he just making it up?" Well, they themselves likely don't know! It's a mix. They're busy finding out what's possible, what can fit when, and how. They're recruiting people. Ideas are flying. Cakes are in the oven. They're keeping a lots of balls up in the air at once, each a different color. They're injecting a super enthusiastic energy. Except for the occasional down day, they are out in the world interacting—usually, there's a lot of chit-chat, hat-tipping, and hand-waving.

These Ne users actively court—not risk, per se, as in actual physical danger—uncertainty. Risk is more Extraverted Sensing, and uncertainty is more Extraverted Intuiting. Ne users are cool with uncertainty, especially the analytic side of Ne. And as a part of this, there is a calculating element, and it can feel sales-like and at the cutting-edge of things. They're adept at marketing, and usually they find the right image or phrase to energize people. I've only seen one episode of the TV show, "Better Call Saul", so maybe I shouldn't name it, but that element, that approach, is unmistakable. This Ne user might be talking about UFOs, a new kind of investment opportunity, stage-plays they're producing, or the next wave in medical innovations that is "right now, just over the horizon". They're out there churning stuff, shifting the situation. And all of it just seems to work, albeit somewhat chaotically, at least for a while, or at least things appear to be working.

Generally, analytic Ne users are like the Wizard of Oz. There is a yellow brick road, a genius behind the curtain pulling strings, a great story, and in general an amazing dog-and-pony-show. They can be wonderful at getting buy-in from others around change, and negotiating a mutually satisfying path to that change. Because life is as much about journeys as it is destinations.

Holistic/Yin Ne – The Catalyst

Then there is the Catalyst Ne user. Let me describe them this way: I had a student in my lab and she was wearing the brain-imaging cap, and clear on her ENFP preferences, and sitting there between the tasks and not doing anything that I've given her. She's not obviously keeping herself busy. She just seems to be sitting there. But, her brain is super active, and I ask her, "What's going on? What are you thinking about?" And she indicates two students on the other side of the lab and replies, "I'm observing those two other students there, and I'm imagining different kinds of interactions they could be having."

This yin of Ne version is more focused on questions like, "What is the world showing me?", "What patterns am I noticing?", and maybe, "What magic can I help draw out from that?" Often, there's a gentle, quiet humor, and perhaps negotiating towards some win-win outcome, an outcome to be decided like magic. It's subtle. It's not circus or stage magic. It's the kind of magic in one of those ENFP romance movies like "Amélie". The main character, cute and unassuming, just smiles, mumbles some vague wordage, and somehow discovers something wonderful, at just the perfect moment, because the character is actually incredibly attentive to what's going on around her.

These Ne users are naturally talented as therapists. They don't even need to say much. They're just like, "Oh!". They ask you a question, or they sort of throw out something, and they hear the words you give back, and they notice how your voice tone highlights certain words over others, and so on. They're pinging you or the whole situation, and they're building up a picture or model of it and then they're like, "Oh!" They notice where they can move a block or shift a thread. They can remove this block from the Jenga Tower, and wow, it still stands, and the story continues. It turns out they pulled out the block that's made of gold. If you ask how they did it, they don't even know!

These Ne catalysts use humor and disguise, hesitation and misdirection, and overall they like to include and promote others. Rather than pushing a lot of different potential possibilities, they're more about quality because yin focuses on quality. And they're more like, "How can I nurture the best quality of this potential possibility? They're not trying to force the magical moments or actively create them, but to be attentive to when the moments can really manifest on their own, and then doing that "little thing" that draws someone attention, and the result is, "Wow!"

Sorting Flavors of Ne

I should say, I'm describing Ne here in a fairly playful way. Both sides of Ne have negative consequences too. Yin Ne can be fairly manipulative; and with its passive style, it may waste a lot of time daydreaming and allowing others to drive events and then these Ne users wonder how they got left behind. Meanwhile, yang Ne can be quite overwhelming. These folks can waste a lot of energy throwing around tons of ideas, and when they're immature, or lack follow-through, or the ideas are just really ungrounded, then it all comes to naught. There was a great amount of talk, amounting to nothing.

To return to Joel and Antonia: Joel the ENFP—marketer and video maker—is more analytic while Antonia the ENTP—coach and type theorist—is more holistic. So these two sides of Ne are not about Thinking and Feeling flavors of Ne. It's not like NFPs are quiet catalysts and NTPs are wild marketers. Those are stereotypes and reasons why people get confused, wondering if they are ENFP or ENTP, for example. Or ENFP or ENFJ, or whatnot. Once you know enough people of the same type, you'll notice there's a lot of variety. If you practice a side of a function that people don't instantly associate with a certain type, they might think that you're some other type—typically an adjacent one—even though you're actually your type. And so this is where mistyping can happen when we know only one side of a function.

Introverted Intuiting (Ni)

Often, Introverted Intuiting (Ni) is described in two ways: as analytic for Ni types with Thinking and as holistic for Ni types with Feeling. But both sides show up for all Ni types, and really, for everyone. Even though Ni is the least commonly favored among the eight functions in the population, everybody has all eight playing out in some way, if even in the shadows. So we can talk here about any person who is reaching into the future, or opening up to the unconscious, even if that person does not favor Ni.

Analytic/Yang Ni – The Visionary

The analytic version of Ni is active, fixated, and focused—a more yang style. This is someone who is driven, maybe innovative, and certainly sticking to a powerful vision of the future to improve themselves or to build something, whether that's through a creative project or a business or to improve society, whatever it is.

There's a special willpower that comes with yang Ni, and there's a certainty around it that's really compelling. The result is a lot of drive, which easily leads to tunnel vision. The person will not water down his or her vision—won't let it go. As part of this, this Ni user has insights—realizations or "aha!" moments—and then they "recruit" those realizations as principles to support the vision and help make it happen. These realizations can feel and look analytical, as if it's something arrived at by logic or deep contemplation, and the result is a complex idea, a concept with an analytical quality. A tip-off is that the idea is often graphical in nature, and the path that birthed it is murky at best. Another tip-off is that the person embodies a purpose and ends up acting as a guiding spirit for others.

Elon Musk is a great example of visionary, yang Ni. He sticks to a singular, guiding vision. His central vision is the human colonization of Mars. But it goes beyond the obvious: building rockets. For example, even the

Tesla car meets his vision for space: "Can we drive these electric cars on Mars?" Musk's solar power storage units also meet his vision. That's what it comes down to: everything serves to manifest the vision. And that which does not serve is reshaped, deprioritized or discarded.

Analytic Ni can fixate on arguments or causal patterns. For example, in a single moment, this Ni user gets a clear image of a whole pattern of behavior they notice going on in a group. If they name it, typically, others will reply that it sounds outrageous. And yet the Ni user sees it including how the situation will play out, where everything will land eventually, and what's needed to correct it. But few, if anyone listens. Then down the line, more often than not, the insight is proven prescient. Of course, this side of Ni can sometimes be way off the mark while overconfident with tunnel vision.

Holistic/Yin Ni – The Oracle

The other side of Ni is the oracle—receptive, reflective, and diffuse. Using Ni this way is like getting into a certain altered state—a curtained state—of consciousness. It means being engaged with, dancing with, a creative muse and the archetypal world in general.

Yin Ni is otherworldly. It's like a Greek oracle, or like relying on hypnosis or working with psychedelics or being a yogi or mystical poet. This is where we get into Jung's description of Ni. While he touched on both versions, he emphasized yin. He himself practiced "active imagination", a technique to invite images up from the conscious. This is not meant to be whimsical, and its purpose is, "Let's meet in the shadowy middle." He describes an "organ of imagination" that is a bridge to the larger, infinite psychic realm, and his dream-like adventures are detailed in his "Red Book". His bias for yin Ni is why some are misled about his type. But a yin bias does not mean he was, for example, an INFJ. An INTJ, ENTJ, INTP, or ISTP or such could have strong yin Ni too. Regardless of his true type, Jung talked about Ni as cultivating an aesthetic and spiritual experience, which is more on the yin side.

Another example is the shaman. This is an ancient embodiment of Ni. The shaman acts as a bridge between the spirit world and the material community. He, she or "they" acts mostly as a bridge, and the spirit world is an archetypal realm filled with all sorts of energetic complexes represented in symbolic form—spirits animals, deities, wise-and-well ancestors, and stranger or not-so-friendly forms. The climax of that process is the white light, as Jung described in "The Psychology of Kundalini Yoga". As for being a medium or oracle, that kind of role—a receptacle or channel—is even more strongly yin, and that Ni user needs great psychological fortitude to engage in it safely.

Yin Ni is adept at holding multiple, blurry (quantum?) visions at once for themselves and others. It's less pointed and less productive than yang Ni. And rather than being future focused, it is timeless. There is a downside. It can be lazy, a useless mystic, and not just disorganized, but mentally confused. Moreover, yin Ni is largely unwelcome, as-is, in the modern world, and thus individuals who would naturally go here instead easily satisfy themselves with dream analysis, tarot, and fantastical books, fairs, films, games, and so on.

Sorting Flavors of Ni

Think of Ni with two sides, akin to light and dark. When Ni is the dominant function, hopefully both sides work together synergistically, as is true for all the functions. Other times, there is a clear bias, such as the innovative science businessman who would not touch the oracle side until maybe much later in life.

Let's compare. With more yang Ni, we hold a vision, have a productive creative process, and are clear on complex concepts—all fine, but we are also not keen to open up and allow ourselves to be transformed in an unforeseen way. We may think we can grow according to a master plan. And yes, that is an option, with limits; and there is a lack of humility and often a lot of expectations. In contrast, with yin Ni, the person surrenders to an open-ended process. When we sit in the "medicine hut", Ni is there to help us cope with the transformative experiences that happen—for us and/or others.

As with any function, when both sides play together, there is magic. They host a potent creative process. For example, a skilled artist, musician or writer produces a beautiful, original piece as if out of nowhere. The piece reflects the organic, messy nature of the unconscious, with numerous compelling symbols, and yet also fits within the person's career vision and holds up under analytical analysis. That said, there is always a challenge of communicating the vision, prediction or insight to other people.

Let's get past stereotypes. Typical portraits of Ni users with Feeling describe a poet, mystic, or psychic. Those are extreme yin Ni. Thus, an INFJ might hold a dream of building a technology company to help society. He reads an INFJ type portrait and thinks, "I am not so artsy or woo-woo, so I must be an INTJ". Similarly, INTJ portraits tend to show an intuitive tech genius like Nicola Tesla. And yes, some INTJs are like that, and society rewards technical marvels. But many INTJs lean into metaphysics and meditation, and immerse in fantasy and science fiction and such. Those INTJs lack an INFJ's innate diplomatic skills, but when yin and yang Ni are well-integrated, the person can help others with keen insights and ideas.

Extraverted Thinking (Te)

Extroverted Thinking (Te) has a certain weight or style that automatically makes it look analytical. But that's not necessarily the case. A fine word to describe Te overall is "empirical". Another is "effectiveness". From there, we can ask how it shows up developmentally, such as in different career areas, organizational roles, cultural backgrounds, and in general demeanor. For example, there are ESTJ tattoo artists, ISTJ psychologists, ENTJ musicians, and INTJ novelists. Te users are not all accountants, administrators, engineers or such. There really is a range in terms of development, in terms of career, and the same holds true in terms of expression, whether the focus is on leadership, a great matrix of details, or everything in between.

Analytic/Yang Te – The Manager

What does Te look like when it is active, fixated, and focused –a yang style? This Te user is out there and on top of things, committed to fulfilling a clear main goal with sub-goals. That goal can get pretty specific, such as building a company and making one million dollars within the next three years. Whatever it is, it is something that can be measurably achieved in steps out in the world.

This person is the one who gets out there and directs others and speaks articulately with logic, evidence, and confidence, often relying upon heuristics and formulas. These Te users often excel if you put them on the spot to argue or explain something, unless it's completely out of their wheelhouse. They will say, "Oh yes, there's that and this, and then there's this and that." There's an order, they marshal evidence and ideas, and they talk quite confidently. Their strong confidence and clarity around evidence, goals, and reasons can make them notably attractive and effective as leaders. Though one should not mistake that bullishness for accuracy, since their data and analysis is often second or third hand.

Overall, what captures analytic Te is "the business of living". These folks hold a business mindset—in a capitalistic sense. There are consequences, they know where they can succeed and fail, where to allocate resources, and the risks and benefits. They make contingency plans with percentages and costs. And they calculate and weigh those even when they're talking about "soft" things like marriage. There's a seriousness to it, though not necessarily a stone face. Companies can go bankrupt, and so can people, not just in a monetary sense, but also in a moral, emotional, social or physical sense—whatever variables we look at. So they're managing and driving themselves and others, and utilizing resources to get things done actively toward fixed goals in a focused way, usually with an eye on likely consequences and contingency plans.

There is a telltale sign: In general, Te users sort on empirical factors such as speed, usefulness, profit, and accuracy, but yang Te users tend to really prioritize speed and profit. Think of how Jeff Bezos has run Amazon, where low-level employees must wear tracking devices. Yang Te can bull-doze and even deliberately build in suffering and failure, structurally. There's easily an efficient inhumanity to it.

Holistic/Yin Te – The Builder

The holistic or yin version of Te is more receptive, flexible, and diffuse. It's not big on just one thing. It shows up in all of the small things everywhere in a person's life.

It shows up most at the task level with attention to details, facts and figures, charts and diagrams, as well as restraint, thriftiness, and responsible fulfillment of tasks. These people are hard workers, often doing detailed work themselves, whether it's art or electronics or nursing or whatever. And they are comfortable working with a huge mass of logical structures. Maybe there are eighteen spreadsheets and thirty different accounting forms, and there's this and there's that—and keep in mind, they might be working with song structures, not tax structures, but it's the same idea. They make and select templates, fill out the templates, and focus on details and optimizing functionally and arranging every-thing in boxes and along procedures. They easily manage relationships the same way: boxes and procedures. This can get out of hand, becoming pedantic, fastidious or compulsive around facts, details, and order.

All of this may sound very "analytic". But think of the definition of a "holistic" function, and we see this Te quietly crafting a fine watch un-der moonlight. The tell-tale sign: They stick to a budget—not quick and potent wealth building—but of frugalness, economy, timeliness, and ef-ficiency. They look to see that everything is in working order, especially on a personal or one-on-one level. They maintain a practical, predict-able, and somewhat impersonal kind of integrity.

Ultimately, there's a receptive quality: This person is subordinating Te in service of something else. For example, let's say I have a project in front of me. I ask—or I just notice—what the different forms of com-plexity are here and which form fits this particular project, this task. And I have multiple projects available that I'm working on, and I want to optimize my resources to get the right results. How do I min-max all of that while I'm still accommodating the surrounding circumstance? When it comes to factors like speed, profit, usefulness, and accuracy, the yin Te user is prioritizing usefulness and accuracy.

Sorting Flavors of Te

We might think, yang Te sounds like extroverted Te users and yin Te sounds like introverted Te users. But the brain data says otherwise. There are yin and yang versions for all four Te types.

Among those with Sensing, there are both. There is the yang ESTJ military general. And then there is the yin ESTJ accountant—she doesn't want more responsibility than the full plate she already has, and she sees great value in what she does, and she knows all of the rules and regulations to meet. So, she doesn't call shots on a high level, but she is dealing with a lot at the ground level. Imagine, building a pyramid is a long and complex process that requires eyes, hands, and feet on the ground, with measuring sticks and other tools. And there's an element beyond building, to maintain things well, or at least thinking ahead about how to keep things functional.

Among those with Intuiting (N), there are also both. Some INTJs are comfortable acting as corporate directors, though usually not the head honcho. They direct to optimize the whole organization, often with an Ni vision behind it. They are more yang. In contrast, other INTJs are like, "Yeah, I have three music albums that I'm working on until I get all of the details right." There's a very different sense of scope here. The same goes for ENTJs. Not all of them are like Amazon's founder, Jeff Bezos. They are more "small time", and there is also an attention to quality and detail that would be missing otherwise.

It can be somewhat challenging to parse these two sides of Te, especially for those who don't favor it. The analytic yang style is driving others, and it strives to go "big time" quickly, usually around a singular obvious goal. They proactively push the external world, even using and consuming people as widgets. In contrast, the holistic or yin style tends to stay "small time", and is usually personally attentive to numerous diverse tasks on the stove. They are allowing others – or the data, project requirements, or whatever in the outer world – to drive them, and drive others, in a generally impersonal way.

Introverted Thinking (Ti)

Introverted Thinking (Ti) has two sides: analytic and holistic (aka yang and yin, respectively). In a nutshell, analytic Ti is critical, fixed, and at times aggressive around ideas. Say something the wrong way, and this person will correct you. This flavor is easy to spot. In contrast, holistic Ti has a passion for a diversity of ideas—methods, principles, practices, hypotheses, frameworks, designs, and such—with a flexibility around them, with an inner drive to make sense of it all, and with a lot of discussion, questions, experiments, variations, allowances, and so on. Since everyone has Ti in some way, a bias for one side can explain a bit, particularly for people who do not favor Ti yet seem caught in its grip.

Analytic/Yang Ti – The Critic

Analytic Ti is stubborn on principles. There is a singular most worthy framework or approach that explains everything, at least within a particular domain, though this Ti user tends to extend their area of expertise far and wide to cover as much of life as possible. In a sense, can't math or chemistry, economics or literature, architecture or statistics be used to address anything and everything, at least by analogy? And with their expertise, they have a strong drive, an assertiveness, not just to explain things but to "win" at the game of life.

Using analytic Ti, the person aims to define things precisely and is delighted to figure out a perfect unified theory of everything. Often these folks also have an agenda—maybe even unconscious—to provide expert guidance, whether for their family or an organization or for all of society. (By the way, that's where the opposite function, Fe, comes in.) Using their expertise, the person aims to guide others and answer the central questions or tasks of life. In practice, the results are usually more modest but still quite potent: They can act as reliable experts in a particular discipline and they bring a lot of active problem-solving power.

A tip-off to this subtype: They like to correct errors. That includes their own, at least with respect to the central framework they rely on. And of course that includes others' poor thinking and wrong approaches. Thus, they can easily come off as difficult to talk to, obnoxious, know-it-alls, or thick-headed. They often have an authoritative voice tone, steady and forceful. Conversely, listening is also a big challenge because they are usually focusing on how the other person's input fits into their expert model, not for what that person's model is. In a situation, they focus on what they see are the relevant variables. What doesn't match is discarded, force-fit into something they know, or ignored. And because this Ti user has a lot of experience with their favored area, their analysis from that point on is very likely correct, at least in their mind. The process is self-reinforcing. Thus, they can get stuck and not see what they're missing, particularly when a base assumption is off.

Overall, these Ti users are confident. They are hard to intimidate, particularly when they focus on understanding how power dynamics work between people. They also easily resist a lot of impulsive group think and mental missteps that easily mislead others. They can respond quickly to answer a problem, and often do so with a firm voice and solid body language. Thus, they are often successful, at least as they define success to be.

Holistic/Yin Ti – The Systemist

Systemist Ti takes a holistic approach. These Ti users talk about taking different points of view, shifting their approach or perspective, using multiple models, finding patterns in chaos, and so on. So they're not married to just one model on the world. Rather, they notice interactions around them—this, that, and those other things—and they pick up on likely significant factors. They can walk through the woods, so-to-speak, and find themselves analyzing things in five different ways.

These Ti users have a fluid approach. They may say, "Here are a few relevant models we can look at to clarify and gain understanding." They refer to broad themes over rigid definitions. And they very much notice how things shift, scale, or develop. Among human beings, for example, there is the individual psychological system, the family system, and the tribe and nation systems. Holistic Ti is comfortable holding different models around these and analyzing how they're all interconnected without trying to force fit everything into a favorite model. The way they apply principles also tends to be organic. They invite discussion, and along the way, they may notice a new point they had not considered, and they are willing to set aside an existing viewpoint for a moment to try on that new point. Thus, unlike analytic Ti users, they don't come off as insulting. Well, they may accidentally—at times anyone can. But because they are more open, people feel more interested and welcome. Finally, this approach fosters a bit of creativity, though it can take time for an innovation to bear fruit.

When they're less mature, holistic Ti users can be really scattered with no clear expertise, much less goals. There is only a weak inner push to success. They may allow themselves to be carried off in whatever direction the rivers of life take them with a bunch of ideas floating around.

Maybe they dig into various ideas here and there—first one thing, then another. And because analytic vs. holistic is about development, any Ti user may fall into this space over time, and if they use this space to actively explore, experiment, and educate themselves, they can really grow in their expertise and creativity.

Sorting Flavors of Ti

The contrast of Ti flavors is particularly fascinating. I remember sitting at a lunch table in 1996 with David Keirsey Sr. who wrote "Please Understand Me" with Marilyn Bates. Linda Berens was also there, as she had organized the event. Both have INTP preferences. David Keirsey exemplified analytic Ti while Linda Berens exemplified holistic Ti. And it was odd, because David Keirsey espoused a philosophy around personality that is a holistic philosophy, but he himself was not holistic, at least not that I detected. Admittedly, that was the only time I met him. But there definitely was a contrast. At some point, we've all seen the differences between these two versions of Ti.

The two flavors respond to stress differently. Analytic Ti tends to use caustic humor and argue when feeling threatened or not taken seriously. They will be quick to reply with rhetorical tricks, change the goal-posts of an argument, and so on to maintain a sense of superiority. In particular, a reflex kicks in: until a foreign idea is validated on their terms, it is harshly judged as false. Everything can become a game for them. In contrast, holistic Ti users tend to disintegrate under stress. They are already juggling many different models, definitions, ideas, and so on. It's a messy web. Then when stressed, they might get clumsy, cry profusely, ramble, retreat in silence, suffer brain fog, or otherwise temporarily fall apart.

Like all the functions, Ti is a way to construct and maintain ego. For both variants, when they mature, they find a balance between confident expertise in their domain and humility in the face of everything else that they don't really know, including other approaches to their own domain. This brings wisdom and a strength of character. The person can step forward and think, "I truly am an expert in this area here, and I am also open-minded and willing to learn." For analytic Ti, the trick is to keep questioning their underlying paradigm, and for holistic Ti, it is to locate and work with one.

Extraverted Feeling (Fe)

Extraverted Feeling (Fe) is often portrayed one way, especially in type literature. In contrast, people who report Fe preferences often don't behave so stereotypically. In fact, they may easily behave in the opposite way. Specifically, the idealized Fe user is a paragon of empathy, friendliness, and self-effacing support. But they aren't necessarily like that. Firstly, someone who knows how to be super agreeable—just lovely, in fact—also knows how to be nasty, even cruel. That's no surprise. Every function has a dark use. The main point is that, yes, Fe users can be compliant, but they can also be strong, dominant leaders. So what's going on? The answer is analytic (yang) versus holistic (yin) versions of Fe.

Analytic/Yang Fe – The Shepherd

This is an active, focused, fixed, analytic version of Fe—life's Shepherds. They're that person—especially if it's their dominant function—who radiates an aura or field of needs and values, their own or society's as they define them. And they announce those. They voice those given suitable opportunities, and they prescribe those values. That is, when they notice people who are not going with the vibe, the value, they will do their best to corral those outliers and encourage them to join the group, to behave according to some standard of values and socially relevant behaviors, for their own and everyone's good.

When these Fe user see problems in a relationship, they take an active role. They easily speak diplomatic language, as in, "Let's sit down and talk with each other, shall we." And underlying this is a desire to fix the relationship, and maybe "heal" the person, based in a matrix of needs and values that feels very rational to them. Likely, they'll genuinely strive to find a win-win result. But the fact is that they hold certain values, and the other person needs to understand and honor those.

These Fe users can be really inspiring orators and shepherds in any kind of environment. In an organization, they will help everyone be aware of the organization's values and to get in sync (for or against!) as best they can. A church pastor is an obvious example. The extreme is cult-like. Mostly, they're inspiring, advising, corralling, and shepherding. Of course, there will be some black sheep around who don't want to be brought into the pen. This is where maturity versus one-sidedness comes in.

Ultimately, there's an underlying assumption or drive that if everyone joins arms in mutual agreement, consideration, and cooperation—aligning and honoring values and behavior—then any and all problems can be solved. Along the way, to help make this happen, they willingly make sacrifices. They can make huge personal sacrifices, and they ask—or at least hope—that others sacrifice too.

Holistic/Yin Fe – The Host

The holistic Fe user is like a friendly B&B host. The person goes around tending to others' needs. They are particularly empathic, feeling what others are feeling, and at the same time they are also highly sensitive to the nuances of social interactions, the meanings and possible impact of their words. So they tend to tread lightly and not push or embarrass others. Alas, to no surprise, at the end of the day or after twenty years, they may lament that they didn't get many of their own needs met.

Like analytic Fe, holistic Fe can be self-sacrificing, but that tends to be in many small ways rather than in one big way. Imagine all the little sacrifices they make daily as a coworker, friend, parent, spouse, and so on. In these cases, we may call them a caretaker or host (or hostess), and they're "holding space" as well as hosting in a space. Holding space generally means being present, attentive but not interfering, ready to help if asked. Imagine living a whole life holding space for others. Holding space can also mean you don't need to do much for yourself. The years go by, and helping others is an excuse to not step up to one's own potential and be more active. So let's say that at its best, yin Fe is hosting a space for a time.

Let's touch on sensitivity again. Holistic Fe is alert to nuances of social approval. Someone says superficially nice. Was that genuine, an underhanded compliment, or perhaps a joke? And has someone remembered an important day, such as an anniversary? Or kept in mind a small detail about one's life, knowing you are sensitive to it, even though other people normally wouldn't be? Unlike analytic Fe, which foments one big drama, holistic Fe can find itself caught up in numerous tiny dramas.

Sorting Flavors of Fe

These two sides tend to look a bit different from the outside. The more assertive Fe has a right way for everyone to behave, socially and interpersonally, that can be a bit imposing. In contrast, yin Fe is more accepting. And note the words: "imposing" versus "accepting".

When it comes to understanding Fe, the social justice movement is a great example. For those who prefer Fe—in particular, for ESFJ and ENFJ—analytic Fe is about getting people in line with the appropriate language, behavior, and values. They "go big". They may say, "Excuse little ol' us for imposing on everyone but...." while coming across as autocratic. In contrast, holistic Fe is so sensitive to other's different needs and viewpoints, that they shift to allow space and adapt in various situations, making allowances in a very democratic way. They "stay local". And remember, everyone does some measure of Fe, more or less consciously, so this range of behaviors applies to anyone! And of course, social justice is simply one example. There are Fe users in all other corners of the political landscape.

Analytic versus holistic Fe is not about strong-and-hard versus weak-and-soft. Usually, holistic Fe is not just some weakling who accommodates whatever others want. That is a movie trope. Rather, they really enjoy their friendships and close relationships, nurturing those, and being a part of their community, their family, their friends, and their coworkers. They value harmony, and the joys that harmony brings over being right. In contrast, analytic Fe focuses on being right in terms of values and feelings and needs, and even when that Fe user feels, "I have the wrong value, I need to feel differently," it's still about figuring out what's right and sharing that.

Another tell-tale differentiator: Is an Fe user the same in every social situation, or does the person shift? Analytic Fe tends to remain the same in terms of values and behaviors. Their agenda is clear to all, and in general they are far more talkative, even taking the soapbox. They feel, if only everyone paid fuller attention to each other, then we could solve humanity's problems (so true!). In contrast, holistic Fe feels, for example, that "my granddaughter has these needs and I relate to her on her terms," and that other people in my life, like "my neighbor or my boss, have different values from me and that's okay." They ask, "how can we live in simple harmony even though we all have different values?"

Finally, analytic Fe can look a lot like Thinking. These folks have strong organizational skills, value reason, can offer detailed logic, and in general consciously experience Feeling on an intellectual or even academic level, rather than on an emotional or sense level like holistic Fe typically does. However, both versions are still Feeling. Remember: Fe is about both the tribe's values and also the tribe's logic.

Introverted Feeling (Fi)

Introverted Feeling (Fi) has two sides: analytic and holistic (aka yang and yin). This duality helps resolve a paradox among Fi users. It's as if there's one set of Fi users who have strong likes and dislikes, and who seem to really know themselves and focus on being congruent with that knowing. Then, in contrast, there's a second set of Fi users who come off as wishy-washy, as if they're continuously trying new avenues, and they have a vague or multi-faceted sense of identity. These two sides may actually appear in the same person over years, or days. Both flavors are part of the Fi experience.

Analytic/Yang Fi – The Questor

I call analytic, yang Fi the Questor because they're pursuing a particular, singular life quest or truth and their choices and habits are organized around that. Think of a missionary who has a very clear aim and set of values and beliefs. This Fi user can very much come off as—and even score as—a Thinking type, with firm, complex ideas, because they're applying analytical skills to further their moral clarity, to understand and thoroughly sort out their belief system, actions and feelings, with an aim to get everything congruent.

This yang Fi user constantly asks, "Are my actions, beliefs, feelings, relationships, habits, and so on all consistent, regardless of what kind of situation I'm in?" In every circumstance, these people are pretty much the same, with predictable beliefs and expressions, pursuing their quest. They have a consistent personal identity. Hopefully, they're also inevitably listening to some kind of conscience. There may be an external reference like a holy book or a guru, but it comes back to an internal belief system and a conscience and they're following that as best they can.

Now keep in mind, we are all messy, organic human beings and we don't have Platonic moral perfection. So this person has to somehow contain their "sin". The person is often dealing with their failings, grappling with how to contain their mistakes and misalignments.

By now, you might get the impression that analytic Fi is always ideological in nature, but that isn't necessarily so. It's simply a drive, a focus on congruence, and it's active toward a singular quest. That quest could be religious or political. Or it could be artistic, athletic or for business or such. Think of an ISFP who is utterly devoted to a singular practice: music. He or she will say, "It is all about the music" even though fame, fun, money, and travel are a part of the experience too. They believe— maybe fear—that their music will be fake and they will fail if they are not dedicated to a raw honesty.

Overall, yang Fi can come off as highly dedicated, with a firm voice, and fairly black-and-white and even judgmental, even as these folks are actually capable of a lot of analytical complexity.

Holistic/Yin Fi – The Romantic

Ah, the romantic Fi user. This person is particularly existential. He or she lives a life of deep and quiet feeling, full of little leaps and small stories or moving moments, each with its own beauty or sorrow. And nothing is forced. Ideally, everything flows.

With holistic Fi, there are many voices and many feelings that come up every day, many times a day. And rather than trying to push those to align, this person says, "I'm just going to be, with all of these, and whatever emerges from that is what emerges and that is who I am." So there are no big decisions about identity. Rather, "I am the result of all of my processes going on."

Many times this person has multiple soft quests and subtly diverse identities, even within one relationship. Every interaction brings out the so-and-so part of them. So the person is open to connect with whatever comes up and express it in some way. Doing so then evokes a new set of feelings and maybe energizes a goal in this-or-that direction. And then there is yet another relationship that brings out different feelings, and they make room for those too. So there's room for inconsistencies on the outside and on the inside, and they let everything mix around. And that is their identity. You can ask them something like, "What do you believe?" or "Who are you?" Probably the best they can do is tell you a story or joke or invite you on a little adventure with them because there is no one thing they can point to, no one word or idea or system. Indeed, they are non-extremists.

Alas, this Fi user can be a bit wishy-washy. They behave one way for a while in a relationship or on the job and then all of a sudden they move in a different direction and say, "Now I just feel differently." Or, "I love it, and yet I also hate it." Also, they often feel they have quite a hard time being heard.

Sorting Flavors of Fi

To sum up, there are yang and yin versions of Fi. The analytic, yang version is more righteous, and it recruits the brain's willpower to be focused and aligned. In contrast, the holistic, yin version is receptive, diffuse and yielding—it is not one character but many different characters, and it's not just an ocean, but many places and many feelings and many relationships.

We can see the difference in storytelling. The yin Fi user can be a fine novelist, where every character can be their own unique person, including being evil. This holistic Fi does not have so much of a problem with evil, conceptually speaking. They may even say, "Well, what exactly is evil anyway? Let's explore that." Whereas the Questor, the analytic Fi user is going to have a harder time at this task. If you ask them to write a short story, they really want the characters to only do things that they feel are exemplary. Or if a character "breaks bad" it's to serve a narrative purpose, as in, "See what happens when you're like this!"

By the way, remember that everyone uses Fi in some way. For people who don't prefer Fi, it can come up as a deeply entrenched belief system or quest. Consider an ESTJ who has a strong religious faith that never waivers. Always, at the end of the day, amid all of their efficient decisions, everything for them needs to align morally. And because they have a "baby" Fi, this will easily come off as dogmatic, unrealistic, judgmental, and perhaps bullying. In contrast, another ESTJ who has yin Fi can be notably diplomatic. We might even wonder if ESTJ is a best-fit type. Maybe they're ISTJ or a Feeling type? No. Their use of Fi is simply more quiet, and is about a sustainable, subtle, sophisticated harmony. This ESTJ can make a good diplomat, for example, because he or she can easily remain objective and also allow for differences. He or she can be objectively effective even if that means staying friendly with their nation's enemies. On the minus side, a baby yin Fi can also end up morally compromised.

It's a funny thing that Fi, similar to Ni, is about opposites. For Ni, thesis and antithesis can lead to synthesis. For Fi, yin and yang – as in the Daoist religious symbol – are wrapped up in each other, and each contains an element of the other. So for the Fi user, the idea of analytic and holistic can easily make sense, though that doesn't necessarily make balancing them any easier!

What Now?

Now that you've explored the *yin* and *yang* of type:
1. Where are you the most *yang* and the most *yin* in your life (whether favorite processes or not)?
2. Who might you be idealizing or demonizing based on their type expression?
3. How might you diversity your use of your favorite processes for more balance and success in life?

9

Fulfill
Your
Aspirations

Our Hidden Aspirations

As you likely remember from school, a circle has 360 degrees. And we turn around "360" when something really big happens in life. This number, 360, is also the page you can turn to in this book to look again, and again, for ways to make the most of your type's hidden aspirations, to make your dreams come true.

This chapter is all about one big idea: synergy. Our lives are filled with examples all around us of this big idea. Imagine a seed, plus soil and rain; together a tree is born. Similarly, when the two sexes come together, a brand new human life is possible. Or take chemistry: On their own, oxygen and hydrogen are dangerous flammable gasses at room temperature, but when we combine them gently, they turn into something amazing: liquid water. The same can go for opposing groups of people, or opposing teams. It takes two football teams to really entertain a crowd, and it takes two leaders with integrity to transcend hostilities between them and perhaps even birth something new with cooperation.

You surely get the idea by now. Jung had a word for this magical union of opposing forces: alchemy. He observed the tension and resolution of opposing forces within us is what gives rise to healing, growth, and wisdom. Let's discover which alchemical formulas work to bring the magic of alchemy into your life.

This chapter is organized like a play, in five acts:
1. Getting started with alchemy.
2. See all in one place the common hidden aspirations for each type.
3. Learn about the "spine of the personality", how seemingly-opposite functions can synergize with each other to combine into something new and better.
4. Read in depth seven key suggestions for your type.
5. Write down an action plan.

Remember "What's at Stake?" at the start of the book (page 12)? Now is a good time to review what you brainstormed and wrote down there. Or, take a moment to consider a big issue in your life. Then let's get started...

Aspirational Se (mainly INTJ and INFJ)

Yearn to live freely in the present with tangible and immediate experiences. Enjoy trips into nature. Channel abstract visions into tangible projects or actionable plans. Use insights for personal and interpersonal improvement. Use foresight to predict trends and create products and services for these trends. Stimulate inner growth through rich sensory experiences such as travel. Express deep insights about the human experience through sensory mediums like art, dance, music, writing, or yoga. Can get derailed by concrete details or entertaining pleasures.

Aspirational Si (mainly ENTP and ENFP)

Yearn for stability. Find grounding and a sense of safety in past experiences, traditions, and the familiar. Skilled at revitalizing old ideas with new applications, and drawn to reimagine or expand upon established ideas with inventive twists. Ideally, they come to respect proven methods, historical context, and learned lessons. At their best, they acknowledge the wisdom of the past, and existing methods and institutions, as they balance new ideas with universal themes that speak to society at large and the timeless human experience. Can get overly nostalgic or stuck in poor habits.

Aspirational Ne (mainly ISTJ and ISFJ)

Yearn for an exciting life of adventure. Enjoy "risk taking" or letting loose in a safe, set environment such as an amusement park or casino. Willing to try a new idea if it links to the past, an authority figure, or the need is pressing. Can connect the dots and come up with a surprising solution given time to do thorough research. Enjoy cute arts and crafts and small-time entrepreneurial ventures (e.g. lemonade stand). Will lighten the moment with PG humor. Can worry excessively about "what if...", and on rare occasions, may make a big rash decision that's far out of character.

Aspirational Ni (mainly ESTP and ESFP)

Yearn to experience the ultimate answer of life. Can quickly take action based on a realization. Like to sell products and services for personal betterment. Enjoy performing using evocative costumes and imagery. Open to body-mind practices like yoga to connect to their inner spirit. Often foresee the next move in a game or venture, but must learn to foresee the wider consequences of their actions, develop long-term strategy, and hold to a purposeful vision. Fascinated by the mystical and supernatural. Can sometimes get wild or feel things are crazy.

Aspirational Te (mainly ISFP and INFP)

Yearn to channel their deeply felt emotions and convictions into a productive life. Establish a nonprofit, design a set of tools or methods or a platform, follow a strict training regime, or manage an effective business venture—aims that align with their values. Enjoy producing creative compositions (art, music, etc.) to put out in the world. Love to see objective validation, such as scientific measures. Harbor a hidden drive for effective organization, objective structure, and impactful execution. Can occasionally become overly critical, fixated on success metrics, or subtly controlling.

Aspirational Ti (mainly ESFJ and ENFJ)

Yearn for a consistent, universal philosophy underlying life's squabbles and troubles. Try to see an issue from multiple angles and from voices of all involved in order to find equitable solutions. Drawn to use analytical rigor and a logical framework that can help people live better. Willing to specialize deeply to do that. Generally, seek to analyze situations logically, draw boundaries, and balance their empathy and caregiving with objective outcomes. Tend to admire intellect, scholarship, and deep thinking. May over-apply leverage to move themselves up in social systems.

Aspirational Fe (mainly ISTP and INTP)

Yearn to be useful to others and society. Will apply a model, philosophy, set of techniques, or a scientific principle to deal with human behavior. Tend to remain calm and independent when most others fall prey to emotions or group-think. Stay informed about and support social policy causes, often from the sidelines. Uncomfortable in the spotlight. At their best, apply their problem solving skills to aid people, or at least fix things that matter to others. Like to be in a network of fellow experts. Can latch on to someone in a sticky way as an idealized companion.

Aspirational Fi (mainly ESTJ and ENTJ)

Yearn to improve the human condition on a mass scale by the power of efficient organization. Will quickly gather facts, present logical arguments, and organize people and resources for a good cause. Can lead a moral crusade. Secretly really enjoy quiet relaxation. Benefit from self-reflection such as journaling. Want to help people get to know their unique potential and develop into exemplary individuals. Must practice patience. Find that hardship breeds character. Need a good cry in private on rare occasion. Can be childish emotionally, or hold simplistic black-or-white judgments.

How Opposites Work Together

First, let's review how the functions stack: Once we know our first and second favorite functions, we can infer the rest of the stack. This is the genius of Jung's framework. It's a map to understand how the whole psyche works dynamically, "under the hood", as a system. As described in Chapter 2 (page 20), research strongly supports this framework. The figure here illustrates how the functions work together for ENTJ using the metaphor of the body.

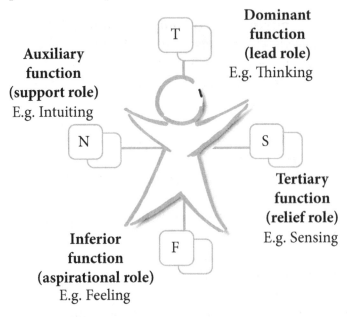

Auxiliary function (support role) E.g. Intuiting

Dominant function (lead role) E.g. Thinking

Tertiary function (relief role) E.g. Sensing

Inferior function (aspirational role) E.g. Feeling

In the figure, the *dominant* function sits at the head. Using it, we figure out what to do and play a lead role like an army general. In contrast, the *inferior* function is our feet. We often need our feet to implement our head's desires, though we may not give them much credit day-to-day as we use our legs unconsciously. Yet their use can save us. Together, in the words of Dr. John Beebe, these two form the "spine" of the personality. Meanwhile, our preferred hand (on the left here) plays an *auxiliary* or support role. We can do a lot with one hand, and we truly benefit by using the other hand, our *tertiary* function, to play a back-up role. Imagine how many daily tasks benefit from two hands. Altogether, a person cannot get much done unless the whole system coordinates in a swift and beautiful way. Jung described a technique, Active Imagination, to help people better integrate their functions.

Alchemy: The Intersection of Opposites

The Venn diagram below is a simple way to look at synergy. There are two opposing circles, black and white, and where they overlap, ideally shown in color, symbolizes their commonalities and also a fundamental change from black-and-white to color.

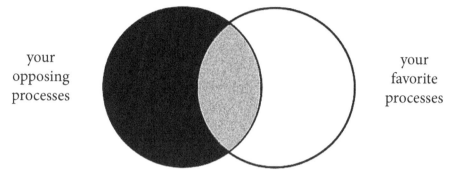

your
opposing
processes

your
favorite
processes

Similarly, when we bring together our dominant and inferior functions—our head and feet, and top and bottom of our stack—or we bring together our left and right hands, or the middle members of our stack, then the result is a fundamental change from simple to complex, from either-or to color.

In the next section, take a look at the pages for your type. There you will find examples and suggestions for what synergy can look like.

From Four to All Eight Processes

There are more than the 4 functions. Notice in the figure that behind each box is a second, shaded box, and in total there are eight boxes, just as there are eight cognitive processes. In fact, we can express all eight processes, not just our favorites or top four, though the later four are often called "shadow functions". They tend to appear only in a defensive way or in times of great stress or change, as described by Jungian analyst Dr. John Beebe. The entirety of this framework is beyond the scope of this book, but it is a fascinating journey to take, to explore how all eight play out in the pattern of your personality. If you want to know more, *The Magic Diamond* is a good place to start. Or you might look at *8 Keys to Self-Leadership*, which focuses on skill building for all eight processes.

Aspirational Se
(for **INTJ** and **INFJ**, and also ENTJ and ENFJ)

Embracing the Moment with Active Adapting

For those who naturally lean towards the depths of introverted Intuiting (Ni), the world is often a tapestry of abstract concepts, future possibilities, and profound insights. However, there's an untapped reservoir of potential waiting to be discovered in the opposite realm: the vibrant, immediate world of extraverted Sensing (Se). By integrating Se into your life, you can enrich your intuitive insights and experience the world in a more immediate and tangible way.

Active Adapting: The Power of Living Now

Begin by relaxing into the sensual details of the present. While Ni often pulls you towards future possibilities and abstract concepts, Se beckons you to notice the sensory data right in front of you. It's the aroma of your morning coffee, the texture of your favorite book, or the vibrant colors of a sunset. By actively tuning in to the present, you become more aware of your surroundings and also develop a trust in your gut instincts, allowing you to take actions that are relevant to the moment.

As you advance in this journey, you might find yourself yearning for tangible experiences. This could manifest as a spontaneous trip into nature, channeling your abstract visions into concrete projects, or even using your insights for personal growth. Imagine the thrill of predicting a trend and then creating a product or service that caters to it. Or, consider the fulfillment of expressing your deep insights about the human experience through sensory mediums like art, dance, or music. Ideally, set aside a special space and dedicate time to enjoy these freely.

However, a word of caution: while Se can be exhilarating, it's essential not to get derailed by its allure. It's easy to become fixated on implementing details, take unncessary risks, or get lost in hedonistic pleasures. Consider a Keen Foreseer scientist who imagines a groundbreaking device but becomes so engrossed in its creation that she misses life's small joys. So remember to balance your willful drive with an openness to life's side-treks, exploring opportunities, pitfalls, and pleasures.

Strategy Checklist to Manifest
Your Energy & Purpose with Se

1) Sensory Awareness: Make it a habit to stop and genuinely experience your environment. Smell the flowers, feel the texture of your old clothes, and if something feels off, change it. It's about being present and reactive to your immediate surroundings.

2) Seek Tangible Experiences: Engage in activities that provide raw, undigested experiences. These experiences become fodder for your unconscious, enriching your intuitive insights.

3) Learning Through Experience: Whether it's a virtual class, an outdoor adventure, or a guided group activity, immerse yourself in learning experiences that offer tangible insights. Imagine setting up a live group exercise, helping others gain insights, and in the process, enriching your own understanding.

4) Manifesting Visions: Look inward, envision a transformative idea, and then take concrete steps to realize it. Dream of humanity's journey into space? Start by designing that spaceship, even if it takes years. It's about making the abstract tangible.

5) Physical Engagement: Find an activity to align your body, mind, and environment. It might be a dance class, trail run, or yoga. When these elements merge, you'll often find a renewed sense of energy and joy.

6) Enhancing Creativity: Consider tools like nootropics or light-and-sound machines to elevate your thinking and creativity.

7) Physical Touchstones: Gather items that inspire you, be it a totem, a piece of art, or any sensory-rich object. Let them be a constant reminder and motivator to fulfill your life's dreams.

While the world of Ni is profound and insightful, integrating Se can offer a richness of experience that's unparalleled. It's about merging the abstract with the tangible, the future with the present, and in the process, discovering a more holistic way of experiencing life. Embrace Se, and watch your intuitive insights become even more profound and practical.

Aspirational Si
(for **ENTP** and **ENFP**, and also INTP and INFP)

Finding Comfort in Cautious Protecting

For those who naturally gravitate towards the expansive world of extraverted Intuiting (Ne), life is a kaleidoscope of possibilities, novel ideas, and ever-changing scenarios. However, there's a grounding force waiting to be harnessed in the opposite realm: the stabilizing, reliable world of introverted Sensing (Si). By integrating Si into your life, you can find a balance between the thrill of the new and the comfort of the familiar, enhancing both your creativity and your sense of security.

Cautious Protecting: The Power of Fine Habits

Begin by recalling facts or experiences from your past. Review some favorite memories! While Ne propels you towards new horizons, Si invites you to reflect on past experiences, grounding you in what is known and reliable. You might then compare what's happening now to what happened before, based on your past experiences and learned lessons. This lights the way for where improvements can be made or where more potential lies.

As you delve deeper into this journey, you might find yourself yearning for stability and safety in traditions and the familiar. Having a reliable "home base" can be a great way to free yourself to do creative activities without constantly worry about logistics. Similarly, stability needn't stifle your creativity; instead, it's about revitalizing old ideas with inventive twists. Imagine drawing from the wisdom of the past, respecting proven methods, and balancing them with fresh, innovative concepts. This balance ensures that your ideas resonate with universal themes, speaking to both the timeless human experience and the ever-evolving present.

However, a word of caution: while Si offers comfort, it's essential not to become overly nostalgic or entrenched in habits that no longer serve you. It's more about upping your standards. Imagine a Excited Brainstormer chef who loves experimenting with diverse cuisines. By raising his standards and drawing from past successes, he can refine his brand and appeal to a broader audience without losing his innovative edge.

1) Pattern Recognition: Relate current situations to images or memories from the past. Instead of just imagining alternative scenarios, draw upon past experiences to see patterns, allowing for quicker learning from mistakes.

2) Research with Respect: When exploring a theoretical problem or creating something new, delve into the background. Understand the pioneers in the field, their ideas, and the historical context. This research can enrich your current endeavors, be it a book, film, or experiment.

3) Embrace Support: Lean on supportive institutions and professionals to handle the details, allowing you to soar in the world of ideas. Let a skilled assistant manage logistics or financial intricacies, freeing you to focus on the bigger picture.

4) Humor and Standards: Use humor to shed light on outdated practices. It's a way to challenge the status quo while leaving room for people to feel relaxed enough to reconsider their thinking.

5) Establish New Traditions: Dream up innovative ways to do things and then set them as new traditions or standards. It's about merging the novel with the familiar.

6) Refinement and Cultivation: After accumulating a plethora of experiences, distill the most refined and comforting ones into habits or practices. It's about cherishing the best of both worlds.

7) Safe Spaces: Find places or moments where you can reflect on the unconscious impacts of your early years and other significant moments. These spaces offer healing and understanding.

While the world of Ne is exhilarating and ever-changing, integrating Si provides a grounding force, enhancing both creativity and stability. It's about cherishing the thrill of the new while respecting the wisdom of the old, creating a harmonious dance between exploration and tradition. Embrace Si, and watch your ideas become even more impactful and resonant.

Aspirational Ne
(for **ISTJ** and **ISFJ**, and also ESTJ and ESFJ)

Broadening Horizons with Excited Brainstorming

For those who naturally resonate with the comforting realm of introverted Sensing (Si), life is often about cherishing traditions, recalling past experiences, and finding stability in the known. However, there's a world of endless possibilities and imaginative potential waiting in the opposite realm: the dynamic, pattern-seeking world of extraverted Intuiting (Ne). By integrating Ne into your life, you can enrich your understanding of the world, infusing your cherished traditions with humor, fresh insights, and exciting possibilities.

Excited Brainstorming: The Power of Open Thinking

Begin by tuning in to events as they emerge around you. What patterns or behaviors do you notice? How are things connecting? While Si grounds you in past experiences and tangible data, Ne invites you to explore imaginative possibilities, connect seemingly unrelated dots, and even shift a situation. It's about seeing the bigger picture, understanding underlying themes, and being open to new ideas and perspectives.

As you continue on this journey, you may find yourself yearning for adventures, even if they're within controlled environments like amusement parks or casinos. It's about safely stepping out of your comfort zone, trying new ideas that still fit with something trusted. Consider diving into books, films, concerts, or museums to safely venture into these. For example, virtual reality or puzzle-like escape rooms offer immersive experiences that can provide new perspectives. Or, living or studying abroad can be a transformative adventure, offering insights into different cultures and broadening your understanding of universal human traits. The world is a big, diverse place to keep learning and growing.

In time, your mind will expand. Imagine connecting the dots after thorough research and surprising yourself with a novel solution, or lightening the moment with some wholesome humor. However, it's essential to strike a balance and not get overwhelmed by the endless "what if..." scenarios, or make rash decisions that are out of character.

Strategy Checklist to Loosen
Your Energy & Purpose with Ne

1) Linking Past and Future: Draw upon your wealth of past experiences to discover patterns and possibilities. For instance, delve deep into the history of a place to unravel mysteries about your lineage.

2) Positive Possibilities: In uncertain situations, entertain positive outcomes to reassure yourself and others, providing a beacon of hope.

3) Traditions and Anecdotes: Use quirky traditions or whimsical stories to convey values and standards to the next generation, blending the old with the new.

4) Imagination and Fantasy: Infuse your routines and relationships with a touch of imagination or humor. Whether it's reading mystery novels to unwind or leaving quirky love notes for a loved one, let your creative side shine.

5) Stable Base for Adventures: Establish a secure base, be it a home or a routine, from which you can explore new horizons, try out hobbies, or even indulge in a bit of risk-taking such as visiting a casino or racetrack, without jeopardizing your core stability. As you consider this, remember to actually schedule it on your calendar, allowing yourself the time try it.

6) Mastery and Fun: Become so proficient in a craft or subject that you can playfully experiment with it. Like a jazz musician who, after rigorous practice, can spontaneously riff with his band. While this might sound like it would take years, consider there are specific techniques, such as learning the four key chords on a piano or guitar, to play many fun songs.

7) Coping with Surprises: Equip yourself with tricks to handle unexpected events, or indulge in daydreams and jokes to alleviate stress.

While the world of Si offers comfort and stability, integrating Ne can provide fresh perspectives, adding enjoyment and a broader understanding of the world. It's about cherishing the known while embracing the new, creating a harmonious blend of tradition and flexibility. Embrace Ne, and watch your world expand with new possibilities and ideas.

Aspirational Ni
(for **ESTP** and **ESFP**, and also ISTP and ISFP)

Discovering Depth with Keen Foreseeing

For those who naturally resonate with the vibrant and immediate world of extraverted Sensing (Se), life is often about immersing in the present moment, experiencing the tangible, and reacting to the environment. However, there's a profound depth and transformative potential waiting in the opposite realm: the introspective, visionary world of introverted Intuiting (Ni). By integrating Ni into your life, you can enrich your sensory experiences with deeper insights, foresight, and a broader perspective on life's mysteries.

Keen Foreseeing: The Power of Deep Insight

Begin by tuning into those "aha!" moments of realization. While Se draws you to the external world and its sensory delights, Ni beckons you to delve deeper, seeking greater awareness and transformative insights. It's about understanding the underlying patterns, foreseeing potential outcomes, and aligning with a purposeful vision.

As you journey deeper into the realm of Ni, you might find yourself yearning for answers to life's ultimate questions. Whether it's through selling products for personal betterment, evocative performances, or body-mind practices like yoga, Ni offers a path to connect with the inner spirit and the mysteries of existence. It's about balancing the thrill of the present with a deeper understanding of life's purpose and potential. However, a word of caution: while Ni offers profound insights, it's essential not to get lost in its depths or feel overwhelmed by its intensity. It's about finding a balance between the sensory experiences of Se and the introspective insights of Ni, ensuring a harmonious dance between the tangible and the abstract.

There's more to life than meets the eye. Much is invisible. Whether it's through music, nature, spiritual practices, or even extreme sports, Ni offers a gateway to explore deeper realms of meaning and connection. Consider engaging in activities that challenge your perceptions, stimulate your unconscious, and open you up to life's profound mysteries.

1) Anticipate the Future: Stay hyper-tuned to your environment, anticipating what's coming next. For instance, immerse yourself in industry news to catch the next wave of innovation.

2) Transformative Engagement: Engage others in activities that help them discover their potential. Imagine drawing a reserved individual onto the dance floor, unveiling their inner dancer.

3) Visionary Action: Shape your current situation based on your envisioned outcome. Imagine a sculptor who can "see" the final statue within a marble block and chisels away to reveal it.

4) Extreme Experiences: Engage in extreme activities like mountain climbing, or in fetish play, trance music, ice baths, fire-walking, entheogens (psychedelic plants) or the like to tap into hidden realms of ultimate meaning.

5) Dare to be Different: Continuously take actions aligned with a singular goal, even if it means standing out. An aspiring musician, for instance, might wear unique, even outlandish costumes to express an archetypal self.

6) Express Your Inner Artist: Dive into artistic pursuits, be it drawing, painting, or woodworking, to express your innermost dreams, demons, and insights.

7) Mindful Improvement: Study how your mind works and find ways to improve yourself. In everyday activities, when you notice a behavior doesn't work for you, try to shift or improve it. Or during physical activity, find a way to "tune" your mind to push your performance.

While the world of Se offers exhilarating sensory experiences, integrating Ni provides depth, foresight, and a broader perspective on life's mysteries. It's about cherishing the present moment while seeking deeper insights and transformative visions. Embrace Ni, and watch your sensory experiences become enriched with profound depth and meaning.

Aspirational Te
(for **ISFP** and **INFP**, and also ESFP and ENFP)

Harnessing Structure with Timely Building

For those who naturally resonate with the introspective realm of introverted Feeling (Fi), life is often about deeply felt emotions, personal values, and authentic self-expression. However, there's a world of structure, efficiency, and evidence-based reasoning waiting in the opposite realm: the pragmatic, results-driven world of extraverted Thinking (Te). By integrating Te into your life, you can channel your convictions and emotions into productive endeavors, ensuring that your deeply-held values manifest in tangible, impactful ways.

Timely Building: The Power of Timely Efficiency

Begin by doing your best to layout and follow some steps and timetables. While Fi draws you inward, focusing on personal beliefs and feelings, Te invites you to create structure, reason with evidence, and implement complex plans. It's about taking those strong convictions and channeling them into actionable steps that align with your values.

As you journey deeper into the realm of Te, you might find yourself yearning to see your emotions and convictions take shape in the external world. Whether it's establishing a nonprofit, designing tools, or managing a business venture, Te offers the framework to ensure your aims align with your values. Imagine producing creative compositions and seeing them validated through objective measures, or harboring a drive for effective organization and impactful execution.

However, a word of caution: while Te offers structure and efficiency, it's essential not to become overly critical or fixated solely on success metrics. And Te is about more than toughening up. It's about finding a balance between personal values and objective reasoning, ensuring that your actions are both authentic and effective.

You can make a substansive, observable difference! By channeling your Fi through Te, you can create a structured path that aligns with your values while ensuring efficiency and impact.

Strategy Checklist to Structure
Your Energy & Purpose with Te

1) Structured Beliefs: Structure your life around your beliefs, standing firm on what's important. For instance, if you value environmental sustainability, structure your life and habits to reflect that commitment.

2) Objective Evidence: Support your beliefs with evidence and empirical reasoning. If you believe in the unique gifts each individual brings, construct metrics or gather data to validate these beliefs.

3) Time Management: Use time management skills to ensure you follow through on commitments and projects that align with your values.

4) Personal Space Efficiency: Maintain a clean and organized personal space, not just for efficiency but also because it resonates with your inner sense of order.

5) Solicit Feedback: Actively gather data and feedback to test the validity of your reasoning. This objective approach can offer insights and help refine your beliefs and actions. Deliberately gather data and solicit feedback to test the validity of your reasoning. For example, after taking part in an anonymous 360 feedback, you might discover that 75% of colleagues rate an ongoing "problem" is due to some other cause than being your boss's fault.

6) Stay Motivated: Connect with your beliefs, and perhaps others' belief in you, to motivate yourself to tackle challenges and achieve what once seemed impossible.

7) Smart Business Practices: Consider practices like reducing spending and saving for future projects, ensuring that your actions align with your long-term vision and values.

While the world of Fi offers depth and introspection, integrating Te offers a structure to channel those emotions and convictions into tangible results. It's about cherishing personal values while harnessing objective reasoning to make a meaningful impact. Embrace Te, and watch your core convictions manifest in structured, impactful ways.

Aspirational Ti
(for **ESFJ** and **ENFJ**, and also ISFJ and INFJ)

Deepening Understanding with Skillful Sleuthing

For those who naturally resonate with the empathetic and harmonious realm of extraverted Feeling (Fe), life is often about connecting with others, understanding their emotions, and nurturing social harmony. However, there's a world of analytical rigor, logical frameworks, and deep thinking waiting in the opposite realm: the precise, problem-solving world of introverted Thinking (Ti). By integrating Ti into your life, you can deepen your understanding, find equitable solutions, and balance your natural empathy with objective outcomes.

Skillful Sleuthing: The Power of Logical Frameworks

Begin by learning about definitions and philosophical principles, and making some effort to reorder your decisions and routine to fit those. While Fe draws you towards understanding and harmonizing emotions, Ti invites you to analyze problems using frameworks, finding angles or leverage points to solve them. It's about seeing the underlying logic, understanding the nuances, and applying analytical rigor to situations.

As you journey deeper into the realm of Ti, you might find yourself yearning for a singularly consistent, universal philosophy that underpins life's challenges. This can feel like a call to specialize in something of value to society, as a means to rigorously help others. Whatever you decide, the journey is about balancing your natural caregiving instincts with objective, logical outcomes, ensuring that your actions are both empathetic and effective. However, a word of caution: It is easy to over-apply a principle or idea. No "truth" fits all situations, and ideas can make sense logically but not actually work effectively in real life. Pay close attention when people push back against your ideas, and ask them what it is that they value.

In summary, there's a balance to be struck between understanding emotions and applying logical reasoning. By channeling your Fe through Ti, you can create a harmonious blend of empathy and analysis, ensuring that your actions resonate with both heart and mind.

1) *Guided Behavior*: Connect better with others by following guidelines about appropriate behavior. For example, you might follow principles of fair play or the Platinum Rule in all of your transactions with others.

2) *Diplomatic Leverage*: Identify leverage points in situations to help all parties achieve their needs in the most affirming and fair way possible.

3) *Leverage Social Contacts*: Use your extensive network to solve problems or connect with individuals beyond your immediate circle, ensuring that your actions are both inclusive and effective.

4) *Face-to-Face Engagement*: Work tirelessly with individuals, applying your expertise to shift their perspectives and empower them with knowledge. For example, you might tell people know about smarter principles of living such as how to manage their health, appearance, or study habits.

5) *Master Complex Disciplines*: Dive deep into a discipline, understanding its nuances and intricacies, to help others. Whether it's medicine, architecture, or another field, use your expertise to make a positive impact. For example, you might become a pediatric doctor to help sick children or an architect to create beautiful living spaces for others.

6) *Mediate with Objectivity*: When mediating disputes, observe from multiple angles, and help every side receive a fair hearing, ensuring that every party is heard and that decisions are made within a consistent logical framework.

7) *Engage in Complex Strategy*: Invest time in research and preparation, using legal or other maneuvers to achieve ethical outcomes.

While the world of Fe offers empathy and connection, integrating Ti provides a structured framework to analyze situations and find logical solutions. It's about cherishing human connections while harnessing logical reasoning to make a meaningful impact. Embrace Ti, and watch your empathetic insights deepen with analytical rigor and precision.

Aspirational Fe
(for **ISTP** and **INTP**, and also ESTP and ENTP)

Building Bridges with Friendly Hosting

For those who naturally resonate with the analytical, framework-driven realm of introverted Thinking (Ti), life often revolves around dissecting problems, understanding systems, and seeking precision. However, there's a world of interpersonal connection, empathy, and relationship-building waiting in the opposite realm: the social, values-driven world of extraverted Feeling (Fe). By integrating Fe into your life, you can ensure that your analytical insights are not only precise but also resonate with and help the people around you.

Friendly Hosting: The Power of Nurturing Trust

Begin by looking into others' needs and preferences, and honoring those when you can. While Ti drives you towards understanding the intricacies of problems, Fe invites you to connect with people, sharing values and, in the process of helping them with a problem, taking on some of their needs. Asking about preferences helps ensure that your solutions are accurate and also considerate of the human element.

As you journey deeper into the realm of Fe, you might find yourself yearning to be of service to others and society at large. Imagine applying your analytical models and techniques to human behavior, and keeping yourself informed about social causes, maybe supporting them, if even from the sidelines. Or consider, you can find ways to disseminate your ideas and expertise, such as on a forum, to aid people to fix things that matter to them. And bringing in Fe also often involves building a network of fellow experts. However, as you try more Fe in your life, a word of caution: Being nice, following the surface social rules, is fine. But eventually people notice a lack of authenticity or manipulation. Ideally, you find people who enjoy you for who you are.

There's a balance to be struck between analytical reasoning and interpersonal connection. By channeling your Ti through Fe, you can create a harmonious blend of precision and empathy, ensuring that your actions resonate with both logic and heart.

1) Practical Problem Solving: Show interest in others by solving practical problems for them. While the problem might be your primary focus, the act of helping is a gesture of care.

2) Leverage Behavioral Models: Use principles or models of human behavior to manage differences. For instance, a manager might rely on a team life cycle model—forming, norming, storming, and performing—to help her team flow more smoothly.

3) Nurture Peer Relationships: Build and maintain relationships with a collaborative network of respected peers. With multiple minds on a problem and mutual, and congenial openness to others' viewpoints, you can get help with whatever you are figuring out.

4) Personal Disclosure: Share personal experiences to add clarity and depth to discussions. For example, when helping someone figure out a problem with his child, you might share a relevant memory about your own childhood to add to the discussion.

5) Reasoned Adjustments: Use your analytical skills to make small adjustments that benefit others, maximizing positive impact with minimal interference and drama.

6) Communicate Ideas as Gifts: Consider sharing ideas and principles that you believe can benefit society—for example, for better fitness or financial success. Whether it's a life principle or a problem-solving technique, present it as a valuable contribution to others' well-being.

7) Temper Your Critiquing: Offer suggestions over corrections, and allow people time to digest what you are saying, obvious as it may be.

While the world of Ti offers analytical depth and precision, integrating Fe provides a touch of empathy and interpersonal connection. It's about cherishing logical reasoning while ensuring that every insight and solution is considerate of the human element. Embrace Fe, and watch your analytical insights deepen with warmth and connection.

Aspirational Fi
(for **ESTJ** and **ENTJ**, and also ISTJ and INTJ)

Discovering Authenticity with Quiet Crusading

For those who naturally resonate with the structured, objective realm of extraverted Thinking (Te), life often revolves around efficiency, organization, and evidence-based reasoning. However, there's a world of personal convictions and authentic self-expression waiting in the opposite realm: the introspective, values-driven world of introverted Feeling (Fi). By integrating Fi into your life, you can ensure that your actions and decisions are not only efficient but also resonate with your true self.

Quiet Crusading: The Power of Personal Conviction

Begin by reflecting on your convictions and finding ways to better live by your personal beliefs of what's important. While Te drives you towards structured reasoning and objective outcomes, Fi invites you to evaluate situations based on what aligns with your personal identity. It's about ensuring that your actions and decisions resonate with who you truly are.

As you delve deeper into the realm of Fi, you might find yourself yearning to improve the human condition on a broader scale, driven by efficient organization. Imagine gathering facts, presenting logical arguments, and organizing resources, all for a cause that deeply resonates with your personal beliefs. It's about leading a moral crusade of sorts, reflecting on your actions, and ensuring that they align with your values.

However, a word of caution: Reprioritizing doesn't just mean re-ranking the items on your to-do list. It means crossing out items or putting the list aside to relax into your natural self again. It can also mean checking those to-do items against your identity and beliefs. Who are you, and why are you doing all this? What undisclosed beliefs are influencing your thinking? And can you simplify those?

There's a balance to be struck between objective reasoning and personal convictions. By checking use of Te with Fi, you can create a harmonious blend of efficiency and authenticity, ensuring that your actions resonate with efficiency, logic, evidence and also your heart.

Strategy Checklist to Soften
Your Energy & Purpose with Fi

1) Beliefs Checklist: Before making decisions, refer to a checklist of your personal beliefs, ensuring that your actions align with what's truly important to you.

2) Prioritize with Purpose: Sequence and prioritize based on objective measures while following beliefs about what's important. For example, if there isn't enough time in the day to do everything you want to, then select the tasks that personally matter most to you.

3) Humane Realism: Set up a system that realistically rewards people based on actual human behavior to get the best possible result that you (and they) can live with. This includes building in flexibility, and learning from failure rather than trying to perfectly prevent it.

4) Will Power in Action: Apply will power to follow an important procedure or task to completion, implement a life choice, or live up to a moral belief. For example, you wear a metaphorical suit of armor to endure a tragedy to keep helping those who share loyalty.

5) Fair Systems: Structure organizations or systems to honor individual identities, ensuring that everyone is treated fairly and with respect.

6) Decision Authenticity: When making a decision, if you see evidence or resources are insufficient, go with what you personally believe while ready to pivot when necessary. At the same time, attend to your own emotions and consider how those are influencing you.

7) Straightforward Advocacy: Gather evidence and present results in clear ways, such as charts, to advocate for issues that resonate with your personal beliefs.

While the world of Te offers structure and efficiency, integrating Fi provides a touch of authenticity and personal resonance. It's about cherishing logical reasoning while ensuring that every action and decision aligns with your true self. Embrace Fi, and watch your efficient actions deepen with authenticity and heart.

What Now?

Please do your best to complete the table below. Scan through your notes on prior pages as needed, namely the chapter for your type as well as the checklist for your type here, to help gather your thoughts and include everything important. After, you might place a copy of this page by your work area or on an inspirational bulletin board.

Reflections, Suggestions, Actions

1. One big insight:

2. One suggestion on the "strategy checklist" that fit you:

3. One small action you can try today:

4. One person you can interact with more mindfully:

5. One task you can handle differently:

6. A practice you can commit to each day for 5 minutes:

7. A practice you can commit to once weekly (or monthly):

8. How you can get regular feedback:

Appendix:

Cognitive
Processes
Assessment

Find Your Favorite Goal-Focused CEO

Instructions: Please read carefully the statements below. For each:

- On a scale from 1 to 5, rate how often you do skillfully what the statement describes. A "1" means no skill, while a "5" means outstanding skill. A range of scores (not all high or low) gives clearer results.
- Use dictionary definitions and go with the overall meaning most comfortable to you.
- Some statements may reflect activities outside of your awareness or experience, requiring extra consideration.
- If you don't understand a statement, then mark it as "1" for no skill.

Here are the questions. Let's start!

1. _____ Determine success by measurement or other objective method such as the time taken.

2. _____ Feel inclined to be responsible for, and take care of, others' feelings.

3. _____ Be guided by a definition, logical deduction, or other nugget of reasoning.

4. _____ Feel strongly that something is good or bad.

5. _____ Construct an argument to convince someone using evidence clearly in front of you both.

6. _____ Compassionately take on someone else's needs as your own.

7. _____ Apply leverage to a situation to solve a problem impersonally using minimal effort.

8. _____ Remain in touch with what you want for yourself, what motivates you, and what is good.

9. _____ Follow a straight line of reasoning.

10. _____ Help make people feel comfortable by engaging in hosting and care-taking.

11. _____ Analyze and critique what doesn't fit with a well-defined principle.

12. _____ Always remain true to what you want for yourself or others.

13. _____ Lay out methods for others to complete tasks in time- and resource-efficient ways.

14. _____ Readily communicate personally to all members of a group to feel unity.

15. _____ Fine-tune a definition or concept to support a theory, perspective or framework.

16. _____ Evaluate what is worth believing in and most important to who you really are inside.

Now, add up the points:

Add #1 ◯ + #5 ◯ + #9 ◯ + #13 ◯ = _____
Timely Building

Add #2 ◯ + #6 ◯ + #10 ◯ + #14 ◯ = _____
Friendly Hosting

Add #3 ◯ + #7 ◯ + #11 ◯ + #15 ◯ = _____
Skillful Sleuthing

Add #4 ◯ + #8 ◯ + #12 ◯ + #16 ◯ = _____
Quiet Crusading

Highest Score? Circle the highest scoring result as your likely favorite "judging" process—your preferred way to organize and decide.

Note: These questions from www.keys2cognition.com are validated with ~130,000 subjects ages 25-65 with Chonbach alpha of 0.70+.

Find Your Favorite Open-Ended CEO

Instructions: Please read carefully the statements below. For each:

- On a scale from 1 to 5, rate how often you do skillfully what the statement describes. A "1" means no skill, while a "5" means outstanding skill. A range of scores (not all high or low) gives clearer results.
- Use dictionary definitions and go with the overall meaning most comfortable to you.
- Some statements may reflect activities outside of your awareness or experience, requiring extra consideration.
- If you don't understand a statement, then mark it as "1" for no skill.

Here are the questions. Let's start!

1. _____ Freely follow your gut instincts and exciting physical impulses as they come up.

2. _____ Offer various unrelated ideas and see what potential they might suggest.

3. _____ Notice whether the details in front of you match what you are accustomed to.

4. _____ Experience a premonition or foresee the distant future.

5. _____ Enjoy the thrill of action and physical experience in the present moment.

6. _____ Enjoy playing with random interconnections and patterns.

7. _____ Compare an experience against a storehouse of familiar experiences to find what's reliable.

8. _____ Achieve a metamorphosis, definitive insight, or a powerful vision of change.

9. _____ Instantly read visible cues to see just how far you can go.

10. _____ Keep following tangents and new ideas without limiting yourself to one.

11. _____ Review a lot of information over time to confirm what is customary or standard.

12. _____ Feel attracted to the symbolic, archetypal, or mysterious.

13. _____ Spur action and pull off results simply by making your presence felt.

14. _____ Weave into the current dynamics of a situation aspects of other, random contexts.

15. _____ Fulfill the same regular work or activity every day at a comfortable pace.

16. _____ Transform yourself by focusing inward on a specific way you foresee you will need to be.

Now, add up the points:

Add #1 ◯ + #5 ◯ + #9 ◯ + #13 ◯ = _____
Active Adapting

Add #2 ◯ + #6 ◯ + #10 ◯ + #14 ◯ = _____
Excited Brainstorming

Add #3 ◯ + #7 ◯ + #11 ◯ + #15 ◯ = _____
Cautious Protecting

Add #4 ◯ + #8 ◯ + #12 ◯ + #16 ◯ = _____
Keen Foreseeing

Highest Score? Circle the highest scoring result as your likely favorite "perceiving" process—your preferred way to get information.

Note: These questions from www.keys2cognition.com are validated with ~130,000 subjects ages 25-65 with Chonbach alpha of 0.70+.

Find Your Likely Type

Given your highest and second highest scoring processes from the questionnaire, you can use the table below to look up a likely type, or types if there's a tie, to explore further. Simply look up the highest scoring process and then consider the second highest process. There will find the corresponding type code and page to start that type's chapter.

Highest	Second Highest	Type Code	Page
Sensing			
Se	Ti (or Te or Fe)	ESTP	65
	Fi (or Fe or Te)	ESFP	93
Si	Te (or Ti or Fi)	ISTJ	135
	Fe (or Fi or Ti)	ISFJ	163
Intuiting			
Ne	Ti (or Te or Fe)	ENTP	205
	Fi (or Fe or Te)	ENFP	261
Ni	Te (or Ti or Fi)	INTJ	291
	Fe (or Fi or Ti)	INFJ	247
Thinking			
Te	Si (or Se or Ne)	ESTJ	121
	Ni (or Ne or Se)	ENTJ	177
Ti	Se (or Si or Ni)	ISTP	79
	Ne (or Ni or Si)	INTP	219
Feeling			
Fe	Si (or Se or Ne)	ESFJ	149
	Ni (or Ne or Se)	ENFJ	233
Fi	Se (or Si or Ni)	ISFP	107
	Ne (or Ni or Si)	INFP	275

Note: If you don't find an exact match in the table, start with the closest possible matches. And/or, you can consider the second-highest scoring process as the highest in the table, and look up a type that way. The online version of this questionnaire at keys2cognition.com offers more questions, calculates for you, and offers three types to consider.

About the Author

Dario Nardi, Ph.D. is an international author, researcher, speaker and expert in neuroscience, personality, games, and body-mind practices.

From 1998 to 2015, Dario taught computing and anthropology at University of California (Los Angeles), where he won UCLA's *Copenhaver Award for Innovative Use of Technology* in 2005 and UCLA's *Distinguished Teacher* of the year in 2011. He also taught in the Honors Collegium for many of his years there.

Dario was certified in the use of type under Dr. Linda Berens in 1994. His books include *Neuroscience of Personality, 8 Keys to Self-Leadership, Jung on Yoga, The Magic Diamond, 16 Personality Types: Descriptions for Self-Discovery, Teaching Tales for the 16 Personality Types,* and others.

His Udemy and Personality Hacker digital courses include *Jung on Yoga,* the *Awaken Your Inner Viking Shaman* series, and the *Psychological Types* series, which takes students from finding best-fit type and learning type dynamics to coaching activities and the neuroscience of personality. Also, Dario is the creator of the *Personality Types* iPhone app and the CPA, or *Cognitive Processes Assessment,* a tool to profile the Jungian framework and validated on over 130,000 people.

Dario has authored tabletop RPG game books and novellas including *Love's Tapestry* and the *Dark Prism* series.

Since 2006, Dario has focused on conducting hands-on brain research, utilizing insights of real-time EEG technology. His database presently holds over 600 subjects. Applications extend to coaching, counseling, education, games, healthcare, leadership development, yoga, and many other areas. Discover more at www.puzzlin.org.

Dario is a co-author of Facets of Ayahuasca, practices kundalini yoga, and trained in shamanic techniques in the Norse tradition through the Scandinavian Center for Shamanic Studies (www.shamanism.dk).

Dario is CEO of Radiance House, a publisher and media store. As a consultant, he usually helps businesses to integrate type or to implement game-like training scenarios into training.

Psychological Types #1: "FIND YOUR BEST-FIT TYPE"
Crack the Myers-Briggs type codes, triangulate to your type and sub-type, and try fun applications of type.

https://tinyurl.com/2p99zzjs

Psychological Types #2: "DEVELOP YOUR PERSONALITY"
Explore the 8 Jungian functions in depth and
develop more comfort and skill around each.

https://tinyurl.com/3snr5s89

Multiply Your mastery in psychological type, with almost 20 hours of video: 160 lectures and 150 downloads, spread over 4 courses.

Psychological Types #3: "COACHING TEAMS, LEADERS & CHANGE"
Facilitate change and growth using professional tools and
fun, challenging, and creative activities.

https://tinyurl.com/mt6hcs7t

Psychological Types #4: "NEUROSCIENCE OF PERSONALITY"
Better understand personality, skills, and emotions in terms of recent
neuroscience discoveries.

https://tinyurl.com/4ymwbjj2

Yet More On the Web

Dario Nardi, Ph.D.
DarioNardi.com
https://www.linkedin.com/in/dnardi22/

Assessments and Products by Dario Nardi
RadianceHouse.com
https://www.careerplanner.com/Shop/NPI-FacilitatorReports.cfm
keys2cognition.com
personalityapps.com
radiancehouse.sellfy.store/
puzzlin.org

Allies: Personality Hacker & Type School
personalityhacker.com | www.facebook.com/PersonalityHacker
https://campus.typeschool.co

Linda Berens, Ph.D.
lindaberens.com
interstrength.org

British Association of Psychological Type
bapt.org.uk | facebook.com/BAPT1989

Australian Association of Psychological Type
ausapt.org.au | facebook.com/AusAPT

Association Francophone des Types Psychologiques
types-psychologiques.com

APTi (the North American type association)
www.aptinternational.org

Myers-Briggs Database and Resources
themyersbriggs.com | CAPT.org

Biotypes by Laura Power, Ph.D.
biotype.net

Top Books

If you enjoyed this book and would like to explore further, here are four books that provide more for self-discovery, skill-building exercises, neuroscience results and body-mind practices.

Contains 160 exercises, or 20 for each of the 8 cognitive processes, plus deep understanding of each process.

Contains coaching packets for each of the 8 Jungian functions. Packets include Jung's words, suggested activities, and more.

Explains brain basics and summarizes results of a pilot study of 65 people in terms of their personality and brain activity.

In 1934, Dr. Jung gave 4 profound talks on kundalini yoga. Through his words, discover Eastern spirituality and body-mind practices.

References and Resources

Free Online Personality Assessment
www.keys2cognition.com

Online Udemy.com Digital Type Courses
- *Psychological Types #1: Find Your Best-Fit Type.* https://tinyurl.com/2p99zzjs
- *Psychological Types #2: Develop Your Personality.* https://tinyurl.com/3snr5s89
- *Psychological Types #3: Coaching Teams, Leaders, and Change.* https://tinyurl.com/mt6hcs7t
- *Psychological Types #4: Neuroscience of Personality.* https://tinyurl.com/4ymwbjj2

Evidence for Jungian and Myers-Briggs Frameworks

- Barimany, Mina E. *The Hierarchy of Preferences in Jungian Psychological Type: Comparing Theory to Evidence* (ProQuest Number 10264427) [Doctoral Dissertation]. The George Washington University. ProQuest Dissertations & eses Global database, 2017.
- Barimany, Mina E. "Evidence for New Dimensions in Type Development." *TypeFace, 41.* https://apti.memberclicks.net/typeface, Sept., 2020.
- Bouchard, T.J. and Hur, Y.M. Genetic and environmental influences on the continuous scales of the Myers-Briggs Type Indicator: an analysis based on twins reared apart. *Journal of Personality* 66(2), 1998.
- Ciorciari, Joseph, Gountas, John, et. al. "A Neuroimaging Study of Personality Traits and Self-Reflection." *Behavioral Sciences*, 2019.
- Nardi, Dario. Strong Evidence for 8 Jungian Functions. *Bulletin of Psychological Type* Vol. 42, 2021.
- Nardi, Dario. *Neuroscience of Personality: Brain-Savvy Insights for All Types of People.* Radiance House, 2011.

Evidence for the Subtypes

- Brown, Luky, Acevedo, Bianca, and Fisher, Helen. "Neural Correlates of Four Broad Temperament Dimensions: Testing Predictions for a Novel Construct of Personality." *PLOS One*, November 2013.
- Fisher, Helen et. al. "Four broad temperament dimensions: description, convergent validation correlations, and comparison with the

Big Five." *Frontiers in Psychology*, August 2015.

- Gulenko, Victor and I.J. Goldman. *Psychological Types: Why Are People So Different?: 64 Portraits in Socionics. How each of the 16 Jungian types varies in 4 main ways.* [Independently published], 2019.
- Nardi, Dario. *Character and Personality Type: Discovering Your Uniqueness for Career and Relationship Success.* InterStrength Press, 1999.
- Nisbett, Richard. *The Geography of Thought.* Fres, 2004.
- Perry, Philip. *This-biological-anthropologist-is-mapping-the-human-personality.* Web article: https://bigthink.com/philip-perry/this-biological-anthropologist-is-mapping-the-human-personality.

Type Theory Popular Classics

- Berens, Linda and Dario Nardi. *The 16 Personality Types: Descriptions for Self-Discovery.* Interstrength Press, 1998.
- Berens, Linda and Dario Nardi. *Understanding Yourself and Others: An Introduction to the Personality Type Code.* Interstrength Press, 2004.
- Jung, Carl. *Psychological Types.* Reprint, Princeton, NJ: Princeton University Press, 1960.
- Keirey, David and Marilyn Bates. *Please Understand Me: Character and Temperament Types*, 5th Edition. Prometheus Nemesis Book Company, 1984.
- Myers, Isabel Briggs. *Gifts Differing.* Consulting Psychologists Press, 1980.

Type Applications in Organizations

- Berens, Linda. *Understanding Yourself and Others: An Introduction Interaction Styles - 2.0.* InterStrength Press, 2008.
- Berens, Linda, Dario Nardi, et. al. *Quick Guide to the 16 Personality Types in Organizations.* Interstrength Press, 2001.
- Nardi, Dario. "What's Your Team's Brain? Brain-Based Assessment for Individuals and Organizations." *Workforce Solutions Review*, July 2015.

Jungian Psychology and Development

- Myers, Steve. *Myers-Briggs Typology vs. Jungian Individuation.* Routledge, 2018.
- Myers, Steve. "The Five Functions of Psychological Type". *Journal of*

Analytical Psychology, Volume 61, Issue 2, pages 183–202, April 2016.

- Nardi, Dario. *8 Keys to Self-Leadership: From Awareness to Action.* Radiance House, 2005.
- Nardi, Dario. *Jung on Yoga: Insights and Activities to Awaken with the Chakras.* Radiance House, 2018.
- Nardi, Dario. *The Magic Diamond: Jung's 8 Paths for Self-Coaching.* Radiance House, 2020.
- Nardi, Dario. *Yin and Yang of Type: Exploring 256 Flavors of Personality.* Presented April 2020 for the French Association of Psychological Type. Radiance House, 2022.

More From the Author

www.radiancehouse.com
https://radiancehouse.sellfy.store/
www.darionardi.com
www.jungonyoga.com
www.neuropq.com
www.puzzlin.org

More on the Web

www.interstrength.org
www.personalityhacker.com
https://campus.typeschool.co
www.themyersbriggs.com
www.aptinternational.org
www.bapt.org.uk
www.ausapt.org.au
www.types-psychologiques.com
www.capt.org

Might you post a review?

Did you like this book? Please take a moment to rate it or consider leaving a review. Even if you didn't buy it online, you can usually leave a review by uploading a photo of the book in your hands. Such reviews can be short and help people know what they will like about the book. Of course, do what's comfortable for you. Cheers!

Made in the USA
Middletown, DE
05 November 2023

41894005R00225